P9-CEY-731

## About the Author

Born in 1970 in Jable, Syria, Samar Yazbek studied literature before beginning her career as a journalist and a script writer for Syrian television and cinema. Her translated work includes the novel *Cinnamon* and *A Woman in The Crossfire*, her diaries of the first four months of the Syrian uprising, for which she was awarded the PEN Pinter, PEN Tucholsky and PEN Oxfam-Novib prizes. In 2010 she was selected as one of the 'Beirut39', the top 39 Arab writers under 40 that year. Following her exile from Syria, she now lives in Paris.

## Praise for *The Crossing*

'Bears comparison with George Orwell's *Homage to Catalonia* as a work of literature. Yazbek is a superb narrator who knows how to pace her text, craft dialogue and convey a universal sense of grief; this is how she crosses the line from journalism to high literary art.' *Observer*

'Brave, rebellious and passionate . . . Yazbek is no ordinary Syrian dissident.' *Financial Times*

'Sheds valuable light on day-to-day life inside Syria, something of which we know little . . . a sobering glimpse of the wreckage that will be discovered when the war is over.' *Sunday Times*

'Samar Yazbek is comparable to Svetlana Alexievich.' Ulrika Mille, Sveriges Television

'A brilliant book about what war does to people . . . should be required reading for every citizen.' Mou'in Al Bayari, *Al Araby*

# The CROSSING

## MY JOURNEY TO THE SHATTERED HEART OF SYRIA

# SAMAR YAZBEK

Translated by Nashwa Gowanlock
and Ruth Ahmedzai Kemp

LONDON · SYDNEY · AUCKLAND · JOHANNESBURG

For the martyrs of the Syrian revolution.
I am writing for you: the betrayed.

3 5 7 9 10 8 6 4 2

Rider, an imprint of Ebury Publishing,
20 Vauxhall Bridge Road,
London SW1V 2SA

Rider is part of the Penguin Random House group of companies whose
addresses can be found at global.penguinrandomhouse.com

Copyright © Samar Yazbek 2015
English translation copyright © Ruth Ahmedzai and Nashwa Gowanlock 2015

Samar Yazbek has asserted her right to be identified as the author of this Work
in accordance with the Copyright, Designs and Patents Act 1988

First published by Rider in 2015. This edition published 2016

www.eburypublishing.co.uk

A CIP catalogue record for this book is available from the British Library

ISBN 9781846044885

Printed and bound in Great Britain by Clays Ltd, St Ives PLC

Penguin Random House is committed to a sustainable future for our business,
our readers and our planet. This book is made from Forest Stewardship
Council® certified paper.

MIX
Paper from
responsible sources
FSC
www.fsc.org    FSC® C018179

# CONTENTS

# FOREWORD
# BY CHRISTINA LAMB

Over the last year many of us have watched a million migrants and refugees streaming into Europe and wondered what would make people leave their homes, families and all they know to make such an uncertain journey where children may drown in unforgiving seas.

We also watched the Paris attacks of 13 November 2015 where an evening out at a concert or bars and restaurants ended in terror, as men with guns and suicide bombs brought carnage to the City of Light, leaving 130 dead in the name of the Islamic State of Iraq and Syria (ISIS).

Seen through the news lens of refugees and terrorists, sometimes it's easy to forget that Syria is a country of ordinary people trying to live their lives. Of girls trying to read bedtime stories to their baby sisters while sheltering from bombs, and mums and dads trying to work and feed their families as war grinds on.

From the moment you read the first sentence of this book Samar Yazbek's writing will hit you like a punch in the stomach. Her literary style is so exquisite that you can even hear the birds in the cages and smell the perfume of the perfectly made-up women. Then a bomb falls nearby and the paint flakes down from the ceiling over them, for this is a damning story.

Damning of a dictator who cares nothing for what he does to his people to stay in power and damning of a world that stands by and does nothing.

Maybe you think you know the story. You've heard it on the news, read it in the newspaper. The Syrian war has after all been going on since 2011. But Yazbek does something none of us foreign correspondents do, for this is her country, as she says, her 'beautiful' country where she grew up, so she bears witness to the terrible changes.

These are the accounts of the people on the ground collected on three journeys between 2012 and 2013, people who are living through the war, feeling as if the world has abandoned them.

This book will remind you of the initial hope of 2011 and the Arab Spring. The earnestness of the early revolutionaries who wanted democracy is heartbreaking. And their warnings of how their fight might be hijacked by well-funded extremists if they continued to get no Western help are horribly prescient.

Today of course the Syrian people find themselves caught between a barbaric regime which uses barrel bombs on its own population and the terrifying death cult that is ISIS.

Living in exile in Paris with her young daughter, Yazbek's journeys back into Syria to bring out the stories of life there are brave by any measure. They are positively heroic when you consider that she is not only wanted by the regime but is an Alawite, the minority sect of the ruling Bashar al Assad, meaning she is suspected as pro-Assad by rebels and seen as a Shia infidel by Sunni militants.

Her life in France means she straddles both worlds. We feel her pain and bewilderment as she lets people tell their own stories. Through her sharp eye and incisive pen, what we get is more than reportage, but a political indictment of Western inaction in the face of a leader who will go to any length to stay in power. It's also a psychological study of how ordinary people are forced into horror and murder from which one wonders how a country can ever recover.

Yet we also see the resilience of a people caught up in what has become one of the great tragedies of the 21st century where, as she says, it seems the only victor is death.

The award-winning Christina Lamb, OBE, is Chief Foreign Correspondent for the *Sunday Times*. She has reported from all over the world, including Afghanistan, Pakistan, Iraq, Libya, and on the refugee crisis. Her bestselling books include *I Am Malala* and *Farewell Kabul*.

# The FIRST CROSSING

## August 2012

The barbed wire lacerated my back. I was trembling uncontrollably. After long hours spent waiting for nightfall, to avoid attracting the attention of Turkish soldiers, I finally raised my head and gazed up at the distant sky, darkening to black. Under the wire fence marking the line of the border a tiny burrow had been dug out, just big enough for one person. My feet sank into the soil and the barbs mauled my back as I crawled across the line of separation between the two countries.

I took a deep breath, arched my back and ran, as fast as I could, just as they had told me to do. Fast. Half an hour at a sprint – that's the distance you have to cover before you've safely crossed the border. I ran and ran until we were out of the danger zone. The ground was treacherous and rocky, but my feet felt light as I sprinted. The pounding of my heart carried me, lifting me up. Panting, I murmured to myself: *I'm back! This isn't a scene in a film, this is real.* I ran, mouthing, *I'm back . . . I'm here.*

Behind us, we heard gunshots and military vehicles moving around on the Turkish side, but we'd done it: we were through and we were running. It felt like it had all been fated long ago. I'd put on a headscarf especially, and a long jacket and loose-fitting trousers. We had a steep hill to climb, before we hurtled down the other side towards the waiting car. On this occasion my guides and I weren't part of a convoy of strangers. At the time I didn't even know if I would ever manage to write about it later;

somehow I'd just assumed I would die, like so many others, when I returned to my homeland. Darkness settled in for the night and everything seemed normal, as expected, or so it seemed.

Later on, after I had made this crossing a number of times over eighteen months, I saw many changes: the chaotic state of Antakya airport, near the border, would be ample evidence of what was happening to Syria. I stowed it all away in the back of my mind, along with everything else that testified to the rapid and profound upheavals taking place in my country. Back then, though, I was ignorant of what was to come as I scrambled down the hill for the first time, my legs throbbing with pain.

When I reached the bottom, I crouched down and paused for at least ten minutes, wheezing and gasping for breath, trying to calm my beating heart. The young men accompanying me must have thought I was emotional at seeing my homeland again. But that was the last thing on my mind. We had been running for so long, I felt like my lungs were being wrenched from my body and I couldn't stand up.

Finally, we reached the car and I started to breathe normally again. I sat in the back with the two men who would be acting as my guides, Maysara and Mohammed. They were two very different combatants from the same family, the family in whose home I would take shelter. Maysara was a rebel fighter who had started out campaigning peacefully against the Assad regime, but had later taken up arms. Mohammed was in his twenties and had been a business student who, like Maysara, had been involved in the peaceful protest movement before joining the armed resistance. As we worked together over the coming weeks he became a lasting friend. In the front were our driver and another young man.

We were travelling through Idlib province, an area only partially liberated from the control of Assad's forces. Between the endless roadblocks set up by the Free Army, we sped along a road lined by olive groves. Everywhere I looked there were armed militants, victory banners. I tried to take snapshots in my mind of what I could see as I stretched my head out of the car window, detaching myself emotionally from my surroundings. The road seemed to go on forever as we drove along with the thud of shelling in the distance. And yet a sense of exhilaration tickled every cell in my body as I looked at this part of Syria, which had been mostly freed from Assad's troops.

Well, some of the land might be liberated, but the sky wouldn't let us celebrate yet; no, the sky was on fire. It felt like I was being bombarded with frenetic images competing for my attention; to take it all in, I needed eyes in the back of my head, on my ears – hell, even on my fingertips. Staring ahead, I tried to make sense of my surroundings. Machines of destruction. The blazing sky. A solitary car carrying one woman and four men, heading through the olive groves to the town of Saraqeb.

The Syria that I remembered had been one of the most beautiful places in the world. I thought back to my early childhood in the town of al-Tabqa (also known as al-Thawra) near the city of Raqqa on the Euphrates river, and my teenage years in the historic city of Jableh on the coast, followed by Latakia, the principal port city of Syria. As an adult, I had lived alone with my daughter in Damascus, the capital, for several years, at a distance from my family, community and sectarian ties. I had lived independently, free to make my own choices, but my lifestyle had cost me a great deal of rejection, criticism and harm to my reputation. It had been difficult to be female in a conservative society that did not allow women to rebel against its laws. Everything had seemed resistant to change. The last thing I'd imagined on my first visit to the rural areas of northern Syria was to see it being destroyed.

Everything I recount in the following narrative is real. The only fictional character is the narrator, me: an implausible figure capable of crossing the border amid all this destruction, as though my life were nothing but the far-fetched plot of a novel. As I absorbed what was happening around me, I ceased to be myself. I was a made-up character considering my choices, just able to keep on going. I put aside the woman I am in real life and became this other imaginary person, whose reactions had to be commensurate with whatever it was she was living for. What was she doing here? Confronting existence? Identity? Exile? Justice? The insanity of bloodshed?

I had been forced into exile in France in July 2011. My departure from Syria hadn't been easy: I had fled with my daughter because I was being pursued by the intelligence services (the *mukhabarat*) after taking part in peaceful demonstrations in the early months of the revolution. And I had written several articles outlining the truth about the actions of the intelligence services, who were murdering and torturing those protesting against Assad's regime. But, having arrived in France, I'd felt compelled to return to northern Syria, to fulfil my dream of achieving democracy and freedom in my homeland. This return to the country of my birth was all I ever thought about, and I believed in doing what was right as an educated person and a writer, standing alongside my people in their cause. My goal was to set up some small-scale women's projects and an organisation aimed at empowering women and providing children with an education. If the situation was likely to be prolonged, there was no choice but to try to focus on the next generation. I was also looking for a workable way of establishing democratic civil institutions in those areas that had freed themselves from al-Assad's control.

Passing along road after road in the pitch-black of night, I was now heading to the home of the family that would play such a fundamental role in my new life. Cautiously we entered the narrow alleys of Saraqeb. The town was not yet fully liberated;

there was still a sniper at the radio tower killing countless people every day.

The building in which I would be staying had several wings, arranged around a central courtyard. It had clearly once been the home of prosperous and hospitable people. These days the large family were 'getting by', as one of the women put it. The oldest, original part of the building had a lovely domed roof and had been built long ago by a previous generation. I would be staying here in a room they called the 'cellar'. To the left of this wing were the quarters of the eldest son, Abu Ibrahim, and his wife, Noura: my hosts. To the right was where my guide Maysara, the family's youngest son, lived with his wife, Manal, and his children Ruha, a very composed eleven-year-old, Aala, aged seven, Mahmoud, aged four, and two-and-a-half-year-old Tala. The building was also home to the sons' elderly mother and their aunt, both of whom were pretty much immobile. They were cared for by Ayouche, Abu Ibrahim's unmarried sister who was in her early fifties.

I didn't know then, but my hosts and I shared the same vision for our country, which created a strong bond between us. As a people, Syrians are extremely hospitable. The moment we arrived everyone was mobilised into preparing dinner for us. We sat down together to eat, cross-legged on the floor on plastic rugs and foam mattresses, the young girls Ruha and Aala never leaving my side. I looked around at their friendly faces. My own relatives lived in parts of the country under the control of the regime, which meant I could no longer visit them.

That evening, I told the women in the family a little about my life and how I'd left home for the first time at the age of sixteen. By sharing these confidences, I wanted to inspire trust and give them an idea of the true meaning of freedom – and the responsibility associated with it. I wanted to show them how a woman's freedom lies in a life lived responsibly, which was the opposite of what Syrian society conceived women's liberation to be, viewing it instead as a chaotic violation of customs and traditions. I talked to them about how I'd lived and worked hard to raise my daughter, to be economically independent after my divorce from my husband, and how I'd been forced to take on various jobs so that my daughter and I could get by. I told them how members of my family and community had cut me off, but that I had done what I had to do to become a writer and journalist. The women's questions kept coming, as I told them a little about my journey to Saraqeb.

I explained how, before crossing the border, I had visited a hospital in the Turkish town of Reyhanli, where there was a special emergency floor dedicated to Syrians wounded by shelling. One room after another reeked of putrefying patients laid out on white sheets, with mutilated feet, amputated limbs, hazy eyes. I was accompanied by Maysara and his brother-in-law Manhal, who was one of the first activists to embrace the revolution in Saraqeb. Manhal warned me to brace myself as we entered the room of two young girls, four-year-old Diana and eleven-year-old Shaima.

Diana had been hit in the spinal cord by a bullet, causing permanent paralysis. She lay there frozen, like a panic-stricken rabbit. It seemed a miracle that her small, fragile body hadn't been completely blown apart under the impact. The little girl had been crossing the street to buy a pastry for breakfast when it happened. What on earth was the sniper thinking when he aimed his sights on her back?

In the hospital bed next to Diana was Shaima, whose leg had been blown off by a shell, and whose left hand had been shattered by shrapnel. Her other foot was also injured and wounds covered her body. She and her family had been taken by surprise as they sat in front of their house. Nine members of her family were killed, including her mother. Her aunt stood at her bedside.

As Shaima looked at me, her gaze was an unsettling mixture of pleading and anger. A white bandage was wrapped around her pelvis, stopping at her upper thigh. There was an empty space where her leg should have been. We are made whole by our imperfections, I thought to myself. And we are incomplete when we are whole. But there was nothing I could say to this child. My fingers touched her forehead. She smiled.

Shaima and Diana were not alone on the floor. In the next room was a young lad waiting for his leg to be amputated after it had been blown apart by a shell. Yet he laughed with his eyes. Another young man was waiting to have his foot cleaned up and shrapnel removed, so he could return to Syria to carry on fighting. He was a group commander called Abdullah who, when I next met him during my second trip back, would make time to talk to me, and we would become friends. I didn't know it then, but my third crossing into Syria would be undertaken with him and, in spite of the falling shells, I would have coffee with his beautiful fiancée.

In the wards of that Turkish hospital, just before the border, lay Syrians whose limbs had been left in the dirt. These young people, lying there with their mangled half bodies, gazed out of the hospital window in the direction of their home country, so near you could smell it. This, I explained to my hosts now, was where I had taken my first real step towards crossing the border.

I told them about sneaking through the barbed wire to the other side. How we had crossed from being lost in one wilderness to being lost in another. It had been a moment of oscillation, of teetering on the line between exile and homeland. There, on both sides of the fence, bodies suddenly emerged from the darkness, shoulders rubbing as they shuffled blindly on. We heard a voice greet us, 'Good evening.' Voices came, voices went. We crept by stealthily, like cats in the shadows. The border beneath which Syrians disappear in the night is just a hair's breadth: no distance to speak of. People go in, people come out; they traverse this distance in the peaceful still of night, although few will find peace at their destination. The barbed-wire fence cannot hold them; it's as useless as trying to contain jelly in a net.

During my first stay in Saraqeb, I gained first-hand experience of the sniper who shot Diana, as I got to know my surroundings and my hosts showed me how to pass through houses to avoid the street that this assassin overlooked. Everyone's door was open to us as we sneaked through the buildings, dodging the sights of the sniper's rifle. Many of the townspeople had torn down the walls between their homes, turning these into thoroughfares. We would pass through these strangers' homes, jump out of windows or climb down ladders to street level, then slip through the courtyard carrying our shoes.

Once I was out with Mohammed and two other young men when we went through an old lady's living room. We greeted her and she greeted us in return, not leaving the spot where she was reclining, not moving an inch. She was clearly accustomed to locals traipsing in and out of her house. Before I jumped out of the window, I glanced across, searching for a sign of surprise, but she simply went back to staring at the ceiling as though she hadn't noticed the four of us. We passed through many houses in this way and managed to stay safe. It was the only way to avoid being shot.

Indeed, I would learn from the local women that on my last day the sniper had shot someone in her genitals and killed a twelve-year-old girl. Hearing that made me freeze: my legs went stiff, I couldn't straighten my knees. 'What are you doing?' the men said to me, raising their voices. 'Come on! You're going to need thicker skin than that!' The incident taught me to postpone my sadness and to keep my distress to myself.

All the same, the only victor in Syria is death: no one talks of anything else. Everything is relative and open to doubt; the only certainty is that death will triumph.

I settled in to my work with the local women, helping them to set up workshops and projects that could support them financially. But it was easy to become distracted. One day, I was getting ready to visit some widows and female relatives of martyred fighters (by martyred, I mean in a secular not a religious sense), when I found myself surrounded by a gathering of beautiful female neighbours all intent on recounting their own stories about Saraqeb. Little Aala was sitting at my side listening, pulling at my hand, while her elder sister Ruha helped her mother and looked at me askance. I wanted to please both of them. I whispered in Aala's ear that we had to listen carefully. She winked at me, put her hand under her chin and listened with me to what the women had to say.

Even without such interesting diversions, it wasn't easy to get to the homes of the women I wanted to meet. Mohammed always accompanied me in the car, but men were forbidden from entering the houses of widows, especially during the *iddah*, the period according to Islamic law of four months and ten days before a widow may be seen by another man. What was striking when I visited women in their homes, in villages scattered around Idlib province, was that their houses were always very clean, even though the water was cut off. They painted their eyebrows, their eyes sparkled, and despite their poverty the aroma of cleaning products wafted from their rooms. Even in the poorest homes, I could smell cheap soap. Women from the very poorest displaced families, those who lived in half tumbled-down, dilapidated houses, took particular care of their surroundings, and were constantly dusting with worn-out cloths or wiping their children's faces with damp towels. You have to adapt your standards accordingly when you barely have a roof over your head.

On the way back from a visit to a widow and her family, Mohammed suggested we visit the calligrapher and painter behind much of Saraqeb's graffiti, one of the most important art forms used by revolutionary activists. No sooner were towns liberated than their walls were turned into open books and transient art exhibits. The man who provided the artwork on Saraqeb's walls was also the man who consigned its martyrs, the victims of bombings, to the grave.

'I bury the bodies,' he told me, holding out the palms of his hands as he said 'bodies'. 'I can tell you the story of each and every one of them. But it would take a long time. I bury Saraqeb's martyrs and paint Saraqeb's walls. I'll never leave this place.'

As we spoke, we were standing in front of the Saraqeb Cultural Centre, its vibrant colours shattering the general drabness of the surroundings. Across the way was a building whose front wall was inscribed with a eulogy to Mohammed Haaf, a martyred local hero: 'It's true, Haaf: an eye never forgets its eyelid, and a flower never forgets its roots.' Opposite, another wall read, 'Damascus, we are here for eternity.' We wandered through the streets. I took photographs of the walls and shopfronts of this city mired in the glorification of death; I saw notices everywhere of the funerals of young men and children, women and the elderly. On we walked in the blazing sun and dry dust. A few men passed us; their eyes were red, but radiant. We could still hear the sound of the sniper's bullets.

That evening a dark-skinned young man called by, a relative of Maysara's, whose cheeks were singed. He sat without saying a word for some time, before telling us how shells had landed in his field and burnt his hay – his bread and butter. That was it for this season. As he said this, he started to bang his head against the wall. The young man's mother was there with us and stared in horror as she realised that she had lost everything too. She gave a low wail, before she fell silent and listened with the rest of us to the sound of the sniper's bullets.

'They're setting fire to the farms around the town to punish the locals,' Mohammed told me the next day as we stood looking at more graffiti. 'But I'm not sure if they'll drop a shell on us now. Maybe they will!' We looked up at the clear blue sky, which trembled with the thunder of shelling. 'When a shell lands nearby, that's a sound you'll never forget,' he said, laughing. A convoy of tanks rumbled by on the outskirts of town, heading to Aleppo.

'Later when the fighting breaks out, Saraqeb will be in the demarcation zone. The shelling won't stop,' he told me as we set off again in the car.

We pulled up in front of a demolished house.

'This house was shelled after being set on fire and after one of the sons was killed,' Mohammed said. 'The son who died was tortured in prison. He has seven sisters and one brother, and they've lost their father. After they killed him, they strung him up to the back of the car and dragged him through the streets, flaying his skin. He'd been involved in the peaceful demonstrations. Another guy was caught filming the demonstrations; they grabbed him, stuck him under the tracks of a tank and told him they were going to drive over him. They fired up the engine while he was underneath. They left him like that for a bit, until they burst out laughing and arrested him.

'We're going to rebuild what they bombed. You see that house on the other side?' Mohammed pointed to the second floor, where there was a huge hole in the wall. 'That's where the sister of one of the dissidents lived. They bombed it purely in retaliation for her brother.'

Even as I recall these events, it seems impossible to write about them in any kind of sequence that makes sense. There's no way I can narrate this in any kind of order. There's nothing I can do but break up time.

There was the day when Maysara and Mohammed insisted I go with them to see the tank graveyard in the city of Al-Atareb: a huge pile of burnt-out machinery, great metallic structures melted to a pulp. Traces of fire were spattered in every direction and the spilled guts of houses had been ripped apart like crushed cardboard boxes. Silence. Desolation. There was not a sound to be heard in the whole of Al-Atareb. Nothing, not even a whisper or the howl of stray dogs. This was where I realised the true meaning of the word 'annihilation'. Only at the end of a side street did we spot candlelight inside a small shop, and from afar we could see the spectre of a woman waving. These were the only signs that Al-Atareb was not an abandoned ghost town, nothing but piles of rubble without structure or identity, where all we could hear was the rumble of bombing nearby.

We got into the car to head back to Saraqeb. A commander was travelling with us, sitting to the left of me in the back. Suddenly he shifted his rifle and started to load it. I shuddered. Then he took out a grenade and clasped his right hand around it. I looked at its green mass, a few centimetres in size, and I touched it. I shuddered again. We were passing through a danger zone; the commander kept a firm grip on the grenade and pressed his gun against the car window. I noticed how, like a wolf, his eyes scoured the burnt-out landscape.

'It'll either be those dogs, the regime,' he said, 'or it'll be the thugs and looters who're plundering the area on behalf of the Free Army.'

As I would soon discover, although the name 'Free Army' might conjure up organised units of men, it actually covers an extremely diverse set of groups, with varying characteristics and attitudes – from the cruel to the compassionate. These fighting men are really just ordinary people such as one might meet in the street; they differ so widely in the extent they adhere to the moral principles of the revolution, or have lost focus of them altogether, that many of the groups seem to have very little in common. The Free Army brigades, or the 'armed people's resistance brigades' as they perhaps ought to be called, with the vast disparity they embody, are a carbon copy of real life in all its diversity – except that in Syria death drifts among them with the lightness of a feather.

In the front seat, Maysara pulled out his gun, while our driver remained steady, focusing on the road with single-minded determination. To my right, Mohammed was also armed and ready. As we made our way through the thickening dusk, the towering cypress trees loomed over the narrow asphalt road and I feigned courage. But the gun at the group commander's side and the grenade, now back inside his jacket pocket, made me think the time had come to breathe my last. The muzzle of the gun was now pointing straight up at me – a tiny, hungry mouth, the barrel right there before my eyes. My fingers needed only to move mere centimetres to pull the trigger, and that would be enough to drown in sweet, eternal darkness. But I was woken abruptly from my trance by the commander's voice.

'We're all here together. No one's going to touch a hair on your head.'

As we drove through the half-light to Saraqeb, the commander told me a story.

'. . . we found him six days later,' he said. 'He was lying in the woods. He'd disappeared on 24 March 2012, the day the army stormed Saraqeb. He was wrapped up and crumpled in a heap, and there was an awful stench coming from him. From far away his body looked like an old rag tossed on the ground, but this rag was actually the body of a young man from the Abboud family. There was a lot of blood, because he had a deep wound in his neck. He'd been slaughtered like an animal. His clothes were intact, a layer of dust clung to them. He was the first to be martyred on the day the army stormed Saraqeb. We thought he'd been detained, like many others, but in fact he was dead. To us, he stayed alive for six more days; maybe that counts for something.

'I'm sure they arrested him in an underhand way. He wasn't carrying his gun that day; he'd left it behind in the house. He went out and he disappeared. If he'd been carrying his weapon, he wouldn't have submitted easily, so they must have tricked him. The incision in his neck was made from behind. He was wearing brand-new clothes, you know.

'The army withdrew very soon after attacking the town. They fooled us. Very few soldiers remained. That was on the Saturday. Then they came back on Tuesday to try to capture Taftanaz and Jarjanaz, and to suppress the entire region again after we'd seized control. They set fire to seventy houses in Jarjanaz and a hundred in Saraqeb. The tanks came in and ploughed into the buildings; when they left, Saraqeb was just a heap of rubble.

'They killed some of our finest young men that day. Sa'ad Barish was confined to his bed with shrapnel in his hand and leg. He was with his sister and her son at her house. They stormed the house and demolished it, then dragged his sister's son Uday al-Amr from his mother's arms. They dragged both of them into the street. Sa'ad, with his shrapnel wounds, was screaming, but they paid no attention and kept on dragging the two of them through the streets of Saraqeb, scraping their skin on the ground, until they disappeared from sight.

'Uday's mother was screaming and chasing after them. They threw her to the ground. Then they left, and we heard gunfire. The mother was running and running, then crawling, towards the sound of shooting. We found Sa'ad and Uday slumped against a wall. Bullet holes were in their heads and bodies, even where the injured guy already had wounds – in the leg and hand. They had been ripped apart by lead.

'This woman whose son had been wrested from her arms and dragged across the ground before they tore him apart with bullets . . . she had a visit from some other soldiers a while later. They came for her second son. The soldiers were hungry, so she cooked them some food. One of them shouted at her, so she cursed them and said, "You're in my house, eating my food, and you're screaming in my face?" The soldier stopped shouting and told his comrades not to harm the woman, but they still took her teenage son. As they were leaving, the soldier who'd shouted seemed sad to see her crying and begging them to bring back her son. But still they went. They did bring back her son, though: dead.

'But still the rebels didn't give in. They weren't afraid of being overwhelmed, or of the shelling, or of being killed, and they continued to defend their homes, even when their ammunition ran out. Six of them were trapped without ammunition, and the army managed to break into the house, which they'd fortified. They set fire to the basement and were about to execute the owner of the house, although he was an old man, when his wife knelt at their feet and pleaded with them.

'"I'm kissing your feet," she said. "I'm begging you, boys, don't kill him . . . I'm kissing your feet . . . Please, leave him be . . . He's a good man . . . He hasn't done anything." They didn't kill him, but they beat him up badly, and threw him in the street. They took the six rebels – all in their twenties – and sat them with their backs against a wall. They opened fire, shooting them all so they fell in a heap on top of each other. And the soldiers left them there, as if nothing had happened.

'The next day, they were patrolling the streets of Saraqeb. They stopped Mohammed Abboud in the middle of the street, shot him and then arrested his brother Zuhair. That was also the day they killed Mohammed Barish, who was known by his *nom de guerre* Mohammed Haaf. They didn't dare confront him, because he was known for his courage and was commander of a very popular battalion in Saraqeb. There was an aircraft circling in the sky ready to assassinate him, with men in it firing machine guns. They had a BMP armoured personnel carrier for support on the ground which launched continuous showers of bullets in every direction. After they'd killed him, and made sure he was definitely dead, they went up to him and started dancing and whooping with joy. As for Zuhair Abboud, he was released after three months of torture, and a few days later he was walking in the street in Saraqeb and taken unawares by a sniper's bullet.

'They achieved a temporary victory over us. We were firing Kalashnikovs, and they were responding with shellfire from tanks and bombs from planes. But, as I said, it's only a temporary victory.'

That's where the commander's story ends, with the first incursion into Saraqeb. His is just one story I've written down among hundreds of others.

Whenever I think of this, my first crossing, isolated moments come back to me, detached from their temporal context. I go back over the many conversations I had with the women I worked with and the young fighters I met. I keep dwelling on the wilderness we passed through as we crossed between the two countries, how we'd been greeted by olive groves and the smell of a different country. Everywhere we drove, the walls of towns were emblazoned with revolutionary posters and flags, and people stared wearily at us. In the car, weaving through the shroud of night, we would pass through checkpoints set up by the Free Army. These roadblocks weren't large and the rebels all seemed to know each other. Both in the liberated villages and the semi-liberated.

We were in the car, heading to Binnish, on our way to join the demonstrations for a free, democratic Syria and to meet one of the rebel battalions later that day. I was determined to get to know the battalions because I knew they represented a cross-section of Syrian society. It was important to understand who they were and what they wanted, why they had taken up arms and how they intended to continue fighting – to gain a proper sense of the situation on the ground. On a practical note, it was difficult to get around in rural Idlib province without the kind of military protection they could provide.

On the way to the city, we passed through a village where we were joined by another car carrying a group of young men heading on to Aleppo in the morning. Most of them were in their early twenties. As we drove, shells exploded around us and sometimes we heard the roar of aircraft. My guides Maysara and Mohammed were quick to reassure me that we were fine, but it was still a few kilometres before we were out of danger.

There wasn't a single woman at the rally in Binnish, where I spotted banners that read *There is no god but Allah, and Mohammed is the messenger of God*. I found myself alone in a sea of men; they stared at me inquisitively, an uncovered female. Although most women in the conservative countryside wore a veil, there were also unveiled women in the region. In fact, before the war and the presence of ISIS (also known as Islamic State or ISIL) and other militant groups, it had been very normal to see uncovered women in Syria. I kept my head uncovered at the rally because I wanted to feel like I was in the land I knew and loved.

In spite of their curiosity, when I was introduced to some of them they were very polite. They chanted and clapped as they took part in the demonstration, and then a sheikh came out to preach. As we weren't going to leave town straight away, I took the opportunity to talk to some of the women who had been sitting in front of their houses watching the day's events.

'We used to take part in the demonstrations, too,' a woman told me, 'but now it's no longer possible. The men are afraid for us because of all the shelling and the snipers.'

Binnish was liberated on the ground, but remained betrayed by the sky, by the treachery of aircraft and tanks. The Syrian Army couldn't confront the rebels on the ground; after severe battles with the locals they didn't dare enter the town. So they came at night and at dawn, firing shells then fleeing. It was mostly the children, women and old people who died, and the locals and the battalions fought on tirelessly.

'This is our destiny,' I heard the young people say.

That evening in Binnish, we were invited to dinner, a lavish affair. I had been the only uncovered woman at the rally, and that was also the case in other towns and villages we went to, though I quickly learned to put on a headscarf so as not to draw unwelcome attention to myself. But when I met with rebels, like the men at this gathering, I sat with them without a veil, and there were some who wouldn't shake my hand. The conversation with them was usually very rational and secular, although they told me there were other battalions that wouldn't accept my presence unless I were veiled. Yet no one spoke about founding an Islamic state. The conversation was always about a civil state, a secular state. At that time, the number of jihadist battalions was still low. Generally speaking there weren't many battalions with Islamist attitudes and they weren't widespread; they only began appearing a few months before my arrival that August, but after each massacre their numbers increased. In Saraqeb at this time it was thought that only 19 of the 750 or so fighters were Arab mujahideen.

The dinner was held in a house set in the middle of an olive grove, and our hosts did their best to offer us their choicest pickings. The group commander was in his early thirties, a very handsome and quiet fellow, originally from the city. I was surprised by how mild-mannered and open-minded he and his fellow fighters were in conversation, and by their desire to discuss the problem of sectarianism and the pressing need for a solution. Our discussion that evening pivoted around several themes, including how important it was not to make way for a sectarian war.

'There have been violent outbreaks in response to the brutality of the regime,' one of the men told me, 'but it hasn't amounted to much, no more than a few isolated cases that were put back in line.'

A few days later the same man told me more, describing how the regime wanted to exacerbate religious differences. 'There's a young guy who's an Alawite who was murdered in retaliation for a massacre, and we spoke up against it. The regime hasn't yet finished what they want to achieve: a Sunni village hasn't yet attacked an Alawite village. This hasn't happened, and it's not going to happen, even if we have to pay the price with our lives. But we can't do anything about people's fury if their entire family is killed, or if their home is flattened. Time doesn't heal when it comes to that kind of anger!'

This young man was killed a few months later by masked mujahideen who were not Syrians.

During the meal that evening and throughout the rest of my stay I heard lots of detailed stories about gangs of mercenaries looting on behalf of the Free Army and kidnapping on behalf of the individual battalions within it. These mercenaries were hired by the battalions to help in their struggle against the regime, and they got involved in some of the skirmishes between armed groups, which sometimes flared up over quite trivial things. These feuds often started out as a personal dispute but spiralled out of control until members of a battalion ended up kidnapping people from the town in question and community leaders had to intervene to resolve the problem. My hosts talked about some of the mistakes they'd made along the way and how to bring the revolution back on track. Perhaps they didn't represent the full demographic spectrum across northern Syria, the provinces of Aleppo and Idlib and Hama, as there were those in the north who didn't think the revolution should be brought back on track, yet all of the battalions I talked to said similar things.

Likewise, I learned that funding and supplies represented a major problem. Time and again, I would hear from defected soldiers that they were struggling to get sufficient ammunition, unlike the new Islamist groups who were well equipped. These groups, which had recently emerged, were described as being extremist and as being well funded by certain states. The rebel battalions spread across northern Syria mostly said the same thing: that the poorly funded fighters were doing whatever they could to avoid having to join the Islamists, such as selling their belongings. They helped each other as if they were members of the same family and sometimes they even sold their wives' jewellery.

When the commander of one moderate militant group was raising money to buy rifles, a woman took off her wedding ring and handed it to him, but he refused to take it. 'If we stoop that low,' he told me despairingly, 'we'd be joining forces with the devil. We'd be on a par with Bashar al-Assad and his regime.' He was clearly angry and despondent. He and his group didn't have sufficient arms to sustain a wider campaign. They wanted to move the fighting away from Aleppo, but they felt helpless. And they had no backing. There were arms dealers out there trading, but the political opposition didn't care about equipping the armed battalions on the ground, and wasn't interested in forming a unified command structure. The official political opposition didn't involve itself in the fighting because it was weaker than the actual revolutionary movement, which had taken shape independently. This political opposition wasn't involved with the struggles of the people themselves. It had also occasionally been mired in the same sort of corruption associated with Assad's regime.

'Under bombardment and siege, with the hunger and the snipers and the arrests, everyone will turn to the well-funded groups for arms,' the commander told me.

'Is this what the regime wants?' I asked.

'Ask the top brass! The opposition big wigs with all their fancy education and culture – where are they?' he replied, angrily. 'The defected senior officers – what are they doing in Turkey? The real battle is here! We are dying every day, and we will continue to die. We have nothing more to offer than our souls, but we will not give up the struggle against the regime. Perhaps we will die, but our children and grandchildren will fight the Assad regime. And where is everyone else while all this is going on?'

A while later I was still listening to the fighters in Binnish tell me about the challenges they faced when we heard the sound of a huge explosion. About ten of us were sitting on the roof terrace overlooking the olive grove, and the moon was bright enough that we could already see quite clearly by it. Then the sky suddenly lit up.

'They're pounding the town of Taftanaz,' someone said, before picking up the thread of the conversation again and urging me to carry on eating. I ate in silence and could hear my heart thumping in fear.

'After you left they started bombing us,' one of them wrote to me later. 'Thank God you left in time.'

Back in Saraqeb, we sat, terrified, listening to the sound of the shelling. We had been up since five that morning. While there was no particular pattern to the timing of the shells during the day, at night it followed a precise routine. A shell was dropped somewhere between every half an hour and an hour. Around 130 shells had landed in the past three days. Manal, Maysara's wife, said that they hadn't had a good night's sleep since the start of the revolution; they would sleep one hour, then they were woken up again. Their eyes were glazed over.

When the shelling started in earnest, I had grabbed Aala and Ruha and quickly led them down to the shelter, with Aala clinging to my waist as we dashed down the stairs and Ruha clutching my arm. We made slow progress going downstairs because, with the girls hanging on to me on both sides, any uncalculated movement could have knocked the three of us over. The shelter was a spacious room formerly used by the family as a storeroom for tools and so on. One of the doorways had been sealed shut with plastic sheeting because, as Manal told me, shards from a shell had once fallen in from the sky. Mostly women and children sheltered here, with just a few men joining them. The rest of the men stayed upstairs with their elderly relatives.

'The old ladies can't move,' explained Ayouche's sister, the oldest daughter, 'and it'd take so long bringing them down that we'd risk getting hit by a shell. They're frail so they stay in their room, listening to the explosions. And when the shelling stops, we hear the wailing song of the muezzin announcing the death of someone in the community. The old ladies just stay up there staring at the little bit of sky they can see from the window.'

I was there three days before the grandmother even greeted me with a 'hello'; until then she was silent and wary of me. Later we became good friends.

Once we were down in the shelter, Aala, Ruha and their baby sister Tala found ways to entertain themselves, including discussing the various types of missiles and rockets. Aala held a piece of shrapnel in her hand which she kept as a souvenir.

Other families from the neighbourhood also came to the large shelter, as many didn't have one. The family whose home was in direct view of the sniper sought refuge here, too. I had seen their house: the walls were sprayed with holes from the sniper's bullets. The day I visited her, as we nervously dashed about, the mother told me that when she moved between rooms in her home and needed to cross the yard outside, she sometimes stood still for a moment, watching the sniper. She would pretend not to notice him, then run on to get a glass of water to drink, or get the children's dinner, or go to the toilet.

'It's like I'm playing a game with him, the son of a bitch,' she said, laughing.

She wore a floral headscarf and an ankle-length dress emblazoned with tropical plants. All the women here wore long dresses, but the mother who played games with the sniper had seemed unusually colourful in the context of her battered home.

The day I'd visited her had been like any other, with the dazzling sunshine and the silence interrupted only by the sound of shelling and sniper fire. Her young son had followed us about, clinging to the skirts of his mother's dress. He put his finger in his mouth and started to cry.

'Don't be scared! At least when they're shelling, the sniper stops and you can play,' the mother said with a laugh, as we crossed the threshold into her house. She winked at me. She picked her son up with one arm and seemed to toss him in the air as she embraced him. Her house was empty, a single rug covering the floor of one room.

This time, a new family of neighbours joined us in the shelter. Aala, who always insisted on telling a bedtime story before going to sleep, pointed them out.

'Their mum is on our side, but their father supports Bashar,' she explained. 'My dad is with the rebels. And those girls support Bashar, too, which means they're not on our side! But never mind. They have to hide with us so they don't die.'

This olive-skinned little girl, my Scheherazade, had the most beautiful brown eyes I have ever seen. Aala walked with a light bounce, combing her hair every hour and putting artificial flowers in her tresses, pink and yellow and red to match her clothes. She was constantly watching people, and seemed more delicate every time we went down to the shelter. She looked after her little sister Tala, who was sick with a strange hormonal imbalance brought on by the fear and anxiety. Aala watched all the children around her; she never let anyone near me, and she recounted for me, in intricate detail, the deaths of various neighbours and stories of young people who had disappeared from the town, one after another.

Shortly before the shelling paused for a while, she retrieved her souvenir piece of shrapnel from Tala. 'Little kids can't hold shells,' Aala warned her, calmly. Although she was no older than seven herself, when we heard shellfire again and huddled together, waiting, she rushed over to cuddle her sister and hold her tightly.

'Bashar's men all came looting – the soldiers and the secret police and the *shabiha*, the armed militias,' said a woman sitting in the corner of the shelter, her children heaped around her. 'They came in a truck packed full of ammunition, started killing people and then went back with the trucks packed full of stuff they'd stolen from us. They killed our children and robbed our homes, but why did they need to open my wardrobe and throw my dresses out in the courtyard, and wipe their arses with them and pee in our drinking cups? They didn't even spare my old wedding dress. It was smeared with shit.'

Nearby sat a woman approaching forty, who was massaging the back of a boy aged at least ten; the only son she had left at home, she explained, but he had a mental disorder. He did not speak, though his deep-blue eyes sparkled. During my visits to Syria, I saw a lot of mute children. This boy had the most beautiful tanned face, with saliva drooling from his open mouth. The woman said she had two other sons. She stared straight ahead as she told me her story, recounting in detail how they had dragged one of her boys from her arms. Her eyes grew bloodshot, and a single large tear fell, landing softly, as she told me she no longer cried.

She said, 'My brother was one of the first people to go out and support the revolution when it took off here. Everyone knew him as "Mohammed Haaf" – he was the hero of Saraqeb.' I remembered the name from the commander's story and the graffiti I had seen.

The woman continued, 'They went out on peaceful demonstrations at first, but the regime bombed us, and executed nine of our children right in front of everyone. My brother carried on fighting until his very last breath. Every day we were dying, and he'd say to me, "We won't die like cowards, we'll die in a way that's worthy of us." They killed my other brother, too. And they set fire to my house as we were trying to escape.

'Two of my brothers have been killed, and my son was dragged from my arms. I begged them to leave him be, but they ignored me. I still have another son alive, but he's off with the rebels. My children are gone. They've all gone, and only this little one is left,' she said, pointing to her boy, the sick child who looked at us curiously and laughed. 'As you see . . .' She continued, with a sigh, 'My son who's fighting for the revolution says he won't come home until Syria is free.'

She pulled out photos of her two martyred sons to show me. The first, his eyes green and his hair blond, was nineteen. Her fingers caressed the photo in a wave-like motion. The second picture was of a smooth-faced young man, with barely any fuzz of a moustache. Then she pulled out a picture of her brother Mohammed Haaf and held it up high. At the fourth image, a photograph of one of her boys, she paused. She bowed to beat her head against the ground.

'They snatched him from my arms. I clung on to him until they surrounded me and dragged him from my arms. I pleaded with them and begged them to leave him alone. I ran out after them, but they took him away. He was an activist in the revolution, and they killed him. He was just a kid . . .'


That morning, the shelter had reverberated with stories. More were to come in the evening when, after we returned from a tour of the villages, a rebel fighter from Jabal Zawiya visited, a commander of a military battalion. His eyes seemed to simmer with life, but now and then he appeared distracted, his eyelids drooped, and his face was overcome by a dreamy calm, almost peaceful were it not for his thoughts of death.

'They took my little brother,' he said. 'They took him to jail and tortured him. Apparently they told him I'd been killed, that they'd chopped up my body and chucked it up there on the mountain . . . They tortured him and burnt him alive . . .

'We're from the village of Ayn Larouz – six of the kids from our village have been killed. My brother was only sixteen – he was alive when they set him on fire. We've had sixteen martyrs in our village so far. My family have left our house and gone into hiding.

'At the beginning of the revolution and all the defections, I was in touch with an Alawite officer; he was my friend. I was also in touch with some non-commissioned officers and their families, and within a month from the beginning of the defections there were about 700 of us. This Alawite officer who'd been helping us helped four of the defecting soldiers to escape. To start with I was a bit scared of him, but then I plucked up the courage to get in touch with him, and he carried on helping us until the last moment.

'Communications between us were strictly confidential. We never talked on the phone. But suddenly he disappeared. I asked about him, and they said he had been transferred to Checkpoint K, but no one knew anything about him. The regime was afraid of potential defections, so they were always swapping officers round. But this one vanished without a trace. After that the army seized control of the entire region. They have since withdrawn tactically to Aleppo, but they'll be back.

'We build some of our weapons ourselves when we don't have enough. Once we tried making rockets from the component parts, and we managed it, but one of the rockets we'd made went missing after we launched it from a wheat field: it went up into the sky and just disappeared. We were afraid so we legged it. I guess it was a failed experiment.' He burst out laughing, his eyes vanishing into his face as he laughed. 'We ran like Tom and Jerry!' he continued. 'We were terrified it would land on one of our houses, even though we were quite far away, because it was sixteen kilos, and that means it lands with the force of sixteen tonnes! But we found it a few days later in the same field.

'We're teaching ourselves everything, and it's possible that at any moment we might blow ourselves up.' The young man fell silent, looking at everyone around him. There were many of us there, sitting in the cellar of the large family house, at least twenty rebels as well as the family and other guests, and all we could hear was the roar of the shelling.

The fighter wanted to carry on telling me his story, but the noise of the shells was never-ending, and Aala was getting cranky because it was long past her bedtime, but she wouldn't go to sleep until she had told me her story. It was a story about some neighbours who were killed, and she wanted to describe them at length one by one, trying to work out who was dearest to her heart.

'So are you going to die as well?' she asked, as we finally left the cellar.

'No, I'm not going to . . .' I began, with a laugh.

But before I could finish my sentence she shook her head, giggling at me. 'Hee hee hee, those people who died all said exactly the same thing!'

The next morning, I decided to keep that day's stories from Aala, and I asked Maysara and Mohammed not to talk about what was happening in front of her. Her eyes pursued me, as though she was aware of my betrayal. The young man who was accompanying us waited outside, and when I told her I was going to Mount Zawiya, in north-west Saraqeb, she frowned and turned her back on me, then turned back to shoot me a stern glare.

'We're going to go up Jabal Zawiya,' I told her. 'We need to visit wives of the martyrs there. We're going to see how they're living and what we can do to help them live on their own. I wish I could take you with us, but it's too dangerous while the shelling is going on.'

'I'm not scared!' she said.

'Girls don't go to places like that,' said her mother, settling the issue. Aala looked at me, quizzically.

I winked at her and whispered, 'I'm a man in disguise as a girl.' Aala laughed out loud. Then she winked back at me, and moved away from her mother to whisper in my ear. 'We'll talk tonight. I'll tell you what happens today.' She laughed and slammed the door shut behind her.

Travelling in two groups and two cars, we were scorched by the sun as we made our way through the countryside north of Aleppo, Idlib and Hama. En route, we stopped at armed checkpoints and headquarters. I was late to discover this part of Syria's identity: the geography of a country made of clay, blood and fire, and ceaseless surprises. There was dust everywhere, the air shimmered from afar as if on fire and an uneasy silence pervaded the villages. It was as though they were ancient abandoned sites: only rarely did you see another person, and all you heard was the occasional drone of aircraft circling in the air. Even so, we were further from the bombing now.

The desolate road, the hushed villages, the armed roadblocks in the midday sun, the salty sting in my eyes: it all brought me to the verge of tears, until I caught a glimpse of something moving. At the far end of a vast field, a set of sprinklers was spraying out water. So, life did go on in spite of everything! On the horizon, at the end of the line of sprinklers, I spotted a girl of no more than fifteen. My heart skipped a beat and I looked up at the sky; could she be targeted by a plane? Leaping about with excitement, she stuck her head under the water. Then she pulled off her hijab, drenched it and her hair, then wiped her face with the wet cloth.

Suddenly we came across a row of small domed mud-brick houses and a small truck passed by. A group of women and young girls were crammed in the back of the truck, standing upright in the blazing sunlight. Their veils concealed everything but their eyes: the best protection from the noon sun. Each woman had a hoe in her hand. The truck stopped and they all got out and walked over to the field. How could these areas be a breeding ground for jihadis and Salafists, when the very nature of the agricultural and pastoral life here required women to go out to work alongside the men?

Weary villages worn down by the raging sun and poverty. Their names had a special ring to them and amusing meanings: Rayyan (lush), Loofah, Ma'sarani (the juice seller), Qatra (a drop of water), Kafr Amim (the plentiful little place), Qatma (a morsel of food) . . . There were other villages that were defying death as it rained down from the heavens.

In the distance we spotted a hill: the site of the ancient 'Kingdom of Ebla' in the village of Tal Mardikh, where civilisation has flourished since the third millennium BC. One of the men told me that the village had been bombarded with several rocket-propelled missiles. How was it even possible to imagine a place such as this – one of the few places where humanity can trace its origins back to the beginnings of history – being destroyed? Here and elsewhere, traces of the successive civilisations that had populated Syria since the Stone Age were being wiped out, and Aramaic, Seleucid, Byzantine and Roman archaeological remains were being destroyed, along with artefacts from many other historical periods. Aleppo and Damascus, two of the oldest cities in the world, were being subjected to destruction while still populated, and now the end of this far-reaching history seemed suddenly to be in sight.

All signs of life disappeared again, but for the occasional flock of birds interrupting the silence. We had to pass by a number of battalions, as the men had no ammunition and wanted to stock up. It was mid-afternoon when we arrived at the headquarters of Ahrar al-Ashayer (the Free Clans Brigade). The men went off to negotiate the purchase of a quantity of arms. I stood by myself, watching them, my face lashed by the harsh sun. Bullets sparkled in the sunshine, and the men rolled them in their palms and spilled them through their fingers like lentils. There wasn't a huge amount, barely enough to defend a few houses, but they still needed to haggle. The cheaper the better, because they didn't have money to throw around.

We entered the building where four men were waiting for us, armed with Kalashnikovs. Their headquarters did not have a landline phone or Internet access, and mobile phones were out of action because the mobile reception for the whole region was cut off, although mobile phone communications were still being provided in some places by Syriatel, the company owned by Rami Makhlouf, a major business magnate and cousin of Bashar al-Assad. Landline phones worked in the province from time to time; nothing is ever predictable in war. For communications and other services, a sort of war economy had been established, dominated by brokers and intermediaries between Assad's men and the opposition. These middlemen ran a great deal of the services for the benefit of their personal wealth.

For months, activists such as these had been buying satellite Internet devices, which were not cheap, but were essential for organisations such as media offices in order to broadcast news and updates of what was happening.

This brigade occupied just two rooms. Armed with very rudimentary weapons, they were facing tanks and aircraft. And yet in spite of the odds, they were managing to put heavily armed military units out of action and force them to retreat. A dark-skinned young man sitting next to the group commander apologised for the mess in the room. There was a table and a few chairs, and the sun burst in. Their faces were tanned a deep dark-brown.

Among all the surprising things I learned in the scattered rural villages, the words of an army defector at this desolate battalion headquarters remain with me most strongly.

'My friend Mohammed and I signed up together,' the rebel soldier told me. 'We did everything together. In Homs we carried out a raid on one of the neighbourhoods. They tell us there are armed gangs and terrorists. So we go into a house and smash everything in sight, while the officer yells at us, cursing his head off. He wants one of us to rape a girl. The family is cowering in the next room. The officer orders us to stand to attention, and he starts inspecting us right up close, poking our faces with his finger, until he stops by Mohammed. He pats him on the back and orders him to enter the room. Mohammed's from the same village as the officer, in the forest region. But he steps back in panic, so the officer starts yelling all kinds of expletives at him.

"'What are you, a girl, for fuck's sake? You pussy!" Mohammed kneels down on the ground, he leans over and starts kissing the officer's shoes.

"'Please, sir," he begs him. "*Ya sidi* – sir – I can't do it. Please, sir, don't make me do it."

'So the officer kicks him over, and then really starts laying into him, booting him over and over. He grabs Mohammed's trousers by the waistband and screams in his face.

"'I'll slice off your dick!" My friend starts to cry at this point – oh, if only you knew Mohammed! He never cried, he was fearless, but I saw his tears that day – he was bawling like a child and I saw snot drip down to his mouth. He was pleading with the officer not to make him do it. He was my friend and we shared so many secrets with each other. I knew he had a girlfriend. But then the officer grabs Mohammed's crotch.

"'I'll show you how to do it, you fucking pussy! You want me to show you how?" And that's when Mohammed lashes out: he kicks him and launches himself on him with all his weight. Man, he's strong and he managed to knock the officer down to the ground. He really lays into him, giving him a sound beating. And then he stops and throws down his gun. The officer gets up straight away and shoots Mohammed. He killed him. I saw it with my own eyes. And do you know which part of Mohammed's body the officer chose to aim at?'

A moment's silence, before he gestured, without any shame, towards his crotch.

'He ordered another of our friends to go in and rape the girl, and he went into the room in silence, and we heard her scream, and we heard her mother and her siblings screaming, because they were all crammed into the next room. Their father was a dissident; he'd been killed two days earlier. That was the day I decided to defect and, by God, not a single day passes without me thinking of Mohammed. He's here in my heart. I've kept his letters to his girlfriend at my parents' house, and if I survive I'll send them to her. I will. It's an oath around my neck – if I manage to stay alive.'

He echoed those words 'if I manage to stay alive' as we felt the blistering heat of the midday sun amidst the thunder of the falling shells. As we left the headquarters behind, when we were some distance away, his story and the look in his weary eyes were still firmly inscribed in my mind.

The next time I visited Syria, I learned that the battalion's headquarters had been bombed.

From the sun-scorched headquarters, we hurried onwards to reach the Ammar al-Muwali clan in Daqra, one of the families based in the rural province around the city of Maarat al-Numan. That's where we met one of the clan leaders, and my eyes were opened to their poverty, as well as their generosity, their sense of honour and their courage. They were concerned about protecting their granaries from looting, so their people did not starve.

We talked with a group of young men, and with Abdul Razak, the leader of the clan, about the importance of having a civil state, of one Syria, where freedom was the only sect. Abdul

Razak was in his mid-fifties, and he was doing his best to resolve a kidnapping case. While he spoke to us, his wife prepared lunch in the kitchen, and her thirteen-year-old son served the guests.

A plane flew overhead. I went outside with everyone to look at it. Fear hung over them like a shadow. This was the moment, as I looked up, that I realised the meaning of exile and of home. Even though I had illegally crossed my country's borders, only at precisely that moment did I truly understand that this was my homeland that I was staring at, with a plane flying overhead dropping its bombs down on it. I looked it in the eye, unwaveringly and directly, without fear. As I watched it pass above me, I thought of when I sat in the Place de la Bastille, in central Paris, sipping my coffee under a gentle sun, with lovers on my left exchanging kisses, when a sparrow landed on my knee making me leap to my feet in panic – that wasn't home, that was exile.

We went back inside to the hospitality of the clan.

'As you see, we're standing up to injustice here,' said the clan leader. 'All we demand is justice in a country which is ruled by law. Yes, we are clans and we are armed, but to start with we went out to protest peacefully. However, if they want to kill our children and our women, then we will fight them. By God Almighty, I'm an educated man, I've been to university, but to me, even the tiny fingernail of one of our children is as important as the entire world, and I will not stand by while they trample on my dignity or the dignity of any Syrian.

'*Wallahi*, by God, you are like my sister,' he said, turning to me, 'and if anyone touches a hair on your head it's like they're touching my sister. You are with us against injustice and against the tyranny of the House of Assad. We are all Syrians standing up against injustice . . .'

The leader spoke at length and I paid close attention to his words, which were intelligent and eloquent, simple and profound.

We laughed at his stories of how much wealth he had lost since the beginning of the revolution, and how he had shared it with his people. He spoke proudly about his brother, a military commander who had joined the battle against Assad.

That evening I returned home in silence, my face burnt from the desert sun. I found Ayouche waiting for us with the women and children. Aala sat herself in my lap, where she combed my hair, and tried to trick me into telling her about my day and the stories I had heard. I was her plan for a future story, and only she and I understood what we wanted from each other. She wanted to turn me into a narrative, a bedtime tale to tell future guests. She said she was storing up all the stories around her. But there was no time to finish the secret game between me and this seven-year-old storyteller. The bombing started again. I quickly picked her up and grabbed Ruha's hand and, terrified, we ran down into the shelter. The noise of the explosions was head-splitting. While the old ladies stayed upstairs, confined to their rooms, staring out of the window, the family from the neighbouring rooms joined us, and there downstairs, under intense shellfire, I called Aala over again.

'Come here, and I'll tell you my story,' I said. Magical words which made Aala's ears perk up. Her eyes twinkled in the dark, and her elder sister Ruha clung to me, staring at me with a look that was both inquisitive and contented. Both girls looked deep into my eyes. The shelter seemed all-encompassing and the roar of shelling never-ending, and I began to tell them my story.

'I haven't always been like you see me now. Originally, in my previous life, I was a gazelle who was badly hurt and whose heart burst with pain.' They both glared at me, disappointed.

'Liar!' they shouted.

But then we laughed . . . we laughed long and hard, and I tried to persuade them that I really was a gazelle. I told them we were going to have to sleep here on the mat, and they had no choice but to listen to the end of my story, because otherwise I was going to go to sleep as I was exhausted. The mood turned sombre, and the whole family was huddled together in fear, but once the girls gave in I finished my story from where I left off.

'The gazelle's heart was in great pain, and a drop of blood fell onto the green grass . . . and I was born!'

I dozed off as I reached the end, the words starting to feel heavy on my tongue. I gazed at them like a ghost, and the women spread a thin blanket over my back before I was out for the count.

I had been planning to embark on a new novel on my return to France. But just as I was leaving Syria at the end of this first trip, something changed. A minor incident set me on a different course and compelled me to compose this testimony in the book you are reading now. On our way back to Turkey, just before we reached the border, on the road from the town of Sarmada, we met two young men, militants, who made me grab my pen and start capturing their words in a small notebook.

It was my final day, a few hours before my last farewells, and we were at a checkpoint set up by the Farouq Brigades. A fighter with bright eyes and honey-coloured hair took a deep breath and told me how he had deserted the 'special units' of the Syrian Army, because he refused to kill.

'I mean, why would I throw myself into the jaws of death?' he asked. 'Who wants to die? No one! But we were already dead and we wanted to live.'

The sky was blue. Nothing clouded our mood, not bullets, not roadblocks, not all the wrecked buildings lining the sides of the road. The town of Sarmada was only a short distance behind us, its walls emblazoned with the flags of the revolution.

'We just want a civil state,' echoed another, slightly older man. And that was the moment I decided I needed to write about my return to Syria.

'Fuck the officers, they're all bloody Alawites,' the younger man added.

'No, not all of them,' the older one retorted, glaring at him.

I listened as the first man continued the story of how he had absconded from the army. His friend came over and whispered something in his ear. Suddenly, the youth with the lively eyes looked at me, embarrassed. He let his gun slump to the ground and dropped his gaze. I caught it again: his eyes were nervous now, as he turned his face away, his weapon resting on the ground.

The sky was unchanged. It was still blue, and the rocky hill, which we had left behind us, followed us with its silent stare. I heard a faint rustling sound and the young man turned to face me. He was biting his lips. His voice trembled as he spoke – and this was the same man who just a moment ago had been brandishing his rifle and venting his anger to the sky.

'Forgive me, ma'am. I didn't realise.'

His face reverted to a kind, forgiving expression, and the armed fighters under the bridge looked at us inquisitively. A white flag fluttered near them, bearing the words 'There is no god but Allah, and Mohammed is the messenger of God.' Two of the rebel fighters had long beards. The sky was still blue, but this soldier seemed childlike as he came closer and spoke to me, hesitantly.

'I don't hate anyone,' he stammered. 'But that lot of Assad's are dogs who want to make us kill innocent people . . . Forgive me, ma'am.'

The older combatant stood at his side. His eyes had an angry glint.

'We just want a civil state,' he reiterated. 'I'm in the Farouq Brigades and I want a civil state. I'm a college student, doing a business degree. I'm in my second year.'

We couldn't stay long to listen to their stories.

'Don't worry,' I said. 'It's fine.' But the young man was determined to explain that he didn't mean to offend me.

'I'm not an Alawite,' I told him, before we set off. 'And you're not a Sunni. I'm Syrian and you're Syrian.' He looked at me in astonishment.

'It's true,' I said. 'We're just Syrians.'

I don't know what else it was about this last roadblock that compelled me to start writing about my home country, apart from the impact of that young dissident soldier reverting to childhood right there before my eyes. This soldier who dropped his weapon to the ground to apologise for an offence he didn't even commit, when he realized that the woman standing before him was from the same sect as the army officers he rebelled against.

Back in the car, as we left the Farouq Brigades checkpoint behind us, my brow was knotted into a frown as I thought about my parting remark. Just who was I trying to reassure? Who was trying to build a state out of blood and fire: this defected soldier who'd turned into a child before my eyes, or those murderers, al-Assad's henchmen? They had looked at me in amazement when I said we are all just Syrians. They laughed at me; they didn't have a clue what I was talking about.

Where do fighters like them get their strength from? Which of us is more a stranger to the meaning of life – them or us? Who gets closer to the essence of life? Those who live their lives in the presence of death and who laugh in its face?

# The SECOND CROSSING

## February 2013

In my mind, I hold a portrait of Syria, but it is no ordinary image. It shows a dismembered collection of body parts, the head missing and the right arm dangling precariously. Then you notice a few drops of blood slowly dripping from the frame, disappearing as they are absorbed by the dusty soil below. This is the catastrophe that Syrians deal with every day.

I realised something as I passed through Istanbul Ataturk Airport Terminal 1 en route to the city of Antakya, the ancient city of Antioch, twelve miles from the Syrian border: despite the familiarity of the journey, I found I was unsettled by this recurring vision of dismemberment, which seemed to fill every inch of the airport. There, I saw bearded young men with sunglasses everywhere I looked. Some had dyed their curious beards red in honour of the Prophet Mohammed, but had shaved their moustaches. They looked troubled, as though they were in a hurry. I didn't know if I would see them again, but I kept trying to catch up with them to find out who they were and where they were from. I could tell one was Yemeni and another was Saudi. They all avoided looking at women. I sat down next to them to hear what they were talking about, but they remained silent, waiting like me to board the plane. The airport was bursting with people, all pacing about anxiously, their minds set on salvation. In both Antakya and Istanbul airports, the lost look in the eyes of Syrians betrayed their sense of foreboding, of the imminence of tragedy.

I lifted my small bag onto my back. I was keen to travel light as far as possible when crossing the border, so I chose to make do with a backpack and few clothes. We boarded the plane to Antakya. There were two Yemenis in the seats in front of me and across the aisle were some Syrian men and women. Most of the passengers on the plane were Syrians and other Arabs. My gaze sank into the window at my side, which became my permanent refuge while I travelled. Here was an entire world limited only by a window frame. A universe concentrated within this rectangle of emptiness. All I longed to do was to float, to swim through into boundless, white nothingness. To drift through it, under it, over it, floating ever further from geography, dimensions blurring till a skyscraper was the size of a blade of grass, colours fading in the infinite blindness of outer space, leaving behind all these bearded faces. I would merge into a flowing stream of emptiness, living nowhere, without borders to define me.

The Turkish border town of Reyhanli, which I would be passing through again on this second crossing, is a fifty-minute drive from Antakya, but it is no mere backwater. It has grown into a small city, from a place where peace and quiet reigned before the revolution. A focal point for Syrian and Lebanese tourists, it has long prospered from smuggling between Turkey and Syria. But these days there is no room for peace or quiet, or good old-fashioned trade and smuggling, as the once sleepy town has been turned into a place where every now and then a shell is dropped; where the hustle and bustle has become suffocating overcrowding; where the locals are overwhelmed by invading swarms of Syrian refugees fleeing the bombing – refugees who aren't counted in the official figures because they live outside the camps. Reyhanli is at once a flourishing place of growth and construction, and a site of ruin and destruction. Here, in this small patch of land adjacent to Syrian territory you'll find all the parties currently engaged in the conflict. The regime has its own men on the ground, conducting its operations and trying to infiltrate the networks of rebels and activists. It's no secret: everyone knows you have to tread carefully here.

Small-time traders benefit from this limbo between life and the after-life, turning the business of death into a tradable commodity alongside the artefacts of life. The town teems with the impoverished and destitute searching for scraps, begging in the streets for their daily bread. There has also been a smaller influx of more well-to-do asylum seekers, and here, too, there are those who are loyal to Bashar al-Assad.

In Reyhanli, I met up with my travelling companions, Maysara and a Lebanese journalist called Fida Itani, and we set off together. We were heading to a border village, but our car moved at a snail's pace through the traffic and crowds. It looked like everything you could possibly want to buy was on sale here, including uniforms for the Free Army, revolutionary banners, trinkets, clothes and household items. Groceries and canned foods were spread out on the pavements, with old men, young men and children – mostly Syrians – hawking their wares at the tops of their voices. In fact, I don't think we saw a single Turkish seller, only Syrians, and the customers who came away with their arms heavy with bargains were also Syrian.

The Turks grumble about the influx of Syrian refugees, but deep down it is a different story: the cash that comes with them lines Turkish pockets nicely. Many Turks have benefited from the rush of capital flowing in from Syria. They rent out their shops and homes, hike their prices and see a doubling in sales. Here, in Reyhanli, I saw shops bearing the names of Syrian towns and villages written in Arabic script alongside shops with Turkish names, as if a piece of Syria had been uprooted and planted here, like another mauled body part, subsumed into the city's sewers and muddy irrigation channels. Lost and displaced – just like everything else in this war.

A child stood to the right of our car, no older than ten, his arms laden with goods. Children ran over to flaunt their wares; they must have left school and home and their childhood for good. The lucky ones still lived with their families, but most of them were orphans who had crossed the border and survived here on the streets.

On the pavement on the other side of the road were some men from the Free Army. We didn't know which battalion, but it looked as though they had just arrived and were waiting for others to join them. Their weapons weren't on display here, as they are within Syria itself. From their pale faces, shaggy beards and sleep-deprived eyes it was clear that they badly need a few days off for rest and recuperation, and that they were only in the town because there was something they needed to do. A car stopped next to them and a young man got out, or rather they lifted him out of the car. He had lost an arm and a leg. They changed cars, then one of them yelled, '*Yallah!* OK, go! Quick!'

'I'll drop you off at the sheep gate,' said our driver as we headed on to the border.

The border villages are spread over an area of six to ten square kilometres along the Turkish side, and are inhabited by nomadic Bedouin who, until the revolution, lived off smuggling between Turkey and the Syrian city of Idlib as well as raising livestock and growing crops. Today, these villagers, who speak fluent Turkish and Arabic with a Bedouin dialect, are closely involved in smuggling to and from places such as Atma, the village nearest to one of the most important and most desperate of the Syrian refugee camps.

To the south of the border villages are the mountains that divide the two countries, where, with the help of a network of relatives, the Bedouin now operate an industry of human trafficking, smuggling people through the hills. The Bedouin themselves form a physical network of contact points along the border, some standing at the top of the hills, others in the valleys. They know all the gaps in the border, all the openings in the barbed wire, through which you can slip into Syria; and you are accompanied right up until the point of crossing. They have a solid relationship with the Turkish Gendarmerie and communicate by mobile phones or, if they are in line of sight, by shouts and signals agreed in advance. They are lean, dark-skinned, light of foot and quick; they possess a mysterious ability to disappear among the trees, to merge with the land they know so well.

The car had brought us down a tangle of narrow, muddy lanes. The 'sheep gate', as this unofficial crossing point was referred to, was a grim hamlet. The houses were bare and behind them were sheep pens. Despite the cold, children were jumping about almost naked. When we got out of the car, a tanned young man was waiting for us. I had expected this crossing to be like last time: an exhausting sprint between two fences, then waiting for the breeze to pick up at nightfall, when it would be time to cross. But Maysara had told me that the place where we crossed before was now under observation so we couldn't go that way, especially after the recent bombings on the Syrian–Turkish border.

Ahead were some low green hills where we could see cars parked on both sides of the border. Stretching into the distance were queues of people waiting. We had to walk around a hill nearby and on to another location. I put my bag on my back and we set off along the track, rivulets of dirty water impeding our progress. There were three of us accompanied by our guides. We had only gone a short way before a gendarme appeared. We ran.

'Don't worry,' said our trafficker in accented Arabic.

Then a military vehicle appeared from the right and advanced towards us. The trafficker shouted and turned back. We fled after him and retraced our steps back to the lane where we had set out.

'We'll go and have a cup of tea at mine, and wait till later to cross,' the trafficker said.

So we went to his house, back down the muddy alleys, with the stench of decay and animal dung wafting all around us. The Bedouins' concrete houses resemble their tents: the same colours, the same look of austerity, transience. There were still no women to be seen, only men and children, and no one dawdled.

When we set out again, a few minutes before we reached the border we were joined by the other group that was to cross with us. Of our band of twenty, I was the only woman. Three traffickers accompanied us, and among the men who had just arrived I noticed the Yemeni and the Saudi who had been on my flight from Istanbul to Antakya. They looked ready for action. I moved towards them, keeping a cautious distance away, still hoping to eavesdrop on their conversation. For a moment I wondered about saying something to them, like, 'What are you doing in my country?' But I remained silent. The past two years had taught me to keep quiet. Silence is an opportunity to give meaning to the things around us, to watch and reflect. It gives things the chance to express themselves; even if it's not without ambiguity, silence often creates the space for meaning to emerge.

The Yemeni and Saudi were travelling light, equipped with all they needed for their deaths – which was what they were heading for. As we set off, I tried to catch up with them.

'Hey, brother, you didn't tell me you'd brought a woman with you,' said one of the traffickers, annoyed, as he looked over in our direction. 'Come over here,' he said, glancing at me. 'This way, it's easier.'

We headed into a small wheat field, our feet tramping over mud and the tender green leaves scattered here and there from the olive trees growing nearby. The older of our traffickers watched me nervously. I had hidden my face and head under a black veil and dark glasses. I picked up my pace and caught up with the group, and as I got closer I started to overtake them all. I found myself getting tired, but I refused to let him blame me for slowing everyone down. I walked quickly and once I'd got ahead, even the older trafficker had to ask me to wait. I stopped where I was, waiting for the others to catch up, and when they did I walked alongside them and looked pointedly at him. I took off my glasses and glared, but since I could clearly keep up, the trafficker didn't grumble again about there being a woman in the group, which he had expected would spell trouble and slow progress.

Of course, whenever I travelled back to Syria, most men couldn't resist mentioning the fact that I'm a woman, and that this was no place for a woman. The fighters I was surrounded by this time were tall and thickset, with strong, clear eyes and long beards. They would never turn their heads to look at or say a word to a girl. Yet what many might interpret as signs of manhood and bravery seemed to me like an indifference about life and death. They were searching for the gateway that would lead to the eternal paradise that had been promised them. Rather than be inspired by them, I could only pity them.

We paused a while when we heard gunshots. The border guards were firing bullets into the air; we all knew they were just trying to scare us. One of the traffickers with us had just concluded negotiating with the Turkish Gendarmerie – par for the course, as the gendarmes must have noticed the militants with their obvious fundamentalist appearance. The gendarmes could be harsh if they wanted to, but it wouldn't usually go beyond a rough beating and almost certainly wouldn't go as far as directly opening fire. That in itself was reassurance enough for the traffickers and the trafficked alike.

Ahead of us lay a steep incline. We spread out over several paths to tackle it, the olive trees giving us cover. The foreign fighters were further from us now and there were just three of us with one of the traffickers. The climb was hard going and I moved aside, not wanting to get in anyone's way. I bent my knees, arching my back as I leaned forward, close to the ground as if crawling on all fours. So here we are, I thought, little more than animals. If only we could rely on the instinct for survival and protection of our species that is so strong in other creatures.

Fida Itani, our Lebanese friend, suggested I slow down so I didn't get tired.

'Listen,' I said, my voice trembling, 'if I don't keep going, I'll slip back down into the abyss.' He laughed.

Then Maysara came over and took my bag for me, and we ran to the top. I didn't even turn round when I heard shouting behind me. I could hear my heart beating. The air whipped my lungs. The ground was muddy and the soil on the mountain red and fertile. At what we supposed was the summit, the scene was different: the hill culminated in a kind of broad cliff edge with a road winding steeply down between the trees. We saw a car waiting for us, but at that moment a group of Turkish gendarmes emerged from among the olive trees and came towards us. Police patrols were dotted around the area and could appear suddenly out of nowhere. The gendarmes searched our bags and spoke to one of the traffickers.

Their search completed, we crossed the border. It was not clearly demarcated: there was no fence to crawl through or barbed wire to avoid, and the appearance of the gendarmes had been the only hint that this was an international boundary. The points where people were trafficked across the Syrian–Turkish border were usually like this, I discovered, and represented opportunities for moneymaking, especially as the number of jihadist fighters wishing to be smuggled into the country was on the rise.

Here our groups went their separate ways. The fighters began to disappear – there was another group waiting for them. The man accompanying us told me they were off to join the battle, that there was a French guy among them, of Tunisian origin, and that they were most likely heading for Aleppo now. My guide, who insisted on anonymity, told me they would probably go to join Jabhat al-Nusra (the Nusra Front), a new faction made up of young men with long beards. The existence of the Nusra Front hadn't become public knowledge until recently; early on, they had been an invisible underground movement, and their presence hadn't been tolerated in the villages.

'You'll notice now that they've become much more powerful and more widespread,' said Fida. 'The next phase is going to be harder, because these groups will have more influence and will emerge in a stronger and more violent form. We're going to see videos of floggings and beheadings.'

Gunfire rang out again from the border villages and the Salafists vanished into the trees. The files of Syrians had formed meandering threads, like cracks on an old oil painting, with columns heading in various directions. When the sound of bullets rang out we scattered like a herd of frightened animals fleeing from a huntsman.

The hills were behind us and before us rose olive groves and plains. All around there were signs of drought; even the olive trees planted at the sides of the road looked withered. The houses disappeared as we meandered along twisting roads. There were hardly any signs of life in the landscape; only a few cars passed and in the distance we could see the occasional village.

The city of Binnish was empty. Not crowded with demonstrators like the last time I'd come here. Since then, it had been bombed by al-Assad's MiG aircraft and abandoned by its residents. Only very few remained. The newly confident Nusra Front had taken over and many people in the city had joined them. The movement now controlled state property, but it had been interfering in people's lives and had declared wearing trousers a heresy, even for men, promoting instead the 'Afghan style' of dress. The military infrastructure had also changed. There were now fewer roadblocks.

'O God, what else do we have but You?' Maysara shouted, when we drove past Taftanaz airport. 'O God, how much life has been lost ... how much life has been lost ... This is where Amjad Hussain was killed.'

I had known Amjad, a battalion commander in Saraqeb. A young man of twenty-five. He was courteous, and didn't look you in the eye when he was talking to you; and he was furious about the turn the revolution had taken, the mess it had descended into. He was a conservative Muslim, but he wanted a secular state. He had died in the battle for Taftanaz airport. Many of the young people I'd met previously had since died. We remembered them one by one, as we traversed the villages on the way back to Saraqeb. We passed fields of broad beans and green plains dotted with stone-built villages. The road was muddy and pitted by exploded bombs and shells, making it a challenging drive.

'Since you were last here, the regime has seized Idlib,' said Maysara, 'and it's become isolated from the surrounding countryside. The battalions are engaged in combat as we speak.

There are more thieves in the revolution now than rebels. It's one family against another. Mercenaries against mercenaries. O God, what else do we have but you?'

The house felt empty without my little enchantress, whose company I'd got so used to. Aala and her siblings had left Saraqeb and were now settled in Antakya, over the border, although Maysara still came back to visit their hometown from time to time. He explained to me that the fear of shells and of indiscriminate death had compelled him to take his immediate family to Turkey. So, this time round, the house would be home to me, Maysara's sister Ayouche, my hosts Abu Ibrahim and his elegant wife Noura, and the old ladies. Members of the extended family, including two of the sisters and their young children, regularly came and went; the building was busy with different branches of the family and kinsfolk displaced from their homes. Some had had their houses broken into and vandalised, others were in range of the shelling, or fell within the demarcation area, which acted as a buffer zone between the opposing sides. Some houses were located under the gaze of snipers and some had become hideouts for dissidents. A lot of people had opened up their homes in this way to relatives, friends and acquaintances. Ayouche, too, had given up the basement of her apartment building, in which her own flat had been burnt out, to accommodate a displaced family.

The next morning, Ayouche and I set off in her car to visit the family living in the basement under her flat and to see various places in Saraqeb that had been shelled. A police officer was directing the traffic, so an attempt was being made to bring order to the town, though it was difficult and they were struggling. Most of the roads looked very different now, while many had been destroyed completely. The biggest change was the increase in the number of houses that had been damaged or flattened by bombing, and the fact that there were so few people about. The city looked lifeless and deserted. There were construction sites everywhere as they tried to repair buildings that had been hit. On walls, I glimpsed graffitied lines from the poetry of Mahmoud Darwish and for the first time I saw written next to them sentences glorifying the militant groups Nusra Front and Ahrar al-Sham. These two groups, while separate from the Free Army, coexisted rather than cooperated with each other. One of the phrases, in bold letters, read: 'Nusra Front and Ahrar al-Sham: our beating hearts.'

These days, police salaries were paid for by the armed battalions. The police ticketed traffic offences and, where possible, the battalions enforced the penalty. Ahrar al-Sham was so deeply entrenched in the social fabric that they even owned a bakery, which was both a source of funding for them and a means of control over people in need of supplies. The Nusra Front held sway over the Sharia Court and its judges and clerics, where the law that was upheld was Islamic religious law. The security forces consisted of several battalions, including Suqoor al-Sham (Falcons of the Levant Brigade), Dera' al-Jabal (Shield of the Mountain) and the Shuhada Suriya (Martyrs of Syria).

Ayouche said she wouldn't show me the whole town because the shelling was relentless and it was too dangerous to be out and about in the car. But she still stopped in front of each bombed-out house and told me its story. Houses with no doors, houses without roofs or walls, mountains of piled-up rocks.

'This is where Abu Mohammed died with his children,' she told me. 'And that one,' she continued, pointing to another house, 'was where some of our relatives lived. Their young son died. And that house was completely bombed out – the whole family was killed.'

We stopped in front of the house and I took some pictures, then we headed back to the car. Saraqeb looked even worse than I remembered, with signs of destruction all around.

As we arrived at the basement refuge of the displaced family who were being sheltered by Ayouche, we stopped to talk briefly to her neighbours, but then a plane flew overhead and we had to make a run for it. The cellar was a spacious hall, its sides lined with bedding laid out in groups for the children, women and men of the family, each group in a separate corner. The family matriarch was a beautiful woman, curvaceous with reddish brown hair. She was surrounded by her four daughters, two of whom were studying at university. The eldest was married and had her three children with her. Other relatives sat here and there. Most of their possessions had been lost. There was just a rug and a few teacups, and a small cage holding two little birds.

Suddenly the ceiling began to vibrate and we heard a loud noise. We froze in terror. The plane had dropped its bomb on the house next door. It was only a few metres away; we had been talking to the women of that house moments before as they cleaned up after yesterday's bombardment, washing the floor with water and picking up shards of glass after an explosion that had claimed the life of one of their boys.

After the second bomb, we stayed in the basement, waiting. The bombs were being dropped in the vicinity of a tank parked behind the neighbour's house, left there by one of the battalion commanders. That was what the regime always did: they bombed civilian homes where the rebels were based, to undermine their popular support. As I asked the mother of the family how they had been forced from their home, I shuddered as the force of the exploding bomb sprinkled peeling paint down on our heads like snowflakes. The other women listened with me as the mother hurtled through her story.

'The planes have been bombing us since the beginning of the revolution,' she said. 'Our village, Amenas, is next to the brick factory, which was turned into a major barracks for the army and their mercenaries, the *shabiha*. A lot of people from the village were killed when they bombed our neighbour Naasan's house. A shell hit his olive grove and killed the workers, his wife and son. He was out at the time fetching water and when he got back he found a massacre in his garden.

'The *shabiha* raided another family's olive garden, and they all disappeared. The men of the village found the entire family massacred: the mother, the daughters, the brother, a young boy and a daughter-in-law. Sometimes the *shabiha* went out in gangs. Once, they caught one of our sons and we found him with his eyes gouged out and his fingers chopped off, but he wasn't dead. There was another man who they grabbed and sat on a brazier of burning coal. His backside was burnt to a crisp like roasted meat. His wife ran away . . .

'I didn't want to leave our home, but the army entered Mastuma, a neighbouring village, and warned anyone from the Free Army to leave immediately because the *shabiha* were coming. When they entered Mastuma, they massacred entire families. A mother was weeping for her son because they'd slaughtered him before her eyes, so they killed her too because she was crying!

'I hid my daughters so they wouldn't be raped. Then a rocket fell on the house of one of my brothers, and we thought he must have been blown up, but he came out from under the rubble, shouting: "He who gave me my soul shall be the one to take it away!" How I laughed!

'We paid someone seven thousand five hundred lira to help us get out and we fled in the night. There were long lines of other people fleeing. They were barefoot, some of them half naked, and the shelling didn't stop.

'In the night-time, the rebels came to us and brought us food for *suhoor*, the meal before daybreak, as it was Ramadan. Along the way, one of the women gave birth. We were all homeless, my husband and his eight brothers and sisters – everyone had to go. Then we learned our house had been obliterated. We have nothing left.'

Another deafening noise, another bomb. The woman stopped in mid flow and more flakes of paint trickled down. The basement was damp and full of cracks, and as the building trembled white chunks of plaster fell down on our heads. The birds thrashed about in their cage.

'They can sense the danger,' said one of the older daughters, putting her arms around the cage. Then she opened the cage door and took out the two birds, hugging them close to her chest. Ignoring the shelling nearby, she carried on talking instead of her mother.

'Will you write down everything I tell you?' she asked.

'Yes,' I promised. 'I will.'

She was a beautiful young woman, slender, about twenty years old, with bright green eyes and rosy red cheeks. She wore a simple, coloured headscarf. Her fingers were delicate and soft. She stood up. Her siblings huddled around her. Still clutching the birds, she held out a hand above my head.

'Do you swear by God that you'll tell the world what I have to say?' she asked.

'I swear.'

'Swear by the thing you hold most dearly deep in your heart.'

I swore quietly, and as her palm came down on my head it felt like a rock might have shattered from the force.

'Write about the village of Amenas . . . the place where I was born.'

She told me she loved to draw and write poetry, and retrieved a notebook, which she opened. Then she started to read out her diary, and I began to make notes.

'This happened on the 5th of January 2013. We heard about the deaths of six girls and a young man and his wife after they'd been kidnapped. On the same day another family was killed – they had gone out for the olive harvest – and they killed a woman and her two sons. And in our village, they kidnapped Abu Amer's family and started to torture them; then they killed them all in the same way – shooting them in the head. Amer's wife was nearly nine months pregnant. She gave birth while it was happening. When the men from our family went to look for Abu Amer's family, they found her and the baby both dead, along with other bodies scattered among the olive trees,' said the girl with the almond-shaped eyes, staring at me sternly. She glanced down at her notebook, while I waited for her to continue.

'It was the *shabiha* who did it, but they were driving cars with "Free Army" written on them. But we know it was the government thugs, the *shabiha*. Before they left, they sabotaged the land and uprooted trees, they destroyed everything in their path, and took pictures of the corpses and all the destruction they were responsible for. Then they published the images online, saying it was the Free Army who had done it.' She paused. 'Shall I carry on?' she asked me eagerly, but shyly.

'Yes . . . please,' I replied.

Her eyes blazed as she continued: 'On the 12th of January, at two thirty-five, we were at the village of Qabeen, where some relatives of ours live. Since leaving Amenas, we'd wandered for days without sleep. On the night we left, we heard on the ten o'clock news that they were going to bomb our village and annihilate the revolutionaries. A convoy of tanks and soldiers would be passing through on the way to Taftanaz, the airport blockaded by the rebels. So we left at eleven o'clock the same evening. We were scared. We piled some of our stuff into a small car that had three wheels. When we passed the village of Sarmin, we followed the highway for a long time, but the car's engine finally gave out, so we had to push it along the road. Stranded in the middle of the road, we went to the next village. We headed to the first house we saw, but they wouldn't open the door and asked us to leave. Then we went to the second house, and they wouldn't open up either. When we came to the third house, they welcomed us and said we could spend the night with them, but my mother refused and said she didn't feel comfortable, and asked my father if my brother could take us to his friends in Kafr Amim. It was past 1 a.m., and all around us dogs were barking. I was terrified. Total darkness and the sound of barking dogs chasing us! At two in the morning, we arrived in Kafr Amim where we went from house to house.'

She didn't stop talking, ignoring the noise of the shelling, and I didn't stop writing.

'On the 13th of February, a month later, we still had no idea where we were going. Every night we slept somewhere new, anywhere to escape the shells and the missiles. With all that moving about I ended up getting to know the surrounding villages like the back of my hand.'

She looked at me, still holding her notebook and clutching the birds against her chest: they both peered down at me.

'And then?' I asked.

Next to us, her mother poured tea, muttering all the while, 'In the name of the Lord . . . We've no power or strength except through God.'

'On the 15th of February,' she continued in a cheerful voice, 'we reached Saraqeb at exactly ten minutes past three. God protect you,' she said suddenly, looking at Ayouche, 'and keep you safe like you saved us!' Then she said, 'That was the day I was supposed to go to university to sit an exam, but the roads were blocked and it wasn't safe. I've just got two more days to tell you about. It's fine if you want to miss them – I don't want to waste your time.'

'No, I don't want to leave anything out,' I said, transfixed by her gaze, her eyes brimming with tears. She opened her notebook again and carried on reading.

'This is our second day in Saraqeb. The 16th of February. Ayouche came and made a note of what we needed, and then a man came and gave us blankets. We laid them out on the floor. It's a strange place, with paint peeling off the walls. What hurts most is the broken look in my dad's eyes, the look of humiliation, and the expressions of gratitude he repeats to everyone who offers us food and bread. We used to live comfortably and had everything we needed, and now we are living on charity and handouts. We've become beggars and it's humiliating. We have a wood burner. The place is cold and damp, but the wood fire does the job. Sometimes our stomachs rumble from hunger, but we don't beg for food. We've agreed to hold our peace. A missile fell at the cemetery near us. My younger brothers were outside playing. We ran to get them and then we all huddled up in a corner. Their faces were frozen, rigid with terror.

'The 19th of February. I found a sparrow and a nest, and there was a tiny chick that had just hatched. We're keeping them in a cage in the middle of the room. The bird looks after its chick by feeding it food into its little beak. A bomb falls nearby and the sparrows flutter about nervously in their cage. The mother bird's wings bash against the sides of the cage as she flies about, and then she hops back to her chick, but neither of them calms down until the bombing stops.

'My older brothers have gone, they've disappeared. I should have been at university today, but I'm trapped here with my family. I called my friend and asked her to bring me the notes from the lectures I've missed. We've got our car with three wheels, and my father took me to get the lecture notes, but the car broke down again, we arrived too late and my friend had already left. I sat down on the steps and cried and cried. I was determined to keep up and carry on submitting my work. But it's impossible. We went back to the shelter and sat here in silence all evening.'

She stopped reading. Her voice was getting hoarse.

'That's enough,' she said, grabbing my hand. 'If we die now, the world will know our story, won't they?'

'Yes, they will,' I answered, without hesitating or trying to console her.

We left the girl and her family, and went up to Ayouche's burnt-out flat on the second floor. The walls were charred black. A shell had fallen on the house and set fire to it. She started picking things up and telling me what they were. All I could see were unidentifiable black objects of various shapes, but she was able to explain confidently, 'This is part of my sofa, and this is a coffee cup, this is the side of my wardrobe . . .' When we heard a third shell go off, she said, 'We had better head back. That's enough for today.'

We went back out through the cellar. If I were writing a novel, I told myself, that girl would definitely be one of the heroines. I'd describe her flame-coloured hair and the delicate little wings flapping furiously in her heart, and the look in her eyes. And explain how, whenever one of her little brothers or sisters flops onto her in a heap, trying to hug her and lure her away from this inquisitive visitor who interrupts their day even more than the shelling, she just wraps her arms round them, squeezing them along with the birds tucked under her cardigan.

But this wasn't a novel, this was real life, and she held her little brothers and sisters tight, never taking her eyes off them, protecting them like her little wounded sparrows.

The media centre of Saraqeb was located in the middle of the market, which was the focus of Assad's bombing campaign. From the hubbub in the crowded market you would have had no idea at first sight what was happening, but for the decrepit buildings and the massive holes in the streets, the footprints of shells and bombs. Here, missiles fall and people die. An hour later, people go back to their everyday lives, and to procuring the essentials, the food and drink they need to survive. But I found it terrifying, this relationship with death, and how it had become such an integral part of the way of life.

I told the men working there that they should move their office because the location was so risky, and the most important thing was to stay alive. The men in the media centre included activists who doubled as photographers, combatants and aid workers; and journalists who were constantly coming and going. The occasional foreign journalist passed through, but the influx of journalists from other Arab countries hadn't really begun and wouldn't until the province of Idlib was fully liberated. There were only Syrian journalists here at this moment. The office building was in tatters – one of the walls had been destroyed four months earlier.

Back in August 2012, when we had travelled through the surrounding area the villages had not been fully liberated, so we had had to skirt around them using back roads and lanes to avoid the regime's military roadblocks. Even Saraqeb itself wasn't completely liberated in those days. Now, in February 2013, we could move around quite freely on the ground, but the sky was still held captive. The rebels said that if they had anti-aircraft missiles, victory would be theirs.

'The revolution is not about fighting or war,' a newspaper editor told me. He worked on the Zaytoun newspaper, the *Olive*, a publication founded following Saraqeb's liberation from the regime. 'We want to nurture the human side, but we don't have the resources,' he said. 'The constant bombardment makes it hard to get around. We have started the civil society activities associated with revolution, but we are faced with serious difficulties. The biggest challenges are not financial backing and continuous bombardment; no, the most dangerous thing is the way the *takfiris*, the Islamic extremists, are edging their way in and starting to control people's lives and interfere in their business.' By civil activities, he was referring to their repeated attempts to set up enterprises such as graffiti workshops, cultural newspapers, magazines for children, training workshops, privately run community schools and educational courses.

The editor was clearly exhausted, as were the young men around him, who were all zealously toiling away. They were downloading pictures, confirming headcounts of casualties and martyrs, liaising with humanitarian organisations on the phone, letting them know how people were doing, the conditions they were living in. They kept meticulous records of attacks by the regime: how many missiles, what kind, shape and size. Later in the war, some of these men would prepare a dossier on the chemical shells that fell on Saraqeb, which they sent to several government agencies around the world. Sadly their sense of hope and optimism was undermined, because everything they had worked on came to nothing and the world seemed content to leave them to fight on alone.

Abu Waheed, a married man in his mid-forties who was now a battalion commander in the Free Army, came to get me in his pickup: we were due to head out to some villages to visit displaced people with Manhal, the brother-in-law who had accompanied me to the border hospital on my first crossing, and my guide

Mohammed. The sounds of missiles were distant, giving us hope that our share of death would stay at arm's length today.

As we drove from the marketplace, I noticed there weren't any women on the streets. I had seen just one woman, with her husband, wearing the face-covering *khimar* veil. This was the first time I'd seen the *khimar* in Saraqeb; usually women just wore a headscarf that covered only the hair.

We called in at the battalion headquarters where my companions talked to one of the militants. It turned out we were heading to see a mounted gun they'd constructed, a kind of cannon, and that Abu Waheed was driving the pickup because he wanted to transport it somewhere.

The road out of town was clear, lined on both sides with groves of small cypress trees, and with children selling vegetables and fuel. They had various barrels and containers with the words 'black diesel' or 'red diesel' scrawled on them. The prices varied but both kinds were cheap and of poor quality, producing noxious fumes when burnt. We eventually stopped next to a group of boys selling fuel on the Aleppo–Damascus highway: ten boys lined up as though on military parade, standing to attention behind containers of unrefined diesel, known as mazut, and petrol canisters. Most children no longer went to school because of the constant bombardment. The surprising thing was that there were schoolteachers who continued to receive their salaries from the Syrian government.

The sun was out, but there was still a cool chill in the air as we stood at the roadside, haggling over the price of petrol. When Manhal asked the price of a canister, a boy said, 'Two thousand five hundred and fifty lira.' A year ago, it would have been just 270 lira.

'The February sun . . .' Abu Waheed said, looking up at the sky. He turned to me. 'Ma'am, we want justice for our people. But we don't want other countries interfering in our affairs. We'd be better off if they left us to face Bashar alone, without interfering. Their interference only works in his favour. As you've seen, we haven't got rid of that thorn yet. I used to be well off, I was a building contractor and I had studied law. I actually wanted to study at the Institute of Drama. It didn't work out, but I've always been interested in theatre and TV drama. I guess I'm a bit of an aficionado of the arts.' He laughed.

We drove on through the village of Khan al-Sabal, where there was a large quarry. There had once been a large regime checkpoint here, which the rebel fighters had liberated. The people of Khan al-Sabal had returned to their village after Assad's forces were expelled. We pulled up at what was now the Free Army checkpoint. There were no cars besides our pickup and an open-topped truck with three combatants armed with machine guns sitting in the back.

When we arrived at the village of Jerada, I exclaimed in surprise, 'Oh, the whole village is made of stone!' There were huge Roman mausoleums thousands of years old and towering columns crowned with intricately sculpted capitals. This was just one of the many Roman sites scattered around the Jabal Zawiya region and, as I looked around, I was reminded of how most of the jihadist groups are blind to the significance of these ruins; looting is part of their ideology. For them, civilisation begins with Islam.

The village of Jerada is in the province of Maarat al-Numan, a place name linked to the Arabic word for poppies, *shaqa'iq nu'man*, and these scarlet flowers could be seen peeping out amid the clutter of Roman stones. A carpet of red spread far beyond the ruins, opening up to the village of Rawiha in the distance. Stone houses were interspersed among the Roman tombs, like mini palaces. Most of the stones had been looted, my companions informed me.

After another military checkpoint, we saw a woman with three children, and I learned that the people here scraped a living from raising sheep and growing olives. The soil was red and littered with large rocks. Then we reached the other side of Ariha, near to where the regime had bombed the brick factory in Amenas to smithereens. In the village of Sarja, the red soil disappeared, giving way to pebbly desert. Various battalions had set up roadblocks here and the manifestations of power and control were clearly visible. This was certainly the case in Deir Simbel, a village associated with Jamal Maarouf, leader of the Syrian Martyrs' Brigade. Here we saw a tank and passed through various military checkpoints, including those of the Nusra Front and Ahrar al-Sham.

As an officer in the Free Army, Abu Waheed still believed that the foreign mujahideen would return to their homeland as soon as the regime had fallen. I didn't agree with him. 'Time will tell.' That was all he said.

'But they don't have a homeland,' I said. 'Their home is their faith.'

We were let through the checkpoint without any hassle because the soldiers knew Abu Waheed; you could only travel around safely if accompanied by someone from a well-known battalion. Ahead of us was a truck carrying tents for refugees, and the road was lined with houses that had been completely destroyed; yet almond trees and olive trees still grew in the wreckage.

We arrived in Rabia, a village whose cavernous underground Roman tombs had become shelters for refugees. We stopped so that I could meet the women and find out what conditions were like for those living in the caves. The Roman site was surrounded by olive groves, but many of the trees had been cut down or burnt. A lot of displaced people had resorted to felling trees to use as fuel. Some of the olive trees had been burnt by shells, but several remained around the caves, which were inhabited by some thirty families. There were six or seven caves, each one accessible through a deep, dark hole, where worn-down, dusty steps led to a cavern beneath the ground.

A girl aged about sixteen, wearing a hijab, a headscarf covering the head and chest, was sitting at the entrance to one of the caves. She had lost both her legs when she had been hit by a shell. One had been cut off at the thigh, the other at the knee. Her eyes were nevertheless serene. She said she was teaching her sisters and brothers to draw but they had hardly anything to draw with. The girl explained she would need several operations because her wounds had become infected and she was likely to succumb to blood poisoning. Yet she appeared indifferent watching us descend into the cave where her mother and siblings lived. She tilted her head and went back to drawing lines in the soil.

Inside the cave dwelling we met the girl's family. The mother, Oum Mostafa, was the second wife of a man who had five other children with his first wife, and who lived with her in the cave opposite. The family was originally from the village of Kafruma.

There was no natural light in the cave. Day and night, they filled an empty medicine bottle with oil and dipped a wick into it, which they lit. This makeshift lamp gave off pungent fumes and didn't burn satisfactorily. The children closed in around me and stared inquisitively, hovering around the candles we had brought with us. Their ages ranged between three and fifteen, and I talked with them about what they were doing while they were off school, during these seemingly never-ending holidays. The mother told me that her husband had pilfered the aid intended for her children and given it to his other wife. She held a baby in her arms, and her belly was swollen with another. This would be her ninth: she had eight children living with her in a cave with a dirt floor and rainwater leaking in. She and her children hardly ate one meal a day. All the children were barefoot and poorly clothed. Their faces were pale, crusty with dirt and snot, their eyes blue or deep bluish-black, their skin dry and chapped, and their naked toes seeped blood and pus. In the bitter cold their swollen stomachs protruded like small hills.

The woman's middle daughter had been deafened by a shell landing near her, but she took care of her sister with the amputated legs. When the older girl eased herself down the steps to join us, the deaf child held her hand tightly, and it struck me that despite the darkness, their faces seemed to glow with astonishing beauty. All this beauty amidst such hideous misery.

As we were leaving, I told Abu Waheed about Abu Mostafa stealing his wife's aid money. He laughed. I could not laugh.

In the other caves things were no better. Scores of people lost in the dark bowels of the earth, like animals digging their own graves as they sense the end approaching. Yet up on the surface, everything felt normal. In front of one of the caves the kids had made a hole, which they were using as a target for a yellow ball that darted about between their feet in the dirt. This was the only sign of the humans living underground, with their ragged clothes, their hunger and the squalor in which they slept that passed its smell on to them. I could barely stand. It was an unparalleled vision of hell. Not merely a purgatory through which homeless wanderers passed, this was surely a cursed place created by the devil himself.

We got back into the car in silence. Further along, we came to an area of tombs studded with dark crevasses. Here, too, dozens of families were sheltering in the caves. Directly ahead we saw some houses that had been razed to the ground. Total annihilation. It was as though a time machine had turned the clock back to the Stone Age.

The sky was bright blue and the sun burnt even more brightly as we drove through the village of Hass during an aerial bombardment. The Nusra Front Brigades had been here but had moved on. After Hass, we reached al-Hamidiya, a village that looked like little more than a group of towering cypress trees.

'So many of the battalion commanders and peaceful activists have been killed or arrested,' said Abu Waheed. 'The best men have fallen.' He gave a touching eulogy for each and every one of them. I was taken aback by the small details he recalled as he reeled off these men's names, their ages and their experiences. He narrated the stories of their deaths, while from afar the cypress trees seemed to loom so high that the clouds were ensnared in their foliage. I nodded, my eyes fixed on the road and my ears full of the sound of the sky raining shells.

In Taqla, a poor farming village, the landscape changed some-what. The village name derived from the Aramaic and referred to Saint Taqla. Here were rolling hills and valleys teeming with olive trees. We stopped at the quarters of the Freedom Martyrs Brigade, Abu Waheed's battalion. I couldn't wait any longer. I was burning with curiosity to see the gun they'd built. It had been made from the remains of a government tank and put together using the most primitive tools. Now it sat amid the olive trees, its black muzzle pointing up to the sky, mounted on huge wheels also salvaged from battlefield debris. We walked around it. I slipped my hand up and into the round black opening: a source of death.

'This is nothing compared with the arsenal the regime gets from Iran,' Abu Waheed explained. 'We will fight, we have no choice: we either die or we fight. The young men in the Freedom Martyrs are all villagers who have rallied together to protect their community. They are ordinary people. In other groups, you'll see things are different because of their funding and the supply of arms they get. Our mission is to fight for our country, and our battle against Assad is a battle for our country. We don't know who the other groups are or how they ended up here on our soil!'

At the start of the revolution the sight of a tank would make my hands tremble in panic; now here I was, stroking my fingers across the muzzle of a tank's gun. I thought for a moment about how an entire novel could be written about the life cycle of this one gun, from its initial component parts through to the finished product. Here it was, lounging in the olive groves in the hills, enjoying a brief honeymoon before being launched into action. It hadn't cost them anything; it was pieced together from donated parts and the salvaged remnants of war. They couldn't have bought it. They didn't have the money.

'This gun has a shelling range of fourteen kilometres,' Abu Waheed told me, 'and we use Google to set the distance. We make some of the parts here. We've set up a special weapons workshop, but we've barely got the materials for things like this. I've put everything I have into the revolution. I had a state-funded business worth fifty million lira – I gave it all up. They've bombed us, killed us and killed our children, they've displaced our people, and we will kill them. All we're doing is defending ourselves. We're not attacking them. We pick up their conversations, I hear what they talk about in their planes: they want to kill us, every single one of us!'

'I hate seeing a machine of death become the most important thing people live for,' I replied. 'It's not right.'

Abu Waheed was silent. Nobody else said a word. But I told myself, 'Remember that what is just might not be what is right.'

We continued our conversation at Abu Waheed's home. His wife invited us to eat with the family, including his children and his mother. There was no water and the electricity had been cut off, but they treated us to an abundant spread. In fact, everywhere we found ourselves as guests, our hosts would go out of their way to offer the best hospitality they could. I was sure the food was often all they had, and yet there was no hesitation; it was put on the table.

As we sat down to the delicious meal, immersing ourselves in our hosts' generosity, Abu Waheed continued, 'When the regime falls we'll throw down our weapons. I don't sleep at home, ever. I'm a fighter, and I'm needed on the front line. But we want to live as human beings after this is over; we want to raise our children and give them an education. Can you believe that a government and a state could bomb its own people? I'll never understand this for as long as I live!' Abu Waheed's anger welled up, as the words poured from his mouth. He stopped eating.

'Look at the cracks in the ceiling. A shell fell right by my house, missing my family by just a few metres. Our fate is entirely in the hands of God. But where can we go? We even have to buy water to drink! Can you believe that every month I need four thousand lira just to buy water for my children? I left my well behind on my farm, it's there for the people to use . . . We'll share life and death together.

'One thing you need to know,' he added, 'is that each region now has its own administration, and every village looks after itself. Everything has been turned upside down, as if every little community has become a state in itself.'

'This is the devastation that follows tyranny,' I suggested.

'We've entered a strange time. Think about what Islam says about the spoils of war. The Islamists have issued *fatwas* that have justified looting and have given the battalions the green light to go ahead. For example, the people of the village of Kafrouma started picking battles for the sake of looting, not for the sake of revolution. A gun is worth millions, so you're a winner if you can get your hands on one, which means battles end up being started just for the sake of the spoils! And another thing, our village had a population of five thousand, and now there are twenty-five thousand displaced people. We can't talk about one Syria now in the same way as before; everything has changed.'

It was morning and the bombing back in Saraqeb was less intense, so there was time to sit down with the old ladies and reminisce about Aala and her siblings. The elderly aunt sat next to her sister, the matriarch of the extended family. They seemed almost immortal. Their eyes scanned me and my eyes scanned them. Between us was a kind of tacit collusion, the same kind of understanding I had with Aala. It seemed the entire family had a passion for storytelling. They didn't want me to set off for Maarat al-Numan that day, but I promised them that when I got back we'd stay up and chat, on the condition that the aunt told me about her youth in the 1940s, before the military coups, when the Syrians were still building a modern state. It had occurred to me that we were now at a similar transitional point in history, and that the country was once again on the threshold of a great transformation, which first entailed degradation and regression in all areas of life. We were going back to square one in order to rebuild life from absolutely nothing.

Before leaving town, we stopped at the information office in the marketplace to pick up various publications printed by civil society activists, including a magazine for children and two newspapers: the *Al-Sham* (the *Levant*) and several editions of *Al-Zaytoun* (the *Olive*). These sketched the plans for the state the activists hoped to build in the liberated areas, in spite of the bombing: completing this revolution was going to be no easy task. Mohammed, Manhal and I were to distribute newspapers in the villages that we passed through. With us were Fida Itani, the journalist who had crossed the border with me, and two young activists from the city of Maarat al-Numan, who were to be our guides that day. They were from Basmat Amal (The Smile of Hope), a humanitarian aid organisation that had set up a first-aid and medical centre and which administrated various humanitarian projects. They were the kind of revolutionaries who had turned their hands to civilian work.

To reach Maarat al-Numan, we had to drive a ten-kilometre stretch along the front line. This was the site of an ongoing exchange of fire between the regime and the battalions. Assad's planes were constantly dropping bombs, and there were snipers a kilometre away. The sky was clear and sunny, which meant the planes would be out bombing villages, but the villagers knew the routine and the bombers' favourite times of day for bombing. Even the children knew the various types of missiles and shells; they also knew the modus operandi of the snipers.

'There are several snipers operating on the road we'll be driving along,' Mohammed warned me. A man had been shot on it only two days previously, right before their eyes, but we had no choice other than to go that way. The blossom was out on the trees, and the ground was speckled with pink and yellow petals. Ahead of us was a checkpoint belonging to Bayariq al-Shamal (the Banners of the North Brigade). When Mohammed and Manhal asked if we could pass, the response of the armed guard was telling: 'Well, I wouldn't if I were you – if you value your life.' He sat down on a rock, placed his machine gun in his lap and stared at us with a look of resignation.

We bowed our heads as Manhal drove off at an incredible speed. I heard gunshots and didn't move an inch, even when at last they burst into laughter, shouting, 'We did it! We survived!' Eventually I raised my head and for a moment I imagined I had dozed off into a nightmare. Perhaps my descriptions of these images of destruction are getting repetitive, but what I saw in Maarat al-Numan was truly shocking. On the road in front of us was a white pickup truck, badly damaged by shelling but carrying a mother and her four daughters in the back. The oldest of the girls was about ten. All four daughters were veiled and their mother was shrouded in black.

All around, entire buildings had twisted to the ground. They hadn't been blasted apart in the usual way, but rather the iron and concrete seemed to have melted into liquid right before my eyes, curving and bending. A four-storey building drooped so that its roof was touching the pavement, unfurling like a theatre curtain. And beneath it disappeared a mass of human bodies. Buildings leaned in to touch each other, they bowed down to sleep, amid the huge piles of rubble that filled the city. Maarat al-Numan had been completely decimated, the men told me. As it was on the front line it was the target of ceaseless bombing: it literally never stopped.

At that very moment I heard another shell explode. Right in front of us. We swerved into an alleyway. This road was also pitted with craters and potholes from the explosions. Shopfronts quaked with the impact, metal shards flying through the air. The clamour, the noise, was terrific; and it went on and on.

A woman and her daughter were walking up ahead, which seemed odd as I rarely saw women walking outside. The market was a wreck. Boys ran this way and that, and a woman fled into an alleyway. We were approaching the Great Mosque, one of the city's ancient monuments – or at least it had been once. It had been razed to the ground. The minaret of the mosque had been hit and beneath it lay piles of rocks and glass. I learned that the site had been cleared, but then it had been bombed again, as the regime was targeting the minarets in particular.

The Great Mosque dates back to the pre-Christian era. First a pagan temple, it was later converted into a church and then a cathedral. It still had ornamental engravings and capitals atop great columns bearing symbols of Christian and pre-monotheistic religions. The Islamic library was also devastated: copies of the Quran and other books had been flung in all directions, burnt and in tatters.

We got out of the car and walked into the courtyard of the mosque. As we headed towards the prayer room, which had been ravaged by a shell, we heard the roar of a plane and dashed for cover.

'After a bomb landed here, we uncovered an ancient market,' one of the men from the town told me. 'We went down the hole and saw the entrance. They say it dates back to the pre-Christian era. There are doors and the remains of shops.'

It was a sight of utter devastation: dangling electrical wires intertwined with jagged metal poles and splintered shreds of wood. Concrete walls lay in heaps, forming a homogenous block of many strata, layered up like sheets of pastry in a croissant. I took countless photographs, saving each image with a title. Seeing the effort I was making as I tried to work out the range of each shell, the men urged me to wait, because later on they'd show me the damage at the front line.

Back on the street, in front of the mosque just before the entrance to the market, an old man stood and gestured to me. 'Look! Look!' he shouted, pointing at the remnants of the minaret. 'That's Bashar's reforms for you . . . We didn't do a thing . . . We just asked for a few rights . . . That's all we wanted, let God be our witness . . . Just look . . .' He started to cry. One of the young men took his arm and walked with him for a little while. The old man had lost three of his children when the market was bombed. And now he just stood here, weeping.

The wall of the market bore the words, 'We stand defiant despite the blockade.'

Before we left the city, we were able to glimpse the Maarat al-Numan Museum, which used to house one of the most important mosaic collections in the Middle East. The museum is located in the former Khan Murad Pasha, a sixteenth-century Ottoman caravanserai, or inn, for passing travellers and pilgrims from Istanbul to Damascus. It became the city museum in 1978 and had four wings, each housing a particular archaeological or historical period. A former reading room housed a collection of rare books, and an archive of 2,400 square metres of mosaic murals – no one knows what has happened to them. An impressive 1,600 square metres of mosaic used to be on display, a prime example of Syria's artistic heritage that stretches back to the Akkadian era. Only fragments of these murals remained on the walls when I visited.

By the entrance of the museum, I came across a statue of the poet and feted son of the city Abu al-Ala al-Ma'arri – decapitated. This was clearly the work of one of the *takfiri* militant groups – Islamic extremists who accuse others of being apostates. I asked the others to wait while I took a picture of the headless statue. Later they told me that a shell had fallen on it, but the marks on the stone suggested otherwise.

'They stole the head and sold it,' someone told me, while others claimed the head had been severed by shrapnel. Someone else said the Nusra Front had cut off the statue's head because the poet was an infidel, and someone else, annoyed, replied, 'At least they cut the heads off statues and not human beings like Bashar does!'

'The next stage is going to be very violent,' Fida warned. 'Jihadist groups will resort to intimidating people by cutting off heads and mutilating corpses, because this is part of their propaganda.'

While we'd been touring the countryside around Idlib, I'd started to realise that the story that was reaching the outside world was very confused. The reality was that jihadist military groups were beginning to control certain areas, and were forcibly taking over various administrative posts from ordinary civilians. The problem lay with the *takfiri* groups coming into the country from abroad. Everywhere I went, despite warnings from everyone about the danger, people scrambled to protect me from harm and to keep me away from the *takfiris*, but these groups had already achieved a form of occupation in the areas liberated from the Bashar regime. This wasn't happening in any random or chaotic fashion; it was an orderly, well-planned operation to divide up the liberated north as spoils among jihadist incomers; but this didn't mean that the Free Army battalions were just standing by watching them. Many of these battalions were holding steadfast to the initial spirit of the revolution, although fault lines were certainly starting to show.

The museum door was blocked by diesel barrels and to the side of it was written in large, clear letters: *Maarat Martyrs Brigade*. The museum had been taken over as the brigade's headquarters. In the colonnaded courtyard, oil cans and drums of diesel were stacked up next to the mosaics. A rabbit sat peacefully beneath the arches. The only thing this strange scene was missing to capture the insanity of it all was the bloody remains of a young man crushed beneath a minaret. The rabbit didn't move. He sat there quietly, nibbling at the grass in the cracks between the paving, and no one approached him.

We were shown around by Group Commander Salaheddine, a combatant who was friendly enough, though his face wore a stern, distant look. He told me they had collected up the remains of pottery plates, crockery and broken glass, and were storing them for safekeeping in one of the side rooms.

The two young activists who had travelled with us fell silent, as though uncomfortable with this conversation. When the armed resistance started, some of these young men tended to sympathise with the Nusra Front. I didn't argue with them about it, but I couldn't deny my unequivocal hostility to this militant 'front'.

Broken columns and capitals lay strewn randomly on the ground, along with carved pieces of limestone dating back to the second century AD. Any paintings that still hung on the walls had been pierced by bullets and shrapnel. Assad's army had set fire to the books when they entered Maarat al-Numan and destroyed the museum, while the breathtakingly beautiful sculpted Roman sarcophagi remained untouched, resistant to looting because of their sheer size. The reading room was devastated: the books were burnt even before the bombing, and what remained of them was smothered in dust. I brushed away the dirt to reveal some of the titles: *Uncovering Enigmas* by Zamkhashari, *The Universal Orbit of the Radiant Astronomical Body* by Abdul Rahman Al-Ahmad and several editions of *The Archaeological Annals of the Arabs*; also *The Encyclopaedia of the Oceans* and *Exegesis of Pride* in Razi's 138th edition, from the Eastern Metropolitan Press. So many books, so many in tatters.

'We are busy with the war,' said the commander. 'We can't preserve it all.'

We heard a shell explode. It was very close.

Many statues had disappeared from the museum courtyard, stolen. Almost the entire contents of the glassware room had been looted. The doors of the basalt tombs were still in situ, and occupying pride of place in the heart of one room was a complete mosaic panel depicting the blessed grapevine, discovered in the village of Mazakia and dating back to 2000 BC.

I sat down under a lemon tree in the courtyard. My head was spinning; I needed a moment to take in this colossal destruction, this ruthless sabotage of history. Before me I read the words, 'There is no god but Allah. Maarat Martyrs Brigade.'

Another shell fell.

'They're pelting the city at random,' said the commander.

He took us to the place where horses were tethered in the days of the old caravanserai. Every single artefact had been looted. All we could see were broken chunks of Roman capitals strewn messily around the yard and one fragment that remained on the wall. The commander walked over to an armoured vehicle stranded in this courtyard at the heart of the museum. It gave off a burnt smell, reeking of oil and petrol.

'We won it as booty from a military convoy when we hit Wadi Deif,' said the military commander. He continued, in an earnest tone, 'Listen, sister, we were at the front line, the Free Army, and when we came back they told us that the Nusra Front had chopped off the head of the statue of al-Ma'arri, because they say statues are *haram*. I know you're going to ask me about it.'

Outside the museum, on the way to the city prison, we heard the voices of women and children echoing from within the distorted ruins of a building. Amid the concrete beaten to powder by shelling, among the twisted iron, the wreckage, the disembodied parts, there in an almost entirely ravaged house, in some of the rooms that were still standing, people were living inside the destruction. If I were to read this scene in a book I wouldn't believe it.

Men were picking up shattered glass by the windows. 'A shell fell here yesterday,' they said. 'Today shells have fallen on the other side.'

'We're going over there now,' said the commander.

I looked up. A young boy was pulling some clothes out of a wardrobe that stood against a wall in a room on the second floor. Miraculously, the colourful clothes seemed to be clean and not covered with dust. They were pouring out of the wardrobe as if strung on a long washing line. The boy was trying to reach the sleeve of one of the shirts when his mother shouted from inside the house. The wardrobe toppled over and with it came the entire wall. The boy ran. I screamed and shut my eyes. My scream was more of a wail, the only way I could keep my brain from exploding. When I opened my eyes, I expected to see the boy's body crushed beneath the wall. But he was standing there staring at me – a look of both surprise and ridicule! If it weren't for the noise of the collapsing wall making me close my eyes, I'm sure I'd have seen him fly up above the scene on two wings – that was the only explanation for his survival.

Salaheddine, the group commander, led us to the prison and the municipal administration building. I could see that the public records and archives had all been lost to fire. The offices were abandoned, their ceilings collapsed under the bombardment. The commander tried to explain what had happened here: they had liberated the municipal building from the forces of the regime and broken into the prison, but Assad's forces and their staff had fled. They'd captured a number of Assad's soldiers. Two of them joined their battalion, twelve of them were sentenced to death by the Sharia Court, while two were acquitted and went back to their families.

'There were two from Raqqa, one guy from the coast, one from the cities of Al-Bab and Deir Ezzor. But we killed twelve soldiers,' Salaheddine told me, going on to explain their respect for the law.

'It happens in war,' I replied.

'This isn't war,' he said.

'It's a war between your people and Bashar al-Assad,' I replied straight away.

'Isn't it your war?' he asked.

'Yes, it's my war too, but in my own way. I have my pen. I'm a writer and journalist.'

'Do you want to hold a gun?' he asked with a smile.

'No, although the guys have tried to teach me how to hold one,' I told him. 'I was going to carry a gun to protect myself, but then I thought about it long and hard, and changed my mind. I decided I wouldn't carry anything. Touring around these places is dangerous enough without a gun, but I've nothing to be afraid of when I'm with these guys: they accompany me everywhere and do everything they can to protect me.'

We entered a long, dank and dirty basement. The group commander was a straightforward kind of fellow; he had worked in construction before the revolution and had never imagined he would take up arms, but he said he was forced to. Yet, in spite of the chaos, Salaheddine was trying to enforce the law. He watched me dispassionately. He seemed preoccupied and worried. I would certainly say he was brave.

'This prison was empty when we liberated it,' he said, leading us along a dark corridor lined with prison cells. 'They'd taken the prisoners with them!'

Small cells lined both sides of the passageway, with phrases inscribed high up on the walls. 'Oh time, you are treacherous' read one. Another read 'Abu Rodi, the rose – you are my life, my fate, my choice'. A verse of poetry was inscribed on the wall of a particularly squalid cell: 'Can an age in which you live wrong me, And can wolves devour me when you are a lion?' The prisoners' charred possessions – trousers and shirts, underpants – lay strewn across the floor and there was a distinct smell of burning. Soot stained the ceiling. It looked like the prison had gone up in smoke very recently.

'They bombed the place after we liberated it, and they set fire to the prison and the municipal building,' the commander said. I stopped at a cell that seemed less covered in soot. The clothes on the floor were torn, but for a moment I imagined they were clean; the articles that had belonged to this cell's occupant seemed fairly tidily arranged, although someone had clearly been rifling through them: a shoe, a ripped bedding mat, a few spoons. Next to a pair of black trousers were a few pieces of paper, some charred and some dusty with soot. I picked them up and tried to brush the dust off, but they crumbled to ashes in my hands.

The word 'Allah' was engraved on every wall, and wherever we went the ground was spattered with dried blood, which looked like a layer of wax. Many feet had trampled through it, and I couldn't wipe it off my shoes. I tried to avoid stepping on it – the smell was suffocating, a stench of decomposing bodies – but we couldn't avoid treading on the broken glass. We could only just see by the weak light bulb hanging at the end of the corridor. When we went out into the daylight, the sun was blinding. I stumbled and tripped over onto the ground, where my nose hit a crusty spot of blood. I felt as though I had swallowed a corpse, but got up immediately, not wanting the others to see me in such a state, and ran to catch up with them.

'The guys will take you to the front line in another part of town,' said the group commander. 'Be careful.'

We went on towards the front line. A large bannister was swinging in the air like something in a scene from a science fiction film. It completed a full rotation in the air as it tumbled from the fourth floor of a gutted house, crashing with a thunderous, deafening noise into the rubble below. This concrete building had been drawn and quartered, ripped apart at the seams; it was split into sections like a ripe fruit. On the second floor you could see a bedroom, on the third you could see pots and pans precariously lined up on the shelves in the kitchen, next to that a bathroom where lingerie still hung drying, red like a young bride's, the colour faded with dust. The first floor had been opened up to reveal a large bed, with a child's small wooden cot at its side.

Children's toys, pyjamas on a peg, an embroidered bedspread, once golden but now faded to black. Human life and its most intimate details had been turned inside out, exposed to the world. A shell had literally divided this house in half. The other half of the building had crumbled into rubble.

One of the men with us told me, 'It was pounded by shell after shell. The eastern district of the city was completely deserted, there wasn't a trace of life here after the famous battle to liberate Maarat al-Numan in the autumn last year. The shelling didn't stop for a second after we liberated it. We cleared the area, got the people out, while they were raining shells down on us from the sky.'

The population of Maarat al-Numan was originally 120,000 people. For a while, there was not a single living soul here. The residents fled and sought refuge elsewhere, or were left without shelter. Eventually some of them returned. They preferred death in their own homes to hunger and homelessness.

Another airstrike started and we darted into a side alley, taking cover from the falling missiles. A woman passed by dragging a bag of firewood, and behind her trailed three children also carrying wood, and three other women dressed in black. The electricity had been cut off, and the water too, so people had to rely on drawing water from wells.

We arrived at the Hamza bin Abdul Muttalib mosque to find it was completely devastated, its dome flattened to the ground. Everything was so surreal and strange on this elevated plateau, beyond which the plains extended into the distance.

'This is the front line, so we have to be careful,' said Alaa as we clambered between fractured chunks of stone and concrete, as though embarking on a rocky mountain ascent to reach the dome of the great mosque. With its elegant engravings, the dome remained a thing of great beauty, like an ornate decorative dish.

But the men wouldn't let us climb to the top, right up to the dome, because the bombing started up again. A rocket landed which didn't explode, so they planned to take it to the battalion to reuse.

'This happens sometimes,' one of them explained. 'They fire a missile at us that doesn't go off, so we fire it back at them. We're just seven hundred metres from the front line now.'

The front line consisted of a cluster of cypress trees. We squatted down in the rubble of the mosque's dome. We wouldn't go any further, the men decided. We were scurrying back down, when all of a sudden we saw a small boy. What was he doing here? Should I shout? This six-year-old boy was selling diesel, and he was dragging three worn-down car tyres into his cart to prop up a small fuel can. We walked past him. No one said a word as we went back to the car. We reached Maarat al-Numan town square, where the Martyrs of Maarat Battalion headquarters was positioned on the right-hand side.

We could still hear the missiles, though we were moving further away now. I was in a daze, as our car navigated through this scene of utter destruction. The car pulled up outside the offices of the Smile of Hope organisation.

'They've been battering Saraqeb,' Mohammed shouted angrily, as a message came through on the transceiver in the car. 'Let's get online quickly . . . we might need to go back.' Mohammed was the most dedicated young person I'd ever met when it came to demonstrating his loyalty to his hometown. The thought of leaving Saraqeb was impossible for him. On one occasion, when I insisted he should leave the city to have an operation on his eye, after losing his vision as the result of a blow to the head, he flatly refused to go. He said he knew that things were not as they once had been, that the revolution had deviated from its path, but he would not abandon his people to their fate. As the only treatment he could get was abroad, and he refused to go, Mohammed had been left with sight in just one eye.

Now the car had barely stopped before he leapt out, dashing into the building. The people who worked there were all locals: men, women and children. A doctor was distributing medicines in a large vaulted room, helped by a female assistant and surrounded by a cluster of young men who rushed over to meet us. They were extremely welcoming, generously offering us refreshments.

A young man came in laden with bags of bread, which was being stored in the office so that it could be distributed to people who could not leave their homes because of the intensity of the shelling. The bread had been sourced by the Smile of Hope charity under tremendously difficult circumstances, but this was just one of the many ways in which they were trying to help people living under bombardment.

'We've got a bread crisis,' confirmed the doctor on duty. 'The people are hungry but there's no bread. There's no fuel and the electricity is often cut off. So is the water. Imagine how hard it is to get by for those of us who've survived this far! In the last fortnight, the refugees who left Maarat al-Numan have been returning. Between ten and fifteen thousand displaced people have come back out of the hundred and twenty thousand who fled originally. A large number of them are wounded, including children. We have anaesthetics and we have a field hospital with three operating rooms.' These operating rooms were very simple units with the bare minimum of equipment to remove bullets and shrapnel and stitch up wounds.

Scores of men slept here; they formed rescue parties and teams who documented the bomb sites and recorded the number of casualties. Many houses in the city were more or less devastated, they said, with barely anything left to show for them. Well over a thousand houses had been completely destroyed.

A few young men had returned from the rescue point for the wounded they had set up at al-Hamidiya on the front line. 'Al-Assad's planes dropped twenty-eight bombs in one day,' one of them told me, pouring me a second cup of tea. 'It was like that for a while, but the bombing eased off a bit when two of their planes were shot down.' The men laughed. They crowded around us, whispering and watching me carefully. But they seemed confident and relaxed, eager to speak and share their stories. I asked the men about the circumstances for the women in the area and wondered if I could meet some of them. I told them about the work of the project I was involved in, setting up centres specifically for women. They said they were keen to help the wives of martyrs. We stayed chatting for over an hour, which really tested the patience of Mohammed, who was pacing back and forth nervously, desperate to get back to Saraqeb.

'They're hitting us with Scud missiles,' said a man who had just joined us. 'It's no surprise. We achieved victory on the ground, so now the cowards are battering us from a distance.'

'Maarat is the front line, the line of engagement with the regime,' said another young man in his twenties. 'We will not leave our land, even if we die. If we had anti-aircraft guns, al-Assad would have fallen long ago.' This was the same phrase I had heard repeated endlessly by locals – insurgents, activists, and women and children. It was what everyone said, without exception. They knew that they had managed to liberate the land, but then the air-force planes razed the liberated zones to the ground.

All around us we heard the din of shooting and shelling, as we carried on talking. We were led by a few children to another room, the computer room by the looks of it. Opposite the door was a table piled high with the bags of bread. This room was buzzing with people and a couple of dozen of us sat down in a circle.

Another young man came in, who stood still and turned to me as he declared, 'The Nusra Front is the best group that's fighting.' Some of the men grumbled in disagreement but they let him finish speaking. 'To start with they were mostly foreigners, but a lot of Syrians have joined them, and they have actually got arms.'

'What about the Chechens who joined up recently!' another joined in. 'What have they brought with them?'

'They're our brothers in Islam,' said another, 'and they're fighting against the infidels.' I listened to them but then tried to steer the conversation back to the women and children, and education, and what we would do if the situation dragged on like this for years.

'I support Ahrar al-Sham,' one guy said, interrupting, 'because they don't steal like the other brigades.'

'Of course, because they've already stolen enough,' retorted another. 'Allah doesn't miss a thing!'

Mohammed stopped at the door and raised his voice. 'We need to set off for Saraqeb,' he said, targeting me with a beseeching look.

As we left Maarat al-Numan the shelling began to increase.

'Even the sky is betraying us!' I shouted at the top of my voice.

On the way back, I kept thinking about the family house and Noura and Ayouche and the old ladies, and the warmth that awaited me in their company. They must have been worrying about me.

'It doesn't sound good,' said Mohammed. 'We need to head straight to where the shells are falling, because there are people trapped under the rubble.'

Mohammed drove at an insane speed. We kept quiet, aware of how anxious he was. He muttered to himself the whole journey and we colluded with him in silence. Arriving in Saraqeb, we saw that olive trees had been blown apart by shelling, uprooted from the soil and hurled against the wall of a house. Blocking the road were parts of a tractor that had been ripped to shreds. We turned off onto another road. The scene was horrific. We got out and ran as fast as we could to the bomb site.

'They're digging the graves,' one guy shouted. 'Let's get them buried before sunset.'

A three-storey house had fallen after being pounded by numerous shells. One girl had survived, though she'd lost her mother and brother, and now we were searching for her four-year-old sister. Dozens of young men were clambering over the ruins of the building, which the shell had reduced to a mountain of rubble, and a bulldozer was brought over to drag away the collapsed roof.

The girl's father was sitting on the pavement. His dusty face stared straight ahead, and you would have thought he was a statue were it not for his cigarette. His face was white, and his hair and clothes were covered in dust. He had been out when the shells landed, when his house was brought crashing down in a heap of debris. He had pulled out the bodies of his wife and his son, while his little four-year-old girl remained to be found.

I helped search for her, oblivious to the fact that I was the only woman among dozens of men. I had been warned about this two days previously by the neighbours, some women who said I shouldn't let myself be seen among the men during the shelling, or when out searching for the dead, because this would bring me unwanted attention.

When I thought I had touched a soft, delicate hand under the rubble and a tuft of hair, I screamed. The men noticed me and a young man of no more than twenty came over, a black headband stretched across his forehead with the words 'There is no god but Allah'. He shouted to his friend, 'Get this woman out of here –

this is no place for her among the men. God Almighty forgive us.' I would have listened if I hadn't noticed that he wasn't Syrian, but instead I just stared defiantly into his eyes. His accent was foreign. I stayed where I was. I glared at him again; he was one of the ISIS fighters from abroad. Why should I go back while he was still carrying on? At that moment, my minders' car pulled up. One of them jumped out and waved to me to get in quickly.

'They still haven't pulled her free,' I told them as I got in the car. 'They're going to carry on digging.' Mohammed emerged from the ruins carrying a toy plastic duck. His voice was hoarse; his lips were moving but I couldn't hear him. As he held the toy, we heard a strange sound. He pressed it and it made a quacking sound.

'This burns my heart. Here we are looking for her under these rocks and all I've found is this duck – it's hers.' He went off for a moment, alone.

The bombardment of Saraqeb never stopped. It was a militarily strategic town for the regime, so they wanted to keep it in a state of instability. The people of Saraqeb would bury their martyrs by sunrise: any later and, without power to keep them cool, the bodies would decay. Previously Martyrs' Cemetery had been a garden, and it would be tended as a garden again in the future, each grave planted with a small rose tree.

Every individual buried in the cemetery was a resident of Saraqeb, and among them was Amjad Hussain, a militant I met the first time I was here, and who had been killed in the fight for Taftanaz airport. I tried to keep the image of his youthful face alive in my memory. We had talked for hours and hours at the beginning of the revolution. His presence summarised everything the Syrians have done for their revolution, their struggle for dignity and freedom, but for some mysterious reason when I first met him I had sensed he was ready to die. He was uniquely brave and pure of heart. And his fearlessness had worried me. Now his grave lay before me.

'Hello, Amjad,' I said, treading softly on the soil. I could hear his voice in my head so clearly, and the voices of so many young people who had died like him.

On my left, two men were digging new graves. Beside these pits, dug side by side, was a young seedling, its roots wrapped in a damp cloth. But the sky was not merciful; it wasn't going to let them rest in peace. We heard the bombing, far from the cemetery, and the men carried on with their work. The graveyard was a long way out of town and after the revolution a new mass cemetery was created for the martyrs. The revolution changed the way Syrians buried their dead. The courtyards of their homes became burial grounds and their public parks were turned into cemeteries. They buried bodies among the trees, leaving simple grave markers. In some places they might dig a long trench, a mass grave for dozens of martyrs. Sometimes, a family would turn the scrap of land behind their house into a graveyard for their children. When houses in the city were bombed, they searched for the nearest vacant spot to bury the dead.

Cemeteries began to live among the people, another everyday part of life like the shops and the streets that wind between the houses. Massacre after massacre pitted the soil with craters filled with the bodies of Syrians.

'This cemetery is very organised and tidy,' I said aloud, to no one in particular. One of the gravediggers replied from inside the hole, from where he was tossing out soil, 'They were all in the prime of youth.' I didn't reply. We wandered among the graves, while Fida Itani took photograph after photograph; later on in his pictures I noticed the sun setting behind us. A large sun sinking behind the tombstones and the shadows of me and Mohammed and the others as we turned this way and that between the grave markers. The town had disappeared, reduced to black silhouettes, and we were so tired we staggered, on the verge of collapse. The body is the most honest gauge of exhaustion.

But the light and air and the soil didn't care: we were already dead and decaying as far as they were concerned. Death was so straightforward here, so close and intimate, it lingered even closer than the breath we breathed. I remembered what one woman I worked with on a household management project in Saraqeb had whispered to me about her husband before he died. They had had two children and their relationship had changed so much. 'So much death . . . it brings with it so much love.'

'This cemetery is where we can breathe a sigh of relief,' I heard one of the men say, as he hurled earth from the hole he was standing in. 'We're expanding it and knocking down the wall, so that our boys can sleep in peace under the soil!' I looked at him in amazement, while Mohammed and some other young men walked around the cemetery as comfortably as though it were their home.

'All this soil, this dust is from the flesh of our children,' one man said, barely finishing his sentence before we heard the roar of falling shells. We ran. When we reached a side street, the shell exploded as it hit the next house. The sky was filled with dust as night fell.

In those moments, as bodies were being extricated from the rubble, and others were disintegrating, yet more human beings were being turned into corpses. Where do you even start trying to comprehend this spiralling cycle of endless massacre?

The people did all they could to defend themselves against the bombardment. It became clear that the target of the attack was a school that had been turned into the headquarters of the Ahrar al-Sham Brigades. As we gathered round another bomb site, I listened to a conversation between two militants and tried to make sense of what was going on in the battle of Wadi Deif, the Deif Valley, which lies to the east of Maarat al-Numan.

'The battle for Wadi Deif could have ended long ago,' said the younger one, as they searched through the rubble. 'The battalions that are getting financial support are the ones who are extending the life of the battle, so they can take advantage of it.' The older militant disagreed and started to describe the clashes at Abu al-Duhur air base between Free Army leader Maher al-Naimi and the Martyrs of Syria Battalion. The younger one spat on the ground, tutting. 'And this is what we went out and started a revolution for? For the poor to be taken advantage of? For people to die for the sake of a little money? And who's paying the price now? Those same poor people!' Then, angrily, he climbed the mountainous pile of rubble.

All was still again, except for the screams from the neighbouring houses.

My companions and I drove away from the city centre, the target of the bombing. We headed out of town, to get as far away as possible, and eventually we stopped at the house of some friends. They were sitting by candlelight, but no sooner had we said hello than the preparations began for dinner. I had still been hoping to visit some of the local women that day, especially one of the widows who wanted to open a workshop for woollen goods. But the idea seemed impossible now. It had been a long day and the people whose house we had suddenly descended on insisted we couldn't leave without staying for dinner. My family hostess,

Noura, called the house phone. I was amazed: how did she know where I was? She said she was worried about me.

'I'm not worth worrying about any more than anyone else,' I said.

'No, Samar! By God, you're worth so much more! And you're under our protection.' Her words made me choke as I struggled to swallow the food put before me that night. For all the generosity with which it was offered, it went down as awkwardly as a knife in my throat.

I would have thought it useless to record these events, which often seem to mirror each other and repeat themselves, if it weren't for my conversations with Noura each morning.

Originally from Damascus, Noura was the heart of my small family in Saraqeb, although I couldn't have put my finger on the exact source of the sunshine and warmth that surrounded them all and which made me think of coming back each time. At first, I had been tempted to leave France to settle in the north of Syria and to search for a house in Saraqeb or Kafranbel, but the situation was getting worse every day. I'd started to feel that my movements were a burden on my hosts – the rebels and all the families I knew – who were so concerned for my safety and went out of their way to protect me. There was always that warm welcome, an overwhelming hospitality that gradually started to taste of obligation, day after day.

Each morning, Noura and I used to sip our coffee together on the steps of the basement shelter, where we would enjoy a temporary peace of mind and then the conversation would turn to my favourite types of food. Noura's husband and Maysara's older brother, Abu Ibrahim, was an engineer who'd studied in Bulgaria and was now involved in land management and agriculture. Noura had fallen in love with him when he was in the capital visiting his sister. Like his younger brothers, he'd participated in the peaceful demonstrations but had been jailed at the beginning of the revolution before being released. Yet he never tired of helping with the revolution or with local families in need, and Noura was the same.

She was 'perfect' Noura, as the Damascenes would say; she always did everything just right, with a touch of style. During the shelling, she'd prepare a tray with glasses of water, laying out some small pieces of sweet pastry and the gold-rimmed coffee cups. When I went out on my day trips with the men, she'd stand outside the door of the house and raise her head to the sky in supplication. 'O God, protect her and protect her heart and mind. O God, return them safely,' she'd say, then wave me off. I always waited for her prayer.

But Noura was afraid of the shelling, and never got used to it. Whenever she heard the sound of a shell, she would stand there trembling and was quick to panic. Her nervous reaction would encourage me to stay calm each time, until this calmness became a part of me.

Noura hadn't come to the front door with me this particular morning, as the shelling was ongoing. After another busy day, we were now heading on to the town of Kafranbel, a forty-minute drive away, to see Razan, a female activist who had decided to come back and work in the liberated areas. Razan was a petite woman in her early thirties, who had been detained twice in Assad's jails. These days, she worked in medical relief and at documenting events. She was particularly good at bringing people together, and I wanted to talk to her about a schools project.

It was night by the time we entered town, where Razan and the others were waiting for us at the media office. The banners and posters produced by the office had been seen by people all over the world, and the centre opened its doors to anyone who wanted to communicate with countries outside Syria. However, the phone lines had been cut and there was no Internet access, except via the mobile equipment they had gone to great lengths to procure, which was just about capable of transmitting what was happening to the outside world.

The office itself was situated in a bare, desolate house where the activists and fighters huddled around an old mazut heater in a large central room. Chairs were placed around the edges of the room, with a computer in front of each one. The floor was a mess and some famous paintings by Ahmed Jallal, a local artist, were lying in a heap on a broken chair by the door. The other two rooms were empty but for some plastic rugs on the floor and a few cushions to sit on. This is what most of the media centres I visited in the small towns in Idlib province were like: stark and austere, both in the furnishing and in the way daily activities were conducted.

Sitting cross-legged around the heater on this occasion, trying to use it to make a pot of tea, were my guides Mohammed and Manhal, battalion commander Abu Waheed, our journalist friend Fida, a leading activist called Raed Fares, Razan, Hammoud and Khaled al-Eissa – both of whom I would come to know well – and me. Ahmed Jallal came through to join us. With us were three other activists who were working on laptops balanced on their knees, indifferent to what was going on around them; they stayed for about an hour then left.

I tried to focus; it was easy to believe I was in a movie about the Industrial Revolution or a historical novel because, at first glance, the scene seemed like the romantic cliché of popular revolutions we read about in history books. I despaired that the outside world didn't want to see the truth of what was happening. They wanted to see us as groups of savages who they could not bring themselves to describe as intelligent: they wanted to dismiss everything as religious extremism. And this meant that governments and people around the world could be content to let this dangerous savagery continue to play out between the rival parties.

I realised I lived between two worlds: one when I entered Syria and another when I left. I gave lectures in many cities around the world trying to explain the truth of what was taking place in Syria and trying to understand how other people saw us. I'd find myself tumbling into a deep and futile pit of emptiness that nothing could rescue me from except the prospect of returning to Syria. Then I'd come back here and live with the revolutionaries and the ordinary civilians, and be struck by a sense of despondency and anger at the great injustice that had fallen on us as a people and a cause.

The media centre guys were eager to talk to us. Raed Fares described the chaos that unfurled after the army forces left, explaining how the battalions and the armaments pouring in helped the Nusra Front become more organised and emerge well-stocked with equipment, money and weapons. Who was financing them and supplying the weapons? We didn't know. The situation in Saraqeb was different, Raed said, glancing at Manhal. Ahrar al-Sham was bolstered by money and weapons and they had started to interfere in people's lives. The Nusra Front hadn't yet become as heavy-handed in terms of meddling in people's private affairs as would be the case on my subsequent visit.

A large man, with broad shoulders, Raed had originally been a student of medicine before leaving his studies to work in Lebanon. In 2005, he'd decided to return to Syria to open an estate agency, and now he was committed to the revolution, heart and soul. He was a leading campaigner in the earliest days of the uprising, and a driving force behind satirical posters, banners and videos that had become revolutionary icons reproduced worldwide. I asked him about the idea of an Islamic state, and he admitted that there were people who wanted to build an Islamic caliphate as a response to the excessive violence of the regime; people felt safe with the Nusra Front and their piety, because while their only option was death, according to the Front at least they would be blessed in the life hereafter. The population had developed from a Sufic to a Salafist mentality. For me and many others, Sufism represented moderation in Islam, whereas Salafism represented militancy and religious extremism, with the transformation of religion from a social entity into a political one. The Salafists were counting on their children and young people to carry out their work in the future.

'But this is also dangerous!' I said. The others agreed with me. This change of mentality in the population would very probably lead to the negation of civilian life, as the popular movement evolved into religious extremism and religion took control of the legal system and the state. A secular state would then become an impossibility.

'We started the revolution and it's being transferred to them,' added Ahmed, the painter. As we sipped our tea, I tried to keep track of the different sounds of the shelling.

'This change in mentality shows sheer ignorance of religion and Islam,' added Raed, directing his words to me. 'Ignorance is the basis of extremism.'

But Manhal didn't agree that these were the only reasons. He argued that issues related to how Syrian society had been formed, with its family and tribal affiliations, also played a role. He pointed to what had happened in Binnish, where a dispute between two families was the reason why the Nusra Front had been able to take control of the city. And when Taftanaz was destroyed, the families of Binnish and the town of Haish just stood by watching. The damage ran deep.

'There's no culture of working together for the sake of civil society or a culture of citizenship,' I said. 'That's why regional disputes and rivalries between blocs and groups erupt. It's a direct consequence of totalitarianism. At this rate, we're facing the total disintegration of a society.'

Raed wasn't optimistic, but he wasn't pessimistic. 'We can only continue what we started,' he replied.

'The civilian aspect of the revolution has been neglected,' Manhal added.

Raed looked at me as he nodded sorrowfully and raised his voice to say, 'Yes, we made mistakes but how could we not make mistakes? We had a huge job to do, to help the people and the refugees, and our homes were being demolished over our heads.'

As we talked, Razan and the others had been preparing dinner. There were no limits to the generosity and hospitality of families in the Idlib countryside. We gathered round and started to eat the food they laid out on the floor, dipping our bread into it and alternating sips of hot tea with adding to the never-ending conversation.

Raed was a little irritable but the others listened as he aired his views. He continued, 'We're struggling to cope with the relief work. There's a crisis of confidence among people, and everyone distrusts each other, including the emergency relief workers. Hunger has had its impact. There needs to be more transparency so people can start to see what's going on in this revolution. We want a radio station that we can use to talk to the people of Kafranbel and to establish a sense of nationalism. We're asking the National Council and the Coalition for help with that too! Especially since the Nusra Front has started to interfere with the distribution of bread and mazut, as they have done in Aleppo and Deir Ezzor. There will be catastrophic results.' The National Coalition of Syria, based outside the country, was aimed at representing the political opposition to the Assad regime and had already been recognised by many countries of the world.

I was starting to feel suffocated in the cramped room as I watched my companions passing around plates and laughing, discussing what needed to be done amid all the destruction and death falling from the sky. However, when Abu al-Majd came in, the mood lifted and everyone relaxed.

A good-natured man in his mid-fifties, Abu al-Majd wasn't a political activist or a media professional, but a defected lieutenant colonel from Assad's army, who had become the commander of the Fursan al-Haqq Brigade (The Knights of Justice), which was allied with the Free Army. He carried his laptop with him and had a permanent smile on his face. I scrutinised his thin features to see whether he had the look of a military leader, but he didn't come across like one at all. I'd find out over the coming days and months what it meant to be a military commander with such a highly satirical spirit.

He limped over to join us, sat down and opened his laptop. I learned later that he had been wounded in his last battle, and had recently returned from treatment in Turkey. 'Salaam, guys,' he said. 'I'm here to use the Internet to find out what's happening in the world.'

'You haven't been to a demonstration?' Raed was quick to ask.

Abu al-Majd laughed. 'I'm a soldier; what would I do at a peaceful demonstration? Isn't that what you write on Facebook?' Facebook was very new to Abu al-Majd, and he mentioned it purely as a joke, although it was used by some of the younger activists. He smiled at us. 'Who are your guests?' Raed introduced us by our first names and jobs.

A man leaned across to whisper in his ear, and Abu al-Majd looked at me. 'We're all the sons of one country. May God give you, good people, a long life. Welcome, sister.'

I discovered that Abu al-Majd hadn't teamed up with any side that was offering financial support; he wasn't with any extremist Islamist battalions, and he didn't rely on the money flowing out of the Gulf from capital owned by wealthy businessmen. His battalion was stony broke, he explained.

'We have one thousand nine hundred fighters in the brigade, but only two hundred and twenty of them are working and fighting. The rest are at home. We don't have weapons and there's no internal or external support. Some basic aid comes from the families of Kafranbel. It just about keeps us going. The wolf doesn't die, neither do the sheep!' He was clearly happy to be alive.

He looked at me closely. 'Do you want to go and see a battle? There's one raging on the front line as we speak.'

'Of course,' I answered, but my companions objected loudly.

Abu al-Majd laughed. 'Don't you think I'd protect her with my soul and the souls of my soldiers?'

'Yes, you'll protect her,' one of the others replied, 'but a missile will tear you both apart on the front line. And then only God in the sky will protect the two of you.' Now we all laughed.

'We could be shelled here, too,' Abu al-Majd noted.

I asked him to tell me his story so I could record it as a testimony. He closed his laptop.

'You're going to write about me?' he asked calmly.

'Yes, tell me your story,' I urged him. He gave a troubled smile and nodded. While the others went back to their work, Abu al-Majd stretched out his legs and leaned back against the wall.

'I was a lieutenant colonel in the Syrian Army serving in aircraft engineering at Deir Ezzor airport, but I deserted in the first month of the uprising. At the beginning of June 2011 we hatched a plan to seize the airport, but when Assad's group found out about the plot they jailed me. Although they couldn't prove I was one of the plotters, I was in al-Mazza prison for a year. Some of the officers who were with me got seven-year sentences.

'While I was in prison they tortured me, but I didn't confess. They used the "ghost technique" on me for four days, where you're handcuffed and strung up by your wrists. They electrocuted me.' He laughed. His fine features made him look more like a writer or artist as he continued, 'They would never have released me if I'd confessed. After I was released, I went straight to the headquarters and they reinstated me into service. I knew what the *mukhabarat* wanted, the intelligence services. All they wanted from me was to return a stolen plane from Jordan to Syria. I deceived them into thinking I would talk to the pilot who'd defected, taking his plane with him, and convince him to return.

'Instead, I and a group of officers established an operations room and started to liberate Deir Ezzor. We crossed the Euphrates on three boats transporting ammunition. In July, I came to Kafranbel and set about liberating army checkpoints. Do you think it was those foreign extremists who liberated our villages? No. We liberated them and then they came to us. We liberated them with our blood and the blood of our children. When they asked for help in Haish, we went to them too, but then the regime bombed Haish with their warplanes.'

A fighter came through and, refusing to sit down, told Abu al-Majd he had to see off some combatants who were heading to the front line.

'Tell this lady about the defectors in the battalion,' Abu al-Majd instructed the fighter, who looked at him in surprise. He added, 'The sister is an Alawite.'

'Why did you say that?' I asked him, angrily. I was shocked that he had revealed this about me, putting me at risk. Not only was I unused to having my identity discussed in the context of religion, but I had expected him to keep it a secret because of the sectarian tension.

But he answered excitedly, 'So the kid knows we're all one people.' Nevertheless, I was fuming.

Someone nearby scoffed and shook his head. 'We aren't one people, and her presence doesn't change a thing!'

The fighter spoke up: 'I had defectors with me from every sect: Druze, Christians and Alawites. Some of them are still fighting along with us, but there have been problems. I mean, some people are afraid of them.'

'The Nusra Front wants an Islamic caliphate,' Abu al-Majd said, interrupting, 'and this is impossible in Syria. It's very difficult. This is a revolution of all the Syrians.' He addressed me as he spoke, and stood up. 'We're on our own,' he continued. 'The world has abandoned us and Hizbullah is fighting with Assad against us. We have no way of knowing what will happen.'

The fighter opened the door, letting in a cold breeze.

'Where are you going?' I asked.

The young man had half disappeared behind the door, but came back through and replied, 'We're going to liberate a checkpoint that has eleven soldiers and a tank.'

Abu al-Majd turned to leave with him. He said goodbye to me without shaking hands, simply placing his hand on his chest. 'We'll meet again, if we live, God willing.'

I stood up too as the others bade him farewell. 'Go safely. God protect you,' they said.

'Abu al-Majd is one of our best officers,' Raed told me after he had left. 'Not all of them are like him. Some bring the corruption of their military past with them when they come here. All in all, in Kafranbel we have four brigades, thirty battalions and ten senior officers. But not all of the battalions here are made up of military men, there are some civilian ones. While the military men are more disciplined, they aren't necessarily honest – mind you, nor are the civilian ones. Some of the military men tried to repeat the methods of Assad's army, replicating their corruption and oppression of the people, but we wouldn't allow them. At least until now. Our security battalion as well, some of them were part of the state security apparatus before they defected and brought with them the same old ways of controlling and bullying people. And now we have a revolutionary military council. We're trying to organise ourselves, but people aren't happy because they no longer trust anyone and they've started to lose faith in us.'

Raed stopped talking, at which point Ahmed excused himself, saying he was going to see his fiancée. This prompted a chorus of teasing and jibes, and Razan and I waited till it had calmed down before discussing the schools project. At that point, I still hoped we could complete this revolution with the tools at our disposal, despite all the challenges.

My last day in Syria, in sunny February. As I looked through the car window at a green plain rising to a plateau covered in dense olive groves, I felt anxious because the moment of my departure always filled me with the most intense feelings of exile. This time, I would be travelling over the border at another unofficial crossing point. Mohammed and a young man called Abdullah were waiting in the car with me. I had first met Abdullah a few months earlier, in the hospital in Reyhanli, and would get to know him better on my third trip back.

A group of Turkish soldiers were on patrol. They were pacing back and forth, throwing indifferent glances towards the columns of Syrians approaching the border on the other side. Some Syrians sat beneath the trees, looking through the fence. Some stopped directly in front of the Turkish soldiers, while yet others moved back and forth, almost as if mimicking the patrol's own movements. Cars of every shape and type lined both sides of the road at this sheep gate. Entire families stood around waiting, laden with their few worldly belongings. Now and then, from the olive groves on both sides of the border, gunfire would ring out.

Abdullah, who had been crippled for life after being wounded in battle, kept laughing. He was worried about his fiancée, saying he didn't want to make her a widow before her time. 'I live with death,' he explained. 'My leg was wounded but I'm still a fighter. I don't want to stop fighting Bashar al-Assad but I don't want to make the girl a victim too.'

Children were running about between the cars, hawking their wares. Aged between five and fifteen, the children seemed to be selling just about everything you could think of: gas lighters, bread, sunglasses, cold juice, fizzy drinks, coffee and tea. People would start arriving here in the morning and then wait until night-time to cross, to be smuggled through. Some didn't have enough money to pay the smugglers so they'd wait for nightfall and then try to creep through by themselves. But this would irritate the smugglers, who didn't want to lose any profits, so they'd report these penniless refugees.

Once, the smugglers had sent an old man and his son back, and there had been nothing for the old man to do but stay there by the divide separating the two countries for several nights until he had become extremely ill from the bitterly cold weather. After trying in vain to escape the shelling, which had demolished his house, he had ended up being transferred to a Turkish hospital – and that was how he'd eventually managed to enter Turkey.

For me, the last two days had been exhausting: I was shattered not so much from the tours we'd made of women's houses in Jabal Zawiya, and from constantly having to flee the shelling, but because of events during the last twenty-four hours, which I had spent in the village of Ayn Larouz with Abu Waheed, meeting a group of fighters. Our hosts had been Maan, a battalion commander, and his cousin Mostafa, a lawyer and activist who had stayed in the village to carry out relief work as well as development and media activities. We had met in a house that consisted of two small rooms separated by a yard, with one room being for the men and the other for the women. The surrounding countryside was shelled while we were there, but we weren't too worried as the neighbouring village of Baylon seemed to be the target.

During my meeting with Maan and Mostafa, I wanted to come to a decision about an aspect of the women's projects I was involved in. During this second trip to Syria, I had started to draw up plans for working with women in rural Idlib – an area that would be a challenge to break into. This wasn't due to the particular circumstances of the women there, but because of the general situation in the Syrian countryside, where, over the past decades, there had been a serious decline not only on an economic level, but socially and culturally as well. Women were the first to pay the price in this war, and the situation was starting to seem even more dangerous for them with the infiltration of the extremist militant groups – strangers to Syrian society – and their attempts to enforce a very different way of life.

With Mostafa in particular, I discussed how we could create sustainable centres for civilians, particularly for groups focusing on women and children, to help resist the radicalisation of society through education and economic empowerment. Every new women's centre could potentially become a self-managing organisation.

'We won't be able to if the regime doesn't stop bombing the liberated areas,' he said, repeating a sentiment I had heard so many times: 'We pushed Assad out on the ground but he's made a comeback in the sky.'

His battalion commander cousin, Maan, had brought with him ten fighters, two of whom were from Suwayda, a Druze city in the south-west close to the border with Jordan. The fighters boasted about having Druze and Alawite men in their ranks. One of the Druze fighters said that he hadn't wanted to kill anyone but he was an officer who had defected. He said that now he could only be on the side of the truth. But this combination of men wasn't the situation in every battalion I met; only a few battalions would allow fighters from religious minorities to join them.

Mostafa's wife served food but didn't sit down. During the meal, I had to go and sit in the women's room across the courtyard for a while too, then return to the men's room afterwards. The customs here didn't allow for men and women to sit and eat together. As I helped her prepare the food, I discovered that the wife had been studying law but stopped when the conflict began. Together, we agreed on a schedule of visits I would make to the women of the village.

The trees were in blossom and I went out onto the plateau, where the two small rooms stood like separate little houses. The sky was clear, the sounds of the explosions distant and there was no smoke on the horizon. The fighters inside were talking about the divisions between the battalions and, on the other side of the plateau, a woman was rocking a small blue cot, tucking in her baby with a thick blanket. Beyond the plateau stood a rocky mountain, punctuated by olive trees. Further down the plateau, a few stone houses were scattered here and there between the olive groves, and they hadn't been shelled. The voices of the fighters indoors were getting louder.

Mostafa came out to bring me a glass of tea. 'How beautiful our country is. Don't worry, we'll rebuild it,' he said, before leaving me to my thoughts.

Hearing his words, I fell quiet. I was occasionally struck by muteness and, sometimes when this happened, could stay for days without speaking to a soul. Right now, I couldn't move my tongue.

Instead, I listened to the men talking in the room behind me, the sounds of their voices drifting through the walls and the window. The conversation went on for a long time about the Nusra Front and its media network called al-Manara al-Bayda (The White Minaret), which the Front used to broadcast their suicide operations and killing sprees.

'Don't believe that this huge financial network and the arrival of all these mujahideen have come about by accident. Something like that doesn't happen by accident! And there's nothing random or accidental about our impoverishment and our lack of weapons,' Maan noted, before making one last remark, 'but we won't despair.'

When they lowered their voices, I sensed the conversation had turned to me because soon afterwards Maan shouted out, 'Miss Samar, do you need anything?'

I found the words to reply, 'No, thank you.'

When I went back to the men's room, the talk had moved on to the transportation of fuel and getting electricity to the shelled villages where power and water supplies had been cut off. One of the fighters was criticising the fact that, whereas a lot of the schools had been closed and turned into accommodation for displaced people, many of them had been transformed into military bases, and Abu Waheed urged them to find another solution. As we sat there, more fighters streamed into Mostafa's house while others left because there wasn't room for everyone. They began to talk about the National Council, the Coalition and the official political opposition, and how votes were being bought, all to the benefit of those holding the purse strings.

I sat in the corner, listening. These fighters were men whose ages ranged between seventeen and fifty, some of whom had received a university education and others who could barely read and write. All of them had abandoned everything else they had in life to focus on combat and civil work in the revolution. They were trying to save the liberated areas from future ruin. A fighter from Jarjanaz explained that the situation there was no better than in Jabal Zawiya, where I'd seen the Roman ruins, but that fault lines had started to emerge between the regions, which would become more distinct in the future if things carried on in the same way.

'Financial aid that is unaccounted for can breed corruption,' I suggested. They agreed with me, but said that financial backing was always conditional on loyalty. Generally, there was a lot of turning a blind eye.

'That's the nature of revolutions,' I told them.

'But the dangerous thing,' Maan added, 'is that there's no longer any trust between the military and civilian groups. There's no trust on any level.'

I went outside again to smoke a cigarette. The conversation indoors was becoming increasingly tense. Three gunmen passed by at the lower end of the plateau. Two planes appeared in the sky relatively close to us, but everything seemed normal.

An old man appeared beside me. 'Yesterday they bombed our house with a MiG plane,' he said. Then he asked, 'Whose daughter are you, my dear?'

'I'm not from here, uncle,' I replied, and repeated, 'I'm not from here.'

The old man walked down the slope towards the armed men and asked them if the planes were about to drop a bomb.

'No, I picked up their radio frequency and heard them saying they're going to Aleppo,' one of them said.

The sound of a violent explosion echoed from the village of Baylon. We would find out that evening that it had killed thirteen people.

The old man tutted, scowling at the three fighters. 'You said it wouldn't bomb us . . . Right, it won't bomb us . . . Huh, you reckon?' He kicked the ground as he muttered scornfully, 'Our house is gone, the mother of my children is gone, the children are gone, everything's gone, O God.' He raised his hands to the sky and shouted, 'O God!' Then he carried on trudging down to the foot of the hill.

I always felt a strange light feeling whenever there was bombing. A sense of emptiness fixed me to the spot as I watched the old man's retreating back.

I recalled the old man as Mohammed and I approached the border, having left Abdullah in the car. Many elderly people like the old man were lined up in front of me, waiting for an opportunity to cross. As I walked, I tried to remember what the thermal balloons looked like that were dropped before the missiles. When they were launched, the balloons burnt at very high temperatures and gave off a strong flash of light and radiation, with the intention of repelling any attacks when the rockets themselves were fired. But I had never learned much about them or the different types of rockets or shells.

A group of children started to grab on to the hem of my black abaya, the ankle-length robe covering me. They were urging me to buy something. One of the children walked up to the woman behind me and tried to get her attention in the same way. He looked like a small thief, angry about being left alone like this. I turned my head away because the mere prospect of buying something from him would only encourage dozens of other children to approach us. These boys had shot up like grass all along the streets of the deserted villages, where the bombing never stopped. Besides selling petrol and mazut at the roadside, they crept around the demolished houses, searching for anything to sell, and they'd hover near the military battalions, waiting to join in the fighting. They slept on the ground in the olive groves. Everywhere overflowed with them, as if they had all been suddenly abandoned and had never been anyone's children. They were the children of chance, living in the hope that an opportunity would come their way, which would uproot them from the ground and toss them into a more welcoming world than this one.

Together, Mohammed and I walked past the queues until we ended up not far from the Turkish soldiers stationed on the other side, where various nationalities were sneaking across. And to think the Turks had been saying lately that they had increased their monitoring of fugitives from Syria because of bombings near the border. The Bedouin trafficker who was to lead me to the other side would be waiting for me at the top of the hill looking down on these Turkish soldiers.

'Why don't we hide in the groves? Will the journey take long?' I asked Mohammed.

He reassured me that the soldiers only ever fired towards the sky. 'I know, but it's strange that they allow all these fighters to cross into Syria,' I replied.

In the distance, I saw the trafficker walk down the hill towards us and peer between the olive trees. With a nod, he signalled to me to cross the border. I was terrified. As soon as I got closer to exile I started trembling. Mohammed couldn't go any further with me. The sky was still blue and the sun harsh, but the biting cold refreshed me.

I was carrying my small backpack. Although I'd only brought a few clothes with me, Noura had weighed down my bag with presents – a woollen scarf she'd knitted for me and a small beaded purse for my daughter. The women of the family had also rustled up whatever gifts they could. Now I tossed my clothes out onto the path, keeping their presents, before hoisting the bag back onto my shoulders.

I moved further away from Mohammed. I was afraid he'd die while I was gone, as I worried whenever I said goodbye to any of the men. He remained where he was while the trafficker met me and signalled that we had to set off right away. Thin as a stick of cane, with a gold tooth, the man spoke rapidly as he walked ahead, making me run after him. A Turkish soldier shouted so I froze. The trafficker stopped and lowered his head, gesturing for me to follow. He led me around the base of the hill where I could see the crowds of people surreptitiously fleeing across the border. They were mostly poor, young and male. Among them was a woman covered completely in black. The smuggler signalled with his hand for me to keep up, and I climbed up the slope after him as quickly as I could. I stumbled.

'Please, carry my bag for me,' I asked. The smuggler looked annoyed and didn't move from where he was standing.

'I'll give you whatever money you want,' I said. He glanced down at the border and I followed his gaze. Mohammed and Abdullah were both standing below, looking up at us. In the distance they seemed like two poplar trees. If they knew how rude this fellow was, they would've given him a good beating, I was sure. The smuggler reluctantly came back and picked up the bag, complaining and cursing his luck. I didn't have the strength to move again until I noticed that the crowds of fleeing people had started to rise up the hill and I suddenly found myself alone. I started sprinting. There was an excruciating pain in my ankle. I'd sprained it. I limped on to the brow of the hill, where I turned and waved, before going down the other side.

This was Turkey; Syria was behind us. I turned again and promised aloud, 'I'll be back soon.'

# The THIRD CROSSING

## July–August 2013

I was on my way back again.

As I'd waited to board my flight to Antakya, I'd been taken aback by the large swathes of fighters who I presumed were also heading to Syria. It was the first time I'd noticed how they were beginning to resemble the pro-government *shabiha* militiamen. The heaviness I felt inside only released when, to my great surprise, I found Maysara, the rebel fighter, and his girls, Aala and Ruha, waiting for me at Antakya airport's arrival gate. They'd become a part of my story – not the kind of story with jinns and sprites, but the kind of tale you would imagine existing as a place of refuge inside an enchanted crystal ball. The two girls had both become very thin and had grown up considerably during the course of a year, but Aala still showered me with kisses just like every time we'd met before and she wouldn't stop hugging me. She was eight years old now. Her hair was curly and frizzy and her fingernails were painted in an array of different colours.

On the fifty-minute drive from the airport to the family's new home in Reyhanli, Aala told me every detail of the story of their crossing into Turkey. They had made their escape in the morning and they had taken just a few clothes with them. One of the traffickers had carried her youngest brother when they'd had to cross a muddy cornfield next to the border. She said how afraid she'd been and how she'd screamed and flung herself into her father's arms. Her scream meant that the Gendarmerie had discovered their presence, so they'd been forced to hide in the irrigation channel which formed the border dividing the two countries. They were drenched in so much mud and filth they looked like clay statues when they eventually emerged.

As she told me this, Aala was laughing and pressing her palms against my face. We were friends of the same fate. We had known each other for a year now, we'd grown up together during that time, and ever since those days in August 2012, when we used to hide from the missiles beneath the stairs in their house, or crammed in with the rest of the women and children in the basement, I knew we'd become firm friends. I had presents wrapped for her in my bag and signalled to her with a wink that there was something special waiting for her. She laughed, and continued to tell the story of their escape.

'Then we ran. It was torture. All that running and the mud and the sound of bullets and the smuggler shouting at us to hurry up!'

That day until nightfall, Aala and her family had hidden on the muddy banks of the irrigation channel, before starting to walk silently through the darkness. They couldn't use a torch for fear of attracting attention to themselves. The fighters, in contrast, were able to cross in broad daylight. Although there had been a number of access points for Aala's family to escape through, security in the area was tighter than usual that day and it was too risky. They ended up having to wait for some hashish smugglers to go first. Among these were two women smuggling hashish under their clothes, and the family had to remain behind the barbed wire in the cornfield until midnight when the Gendarmerie arrested the women and began monitoring the whole area. As Aala talked, I imagined them having to keep quiet and wondered whether dust rising from the rustling reed beds in the ditch nearby would have made them want to cough, but Aala told me that she'd held her breath so tightly she thought she might suffocate, and that she'd clamped her hand over her mouth to stop herself from screaming again.

Her twelve-year-old sister, Ruha, continued, 'After hours of waiting, these guys came over from Atma. They carried us across the irrigation stream – it wasn't easy. I was frightened as I watched their feet trudging slowly in the mud. Five smugglers helped my father carry us across. The water was deep and dangerous and we had to stifle our urge to scream. They were walking along the edges of the ditch, trying to save us from drowning in its depths in the pitch-black night. We carried small rucksacks on our backs, and my mother seemed so far behind; she was weary and edged forward so slowly. Then we tripped and fell and were soaked by the mud and water. But the road was great,' Ruha added, laughing. 'Yes, it was wonderful. A tank had passed over it several times before and evened it out. We were really happy: this tank had flattened the road for us, and we could get out of Syria and escape to the other side.'

Ruha had been wary of her father because he'd been so angry with her sister when she'd screamed and exposed them, but later at the house the girls' younger siblings Mahmoud and Tala claimed they hadn't been scared.

But Aala whispered, 'You know, I'm *still* scared, I swear.'

Aala's complexion had yellowed and her eyes had lost their once piercing brilliance, replaced by a new sadness. Ruha looked years older than her actual age. Their mother, Manal, was also so quiet that her voice was barely audible. She was skinny and calm, though her eyes were permanently full of sorrow ever since being forced to leave her home in Saraqeb.

The family's situation was better than that of many other refugees: they hadn't been forced to live in one of the camps or out in the open, like the majority of Syrians who left their homes. And they could afford to rent a house in Antakya and send the children to school. Yet they faced many challenges: besides having to learn a new language, they were much poorer than they had been before, and Maysara needed to work harder than ever to earn enough money for them to get by. They too had become exiles.

Having spent time with the family in Reyhanli, it was time for me to head towards the border where the young men had travelled from Saraqeb to meet me. Abdullah, who'd accompanied me back to the border on my last visit, and his brother, Ali, were waiting for me. Whereas Abdullah had been crippled from a leg wound, his brother had been shot in the eye. The prospect of seeing my old companions again was as exciting as meeting my own family. Every time I said goodbye to them it felt as though I'd never see them again. Then I returned and it was like I'd been living among them for the rest of my life.

We would be crossing the border together: Abdullah, Maysara, Ali, a young man I hadn't met before, and me. This time though, and as an exception, they had decided we would cross the border at Atma, as the majority of Syrians did who'd lost their IDs and papers in the shelling. I hadn't come this way before, because my friends hadn't had the right connections in place to ensure I could pass through without any difficulties. But now they did and here we were. The border area around Atma resembled components of a stage that had been taken apart and, in order for us to cross the Atma camp checkpoint, we had to enter through a point the Turks had established specifically to prevent Syrian refugees escaping into Turkey. In the suffocating heat we approached the first security checkpoint, which consisted of two small rooms stuffed full of border officials. My travelling companions had decided I should use one of their sisters' names to pass through security as it would be safer for me to travel incognito.

It was the middle of July. Not a single white cloud marred the clear sky. The sun was stiflingly hot, as was the dust and the long robe I wore with a veil that, combined with my large sunglasses, concealed most of my face, so much so that I no longer recognised myself. Yet this disguise was crucial to our safe passage. The scorching sun was less of a burden knowing we wouldn't have to scale any hills, or sprint under a shower of bullets fired by the Gendarmerie, or crawl through barbed wire.

When we arrived at the barrier, we began to see long columns of women and their children coming the other way – people were pouring in and out of the country, some to Atma, some to Turkey and on to other places. I saw a woman who looked to be barely twenty, with a swollen belly, who was carrying a baby and holding a boy by the hand. The little boy was wearing large sunglasses and he was bald, his head completely burnt. So too was his skin, which was covered in red, fleshy and protruding scars that resembled pieces of intestine. His face looked like a plastic mask that was wrinkled and torn. Thin threads of scar tissue bulged from his neck, connecting to his shoulder bones. Although he looked no older than eight, he was like a mummified human corpse, and crept behind his mother as she gripped his hand.

Several women overtook her and a young man appeared whose right arm and leg had been severed. He was hopping in a way that reminded me of a rabbit. Two other young men appeared from behind him, hopping in the same manner. They were racing each other to a small shady platform that people were cramming themselves onto, seeking respite from the stifling air. It was impossible at times like this – with the intensity of the midday heat, the dark-blue sky – to take in the crowds passing through: those fleeing the bombing, smugglers and people profiteering from the business of getting people in and out, the young warmongers and batch after batch of Arab and foreign fighters.

It wasn't even possible to see where to step next because we were part of such a dense throng. The brain became redundant as each person was transformed into a robot. The thought of moving from one crowded spot to the next was enough to fill you with joy. Even the vast plains on both sides of the road seemed dense with yellowed trees. I gazed at everything I passed with astonishment, as though I had just been born.

After having our names recorded at the second checkpoint by a Turkish civil servant, we were through and we got into a waiting car. I sat in the front seat while the young men crammed themselves into the back. They insisted on indulging me, or maybe they clung to the same notion I did, still believing that all we had was each other and that we had to protect one another and the sorry ideals we had set out to achieve: freedom and dignity. I suspected that in their eyes I was a concept, and I certainly saw them in the same way. To me, they embodied the concept of a free, fair and democratic Syria. But, in the face of the profound transformations that had taken place since the revolution, believing in ideals like these was now like trying to grasp the wind. Nevertheless, at that moment, as they sat bundled into the small back seat, in the heat of the sun, doing what they could to make me feel comfortable, I felt an awkward lump in my throat. I reminded myself of my favourite phrase, 'Life's too short for sadness', and waved at two of the young men with severed limbs.

Abdullah, Maysara, Mohammed, Ali and many others had a peculiar relationship with irony. They scoffed at everything, including themselves, and I picked up this habit from them: a harsh, biting sarcasm and mockery of death. It was a relationship that seemed chaotic and courageous but it was the only way they could maintain their resistance. They gave death a sound kicking.

On the drive back, the men were criticising the ISIS men in their black turbans and the behaviour of the radical Islamist battalions. They made fun of the fashion-conscious NGO reps and the proliferation of training workshops near the border. These days, there were countless experts, trainees and journalists hanging around recording events.

'But what about the people who are dying – murdered, bombed or being starved to death?' asked Ali.

We entered the refugee camp at Atma. According to my companions, most of its current inhabitants were from Hama. We drove along with the swarms of displaced people carrying their belongings and standing under the glare of the sun. A stench emanated from the filthy sewage channels, which ran between the tents and were covered in flies and other insects. Stalls had cropped up on either side of the road, forming a makeshift market selling food, fixing shoes, and filling up gas cylinders or kerosene lamps. The stalls were just tents held down with a few rocks. Although the camp had a large generator, it was not large enough and there was no electricity at night. While there was a huge water tank, there were no services. But the tents, scattered beneath the open sky, were spotless on the inside. Some of the refugees had even started growing plants around them, but it was the olive trees that protected the tents erected among them from the elements.

We wandered through the camp: all around I saw deep poverty, emaciated bodies, threadbare scraps of clothing. Groups of children played barefoot under the blazing sun. All the women were veiled; some of them wearing a *khimar* which covered the face as well as the hair. I talked to one woman briefly to ask whether it was true that young girls were being married off to old men and she confirmed that it happened all the time. Made destitute by the war, many families were resorting to marrying off their daughters – some as young as fourteen or fifteen – as a means of overcoming poverty and hunger.

I asked if I could speak with a particular girl whose name had been given to me by an activist. The girl had been married off then divorced after a month, then married again to a Jordanian man forty years her senior, with whom she'd stayed for only three months. As I tried to persuade the woman to help me meet this girl, the woman's husband turned me away from their tent.

Before we resumed our journey, we needed to wait for the men who were going to accompany us to Saraqeb. They were late because the town had been bombarded and they weren't able to leave until the shelling, which claimed the lives of four people, had died down. While we waited in the camp for them to arrive, we sat under an enormous olive tree, and a helicopter passed over. It dropped four barrel bombs at different points in the distance. Barrel bombs were basically water tanks, rubbish bins or ordinary mazut cans, stuffed with dynamite, explosives and iron bars, causing indiscriminate death and destruction. I heard the explosions. My mind was still haunted by the image of the man in his twenties with the severed arm and leg, hopping. I had watched him as he glanced at the girls with a broken look on his face, and the thought of his wasted manhood broke me too. Brave Abdullah's booming voice pulled me out of my stupor as he started to joke about the bombing that had just taken place.

'I swear every other house has had a bomb, but we're still waiting,' he said. We laughed and lit our cigarettes, as he continued, 'The MiG plane may as well have a cigarette too while it waits for our turn to die. And so much for the barrel bombs – they're going to need something stronger!' He grinned and added, 'We don't recognise our friends when we bury them, their faces are so mangled. Some of them survive a MiG airstrike, then two days later are ripped apart by a shell. I wonder which is the better death?'

He stopped laughing and the muscles in his face contracted for a second.

'Once a MiG bombed us at al-Sena'a and thirty people were killed. I was there then but I didn't die. I survive every time. Let's see where this waiting will lead us!' he said, and gave another loud laugh.

Behind us stood an ISIS military base – a sprawling one-storey building made up of several sections, situated amid olive trees, and heavily guarded. It was prohibited to go anywhere near it and no one from the other battalions knew what was inside. There were SUVs all around and trucks going in and out, all draped in thick khaki cloth. This time round, the organisation's presence was obvious in the area; they had started to appear in the north months ago. As we headed towards Saraqeb, we were only stopped once, at an ISIS checkpoint, which was manned by five dark-skinned fighters from Mauritania and Iraq dressed in black robes and turbans. They searched us and reluctantly allowed us to pass after the others told them the name of the combat faction they belonged to. How could these strangers occupy our land? I felt outraged at them stopping us and making us identify ourselves when they were in our country!

We passed by the Qah refugee camp on the road between Atma and Akrabat. These days, there were refugee camps spread along the entire border. I learned that the number of horses used in smuggling operations had increased, and that the Bab al-Hawa crossing was run by the Ahrar al-Sham militant group. Then we passed through the camp there. The children dotted beneath the heat of the sun were the most striking feature, especially in Bab al-Hawa market where they seemed to be running the show. Here, the Farouq Brigades were in charge.

They were aligned with the Free Army and they had no dealings with Ahrar al-Sham.

Shops were spread out along a half-kilometre stretch in Maarat Masreen. There were huge areas where rubbish had accumulated among military vehicles, new Jeeps and large Land Rovers, many of which belonged to ISIS fighters. The cars had no number plates. The revolution had created an enormous, profitable black market where a number of entrepreneurs were set to reap a considerable profit. It was almost certainly in their interest to keep the war going.

Paraffin and mazut were being sold in barrels and plastic containers along the roadside, just like they had been at Atma camp. The difference here was that the containers were bigger and were being sold by children, not adults as they had been there. When we were stopped at another ISIS checkpoint the men warned each other to be careful because it was Ramadan. We needed to make sure no one could smell any cigarette smoke coming from the car, because if they arrested us for breaking the fast, there was no telling what they would do. We might be whipped or even killed. The men told the ISIS fighters that I was one of their sisters, and that I needed to accompany my brother to give him medical treatment. I didn't look at them, but each time we passed one of their checkpoints, I felt a surge of trapped anger in my chest that sent me into a coughing fit.

We'd reached the outskirts of Saraqeb when an ambulance stopped beside us. It was carrying wounded people who were in a critical condition. The paramedics in the ambulance informed us that Saraqeb was being bombed as we spoke and advised us not to go there now, before zooming off noisily.

As we stood talking I gazed at the landscape. A sunflower field extended to our right, all the way to the horizon, each yellow disc drooping under its load. The sun was also lowering. Ahead of us lay a dust cloud and in the distance we could hear the ambulance and the screams of the wounded. Suddenly the sound of a tractor emerged from the middle of a wheat field on the other side of the road. The man ploughing his land was indifferent to the sounds of the explosions as he sat on his tractor. We watched as he gathered up the straw and made a fire by the roadside.

'We're going to a bomb site in town. Are you coming with us or going back to the house?' asked one of the young men accompanying me.

'I'll come with you,' I replied, and we headed towards Saraqeb where the flames and dust clouds awaited us.

As we drove through the town, I noticed that the extent of the destruction was even more obvious and widespread than it had been during my previous trips. Yet the changes differed from one street to the next. In the areas where the bombardment had been most concentrated, there were no signs of life; these neighbourhoods seemed completely deserted and most of the buildings had been totally destroyed. In other neighbourhoods, where there had been less shelling and bombing, a few men and children could be seen in the streets, but not many. And in the middle of the market, despite the intensity of the bombardment, a few stalls were open selling certain provisions. Life went on amid the chaos.

The next morning I went outside into the courtyard of the house, ignoring Noura's words of caution. I felt that they were being overcareful by insisting we stay behind closed doors, away from the yard that was so dear to me, especially since we could run inside straight away if anything happened.

'You'll get hit by shrapnel if you stay out there in the courtyard!' Noura shouted out from inside.

There was a knock on the door and a displaced woman whom Noura and her family had been helping came in through the house and walked straight out into the courtyard. Noura felt anxious whenever a stranger came to the house and saw me or asked about me. She wanted to protect me from being the subject of gossip because she was worried about my safety. She hurried out with her cup of coffee to join us and stood between me and the other woman. Her husband, Abu Ibrahim, was upstairs with the old ladies, listening to a portable two-way radio. The two-way radio transceiver or walkie-talkie they used was a device capable of broadcasting across a range of around eighty kilometres. Families used them to determine the location of planes with the help of fighters and battalions, as well as for communicating with each other. However, they weren't easy to come by and only a few people had them. Abu Ibrahim told us that the village of Sarmin had been bombed a short while ago. It was clear that the planes weren't bombing areas indiscriminately, and that there was an organised plan to destroy the northern provinces, not only using aircraft, but with the aid of extremist battalions. It seemed that an entire society was undergoing a transformation, being wiped out then reconstituted once again.

I was keen to get going because I needed to finish all my meetings with the women about their small business initiatives before heading to Kafranbel. Whereas on my last visit, Ayouche had taken me out, Maysara refused to let me go out on my own with his sister without armed chaperones to accompany us, because, as he said, 'There are more mercenaries around than rebels and you're easy to kidnap.' He was very aware that, as an outsider from a different sect, I was a prime target for abduction by mercenaries or mujahideen. It wasn't the revolution or the rebels that made it dangerous for women like me to go out on our own.

Suddenly the earth and the sky shook and a dust cloud rose from the furthest edge of the neighbourhood. A missile had landed. I stood nailed to the spot until Noura screamed at me to get inside quickly, so I followed her in, walking as if hypnotised. After a second passed without any sound of aircraft and nothing announced on the transceiver, we knew it must have been artillery shelling.

Outside, the sun was high and even after the shelling had subsided, the children carried on watching the sky. A fern that Noura had planted in their small garden was covered in dust and shards of the broken windowpane. I wiped the delicate plant and then washed it with a little water, which dispelled the smell of smoke and dust. Our hearts must have turned into stone for us to cope with life amid the madness of all this killing.

Abu Ibrahim appeared.

'Why didn't it sound like a shell this time?' I asked him.

'God is the only Protector. God is the only Protector,' he replied. Then he told me I could go out now because there was no sign of planes in the sky.

'As for the missiles, only God knows what's coming,' he said as he pointed to the sky.

Noura and her guest resumed their daily activity of planning the day's meal and all talk of the bombing dissipated within a few minutes. The conversation once again revolved around discussing the range of vegetables and meat available in the markets, wondering whether bread would be distributed that day or the next, or when they'd be able to source mazut for the generator. They talked about various ways of rationing the scarce water to wash clothes, and wondered how long the family could carry on like this, as resources would run out when the farming season came to an end because it was impossible to store fresh produce without a reliable supply of electricity. Besides this, they worried about what would become of the two old women upstairs, who required constant attention from the wonderful Ayouche, their tireless carer.

Mohammed stood at the front door, waiting for me, so we could head off to catch up with my ladies. We would be meeting them in the home of Montaha, who was the main person helping me in my work with women. Montaha worked so hard; she was constantly busy. Her father had run a charity before the revolution. She hadn't married but had become involved in social work and dedicated her life to helping people.

On our way to Montaha's house, which she shared with her sister Diaa in the centre of town, we passed several groups of people heading out to the countryside around Saraqeb to escape the bombing. Although several rockets had landed outside the built-up areas, death was less likely there. The town centre was the most targeted area and, sure enough, when we arrived, we discovered that two missiles had landed close by Montaha's house, one of them ripping through her bedroom ceiling.

Nevertheless, her home was full of women, around fifteen of them: half were martyrs' wives, and among them were a dentist and a pharmacist. The women were all young, none of them older than twenty-eight, yet each had four or five children. One of those we planned to see later was a widow whose husband had been killed in the bombing as he tended to the wounded, leaving her with seven children. Most of the women were confined to their homes, especially as the majority of them were widows. Our projects focused mainly on home-made crafts and cooking. This was partly because of local custom, but also because of the threat linked to the ongoing conflict, chaos and kidnappings.

Together, Montaha and I created a business plan for each of the ladies. Their businesses were mainly related to knitting, sewing and retail, including opening a small workshop to produce food and sweets that we called the Grocery Store, where seven women worked with their daughters and by which they were able to support themselves. I was excited to see them and to hear how far they'd got with their businesses and how we could develop them further.

We were interrupted when Mohammed rang on the landline to warn us that Montaha's house was in the danger zone because of its central location, and urged us to postpone our work for the day. But I knew that if we stopped now we'd never finish our work since the bombardment was constant. 'I'll call you after I've finished what I need to do,' I replied. Mohammed was hardworking, but deep down he was also full of upset and rage, which left him in a permanent state of anxiety.

I spoke with the women one by one. Many of them told me that their main source of income came from the Al Ihsan Charity Association run by the Ahrar al-Sham Brigades, which gave salaries to the wives of martyrs. In addition to its bakery, Ahrar al-Sham also ran charities, hospitals and schools. Their members were already a well-integrated part of the community because most of them were Syrian and from local towns and villages.

They weren't just a military battalion, but also a religious missionary movement that penetrated the social fabric here in the rural areas of Idlib province. As I'd learned on my last visit, driving around town with Ayouche, under Ahrar al-Sham the Sharia Authority, which was associated with several Islamist military brigades, had become the de facto judicial authority. It was also said that Ahrar al-Sham had started forcing women to wear the face veil and that they planned to establish an Islamic caliphate, bringing over foreign clerics whom they would appoint as advisers and ministers. One of the women complained that her children weren't getting a proper education, and only had a Saudi *mujahid* coming round to teach the kids to memorise the Quran.

But, on the whole, the women concurred that they wouldn't have been able to survive if it weren't for the Al Ihsan Charity, run by Ahrar al-Sham, which was why they would do anything asked of them in order to protect the income they received. One of the women's husbands was a fighter in the Ahrar al-Sham movement and was getting paid two hundred dollars a month. Before leaving the town of Raqqa to ISIS, the Ahrar al-Sham movement had looted a bank to secure funds because, these days, loyalty was achieved through financial dependency.

The ISIS fighters were generally unpopular with the Syrians, and until recently hadn't managed to integrate themselves into the local community, at least not in the countryside around Idlib.

When I asked the women about the local mosque, they said that the preacher was a Jordanian man who came with Abu Qodama of the Nusra Front. ISIS and the Nusra Front had been spreading their influence throughout the border region at that time. They would later control Saraqeb, leading to a war breaking out between them and the Ahrar al-Sham and Free Army brigades, which would result in their departure from Saraqeb, leaving Ahrar al-Sham in charge for some time.

While the relationship between ISIS and the Nusra Front had been cordial at first – a tactic ISIS took with all Islamic military battalions to begin with – it was becoming increasingly fractious and would only be a matter of time before ISIS waged outright war on the Nusra Front as well. The main differences between the two groups lay in the fact that ISIS tended towards extremism and militancy in the application of Islamic sharia law, in terms of killing, slaughtering and *takfir* – declaring others' beliefs to be heresy. Moreover, they wanted to set up a large and borderless Islamic state and were stronger than the Nusra Front in terms of their numbers, arms, finances and media presence. In comparison, the Nusra Front was less extreme in its teachings about the extent to which the sharia should be applied. However, there was not that much difference between the two groups ideologically: both agreed that Islamic law should be included in any system of government. And, as was becoming increasingly clear, both had strong views about the status of women.

Within a few hours, I managed to finish my work with the women at Montaha's house and had time for a brief rest before setting out again. I intended to make some follow-up visits to other women's homes to check on how their projects were going. The missiles sounded close, and Mohammed, my guardian angel, was waiting outside to collect me. Next to a small kiosk in front of the house stood a child with a disfigured face. Dozens of wide-eyed children lined up next to him to watch the outsider: me. The shop, run by a woman who was virtually blind, was empty apart from some low-quality chocolate bars, crisps and some balloons. When I lowered my gaze, it settled on the face of a girl sitting on a chair to the left of the kiosk. She was around seven years old and had no arms or legs. I stood there for a moment, staring at her absurdly. My head throbbed and I thought I might collapse, but the trembling was coming from the sky. The children ran inside and Mohammed yelled for me to get into the car.

It felt like a split in my head was growing and that ants were emerging from it and creeping down to the bottom of my spine. The people here lived side by side with death. This was no metaphor, but reality. They didn't think about any big issues, they weren't interested in understanding the military situation or the political context; they had no space to think. All they could do was struggle to survive. The details that concerned them were whether they would be able to get hold of any flour to make bread. Coffee was a commodity rarely to be found; would they even find any tea or sugar? Would there be any water to wash their faces in the morning? Was one meal going to be enough to feed several mouths? Would any of them reach the end of their natural lifespan?

It was Ramadan and they hoped to break their fast soon before anyone in the family had his or her head chopped off, or before another father was forced to pull the remains of his children out from under the wreckage brought about by a shell or a barrel bomb. The most noticeable thing was that after two and a half years of this daily bombardment, they had forged a new relationship with the sky. They monitored it constantly. No one went out without first glancing up at the sky, or without going up onto the roof of the house to stare into the depths, searching for the source of the next missile to emerge from the blue.

I didn't know why I was seeking some kind of meaning in these recurrences. I had started to sense the futility in this sea of blood. Did I need to drown in it before I could escape into meaninglessness? Should I keep coming back, so I could reach death through my war against it?

We arrived back at the house. Noura was waiting for us. She greeted me with relieved kisses. 'Thank God you're safe.' Abu Ibrahim was sitting near the radio transceiver.

'The plane's gone. It's heading in the direction of Taftanaz,' he said.

We all took a deep breath. Futile questions lodged themselves in my throat.

'Others will die while we are spared,' I said.

Mohammed left us to go and examine the area that had been bombed. Members of the extended family filtered out of the room and circled around the two grandmothers as we started getting ready for the evening's activities. A lavish meal had been planned to break the fast at the end of the day. Who would cook? Who would go and check the scorched farmland? Noura and I started tidying away her needlecraft, some dresses she'd made. She was good at sewing and I suggested she teach girls how to sew and get a small workshop going, but then a voice shrieked from the transceiver, and we jumped up.

'People of Saraqeb, revolutionaries of Saraqeb . . . an aircraft loaded with barrels is heading towards Saraqeb and Taftanaz.'

As we heard the crackle of interference, we froze on the spot. The mere mention of barrels turned everyone to stone. Barrel bombs offered only the slimmest chance of anyone coming out alive from underneath the rubble, which is why we stood there, unable to move. Noura began to scream and I covered my forehead with my hands as the screeching continued from the transceiver. There were potatoes in the oven – I ran and switched off the gas so we wouldn't burn to death. The two old women looked at us in horror.

We could hear the fighter talking through the transceiver: 'I can see it. It's flying at an altitude of six kilometres. We won't be able to shoot it down.'

We could hear the machine gun the rebels were firing in an attempt to fend off the plane's offensive on Saraqeb. The rumbling noise emanating from the transceiver became louder. It was difficult to distinguish whether this was the sound of a MiG bomber plane or a helicopter until after the missile was dropped. There was the sound of a powerful explosion, then the transceiver bellowed, '*Allahu akbar*, God is the greatest! The barrel exploded in the sky. *Allahu akbar!*'

This near miss deserved a small celebration, but we quickly resumed our activities. The men went out to the street, the women back to preparing food and I followed Ayouche into the courtyard to study the sky.

Here is another day I will never forget: 20 July 2013. How could I forget the moment I truly stepped into the void of meaninglessness?

We were in the media centre in Saraqeb, which was split into two separate sections. One room housed the electrical equipment and charging devices, while the other had the Internet and the communication devices. This second room was where I stayed as the fighters didn't tend to go in there. It had also become a guest room for visiting journalists and other media professionals, with technical services available for anyone who needed to use the Internet. In several towns and villages, activists had established similar media centres, which they used to relay news of what was happening on the ground to the outside world.

I was sending emails and writing down some notes about the plan for the women's projects. There were papers scattered around me with details of the women's cases and their personal situations. Suddenly everything seemed difficult. I felt completely drained and when I tried to leave the room to go to the bathroom to wash my face, it seemed as if I was floating. Assad's air strikes had been relentless. They kept us constantly on the run, like wild animals, not to mention the spreading catastrophe of the jihadist groups, who had started to interfere in people's personal lives.

There were a lot of men coming and going in the comms room that day, and the atmosphere was a little odd because there was a woman around. I told them I wanted to stay until it was time to go to the house of the first woman I was meeting. The room was a beehive, full of buzzing activity. The men were young, most of them no older than thirty. One was the editor of a children's magazine called *Zaytoun and Zaytouna*, which was distributed in the north of Syria, another was the photographer for the website dedicated to news from Saraqeb, and another was in charge of recording videos and sending them to media outlets. Sometimes fighters would come in, some from the Saraqeb Martyrs battalion, whose headquarters were only around two hundred metres from the office. As it was Ramadan, we wouldn't eat until the sunset call to prayer according to the local time.

We heard a loud and powerful explosion followed by several others as shards of glass fell from the windowpanes. Everyone rushed out of the room. A cluster bomb had landed on a wall in the adjacent room. There was a hole where the window had been, and the sky and the ground were blazing. The men were shouting that we had to leave, but someone warned us that the plane was still circling above and that we'd been attacked with cluster and barrel bombs. I couldn't grasp what had happened. We couldn't get down to the basement. Cluster bombs scattered little bomblets on the ground that kept on exploding. With us were the Polish journalist Marcin Suder, an English journalist and two Syrian journalists. Marcin immediately went out to the street and began to take photos of the sky.

'I'm coming with you!' I shouted as I gathered up my papers and stuffed them into my bag.

I got into the car with Mohammed, Manhal and Marcin. As we drove, we avoided certain alleyways so that we wouldn't accidentally set off any cluster bombs. One of the missiles that had landed by the office had scorched the earth and the entire surrounding area. Houses had been hit by the three successive barrel bombs and there were young men at work gathering up the casualties. There was virtually no trace left of the buildings that had once stood there. Just rubble and the dust-coloured bodies they pulled out of the wreckage. Everything blended into one colour. I started to take photos of the scene.

'Go to the hospital. They'll need you there,' shouted one of the young men.

As soon as we set off, a cluster bomb landed in the street across the way, unleashing a blazing fire. As we tried to turn away from the bombed area, we heard on Mohammed's walkie-talkie that the hospital had also been attacked by cluster bombs and that a rocket had crashed into the house next door. We set off to the hospital. The only other people on the roads were those who had no choice but to leave; several families were fleeing Saraqeb. The aircraft could still be heard overhead.

'I feel like we're trapped rats and that Bashar al-Assad is killing us just for a laugh,' I said to the others. They didn't respond but this was the closest description I could think of as the regime's aircraft and missiles attacked our town. The hospital lay at the edge of Saraqeb and its proximity to the highway meant it was always exposed to shelling.

At the hospital, we found a group of dusty-faced men, one of whom was collapsed in a blood-soaked chair. People were walking in and out of the building, colliding with one another, everyone in a state of shock and fear. The doctor who was friends with my companions came out and took us to a side room. He was from Saraqeb, thirty years old and angry.

'The other doctors have all fled and there are people outside waiting to be seen. What can I do? I don't have enough drugs. And people are dying. Families are angry. What can I do?'

A man hammered on the door and shouted for the doctor to come with him. A young man had been wounded and they'd taken him to one of the wards. There was a shortage of medicine, equipment, electricity, water – basically everything. The young man was screaming. I went into another side room. There were two beds with a female corpse lying on each of them. I moved closer to them.

'They were killed by the exploding barrels today,' a nurse informed me.

'Can I look at them?' I asked him.

He looked surprised as he replied, 'Yes, OK.'

I moved closer still and lifted the cover from the face of the first corpse. I guessed she was in her late thirties. She would have looked as though she was just sleeping were it not for the blood smeared over her face. I replaced the cover then gazed out of the window and sat on the edge of the second bed next to the corpse of the other woman. The sky resounded with the hum of aircraft.

'What are you doing here?' another young man hollered at me. I realised that I was sitting in between the two corpses, and that I was touching one of them. I stood up calmly. I wasn't myself. It was only because I was cocooned in a bubble of detachment that I could remain steady. I joined the rest of my group in a room with more dead and wounded.

The doctor was still frantic. 'What should I give people?! I have nothing to give them! They're just left here to die. O God! O God!' he kept repeating.

Outside the hospital's main entrance, a man was carrying the corpse of his son in his arms and whimpering, 'Praise be to God, *alhamdu lilah*. Praise be to God. O God, o God!' People scrambled around outside in a frenzy of screaming and commotion. The building next door was on fire.

I approached a white van parked by the hospital gates. In the back of the van lay three bodies: a mother and her two children, wrapped in threadbare bed sheets. The poor were always the first to die. The women's feet were visible, poking out of the tattered sheets and the skin on her legs was dry and cracked. You could see the boy's hazel-coloured hair amid large patches of blood. I later learned that a barrel bomb had landed on them and killed them, even though their home wasn't in the centre of town, and even though the bomb had exploded in mid-air. They'd been killed by falling shrapnel. The van was full of blood.

A man sat on the pavement nearby, staring vacantly at the hospital entrance. He was gazing into emptiness. This was a recurring sight: men sitting to the side of a scene of appalling carnage or next to the corpses of members of their families. Gazing into the void.

I moved closer to the van. 'May God have mercy on them,' I said.

The man looked at me.

'May God's peace be with you,' he replied, before returning to his silence. I walked away from the van when some young men came to carry the three corpses into the hospital. As she was picked up, the little girl's plait appeared and then her face. She was probably no older than four. She had plastic sandals on, but there was no sign of any toes on one of her feet. Only blood vessels and a copious amount of blood. I caught up with the young men and pulled the sheet over her disfigured foot, trying to tuck it in. My fingers were soaked in blood.

'That's the sixth barrel that's fallen,' another man shouted above the noise as we watched the cloud of dust rising opposite us. The same helicopter was dropping its seventh barrel over the centre of town, then spinning around and tossing down another. We couldn't see a thing for the rising dust.

'This is hell!' I screamed and started walking around in circles. All I could see was dust. The thundering sound blasted my ears.

'We're taking you back to the house,' said Mohammed angrily. 'It's too dangerous for you to be here.'

'But the house is just as likely to be bombed!' I answered after I'd stopped walking in circles around myself.

As we headed to the car, the doctor called after us. 'Bring back the days of the MiG planes and the chemical attacks. At least they were merciful compared with these barrels, which destroy everything. There's no escaping them,' he said.

'They want to open up a way through here to allow people to reach the brick factory,' said a rebel fighter who'd come with us in the car. He had been sitting there silently the entire time, crammed into the back seat with the other young men. 'The bombing has been relentless, non-stop for a week. You have to get of here, ma'am!'

I couldn't utter a single word in response. I didn't want to get into a discussion. When the car stopped in front of Abu Ibrahim's house my fury was overwhelming.

'When will you be back?' I asked them.

'We've got to see what we can do for the casualties. We feel more nervous when you're with us. Stay here. We'll get in touch with you later on Abu Ibrahim's walkie-talkie.'

It was becoming clearer to me day by day that it would be impossible for me to even think about coming to live here as I'd dreamed of doing. Although I was living in exile in France, I hadn't learned French yet because I had been resolved to move back to Syria and settle in the north. Until now, Paris had just been a crossing point for me.

That evening, I stayed in the house with Noura, Ayouche and the old women. They were still in the same places as earlier and Noura was in a state of panic. They hadn't gone down to the shelter – there didn't seem to be any point. The old women were silent as usual and Noura was standing up and praying, while Ayouche and I just stared at each other. I went into the kitchen and made a cup of coffee. Just then, Maysara rushed in.

'Come on! Let's go! We're getting out of Saraqeb!' he shouted at us.

The women and I were sent to shelter in a mosque that Abu Ibrahim had established in al-Mashrafiyah, a village that lay about an hour's drive away to the north-west. I was angry because the reason for my being here at all was to bear witness, and I couldn't do that sheltering in a far-away mosque. Scenes like this kept on repeating themselves, each time exactly like the one before: a confrontation with death, with our own helplessness. In situations like these, all resistance meant was staying put to watch death, and then hearing the news afterwards. What could unarmed civilians do in the face of shelling, rockets and barrel bombs? They had no way of defending themselves. The fighters' weapons were futile and it was mostly civilians who died.

On our way to our temporary displacement, crowds of families were still streaming out of Saraqeb. We heard on the transceiver that one of the fighters had dismantled a cluster bomb that had fallen on someone's home, preventing it from exploding. But there were several houses to the right of ours where barrel bombs had flattened everything.

Ahead of us on the motorway, which was often exposed to heavy shelling and pitted with holes that we had to swerve around to avoid, lay the ruins of a car dealership.

A voice screamed out of the radio transceiver, 'Where are the doctors? We need surgeons. We've got a lot of emergency cases here.' And then another voice continued, 'People of Saraqeb. People of Saraqeb. Beware. An aircraft is approaching. An aircraft is approaching.'

I watched out of the car window as people roved around at the roadside looking lost, carrying their few belongings, their heads lowered in despair. We passed three separate families, each turning towards our car as we went by, then an armed man appeared in front of the car and stopped us. He asked us where we were going before allowing us to pass.

'Gunmen kidnapped a woman for the first time yesterday,' Abu Ibrahim said, as we drove off. 'Women aren't usually kidnapped.

And she was from a local village, but they still kidnapped her. They found her husband on the road, murdered. They stole the guy's car and his wife! We have to be careful. These are mercenaries and thieves.'

We stopped briefly near a building with a collapsed roof, which a crane was trying to raise. Five people had been killed in the building, and there was an ongoing search for the body of a young girl. Two of the members of the family who'd lived in the house looked on at the destruction; one was standing in front of the crane, tracking its movements, the other sat on the pavement. We learned that the man was the father of the three children. They had died along with their mother. The second man was their uncle.

On the other side of the street, children were gathering scraps of iron from the explosion, in order to sell them later. The iron bars in the barrel bombs were usually about a foot long at most. A child of about thirteen was clambering over the immense heap of rubble, searching for more pieces, but the men shouted at him to get back down. The child's clothes were tattered, his eyes black and his hair full of dust. It was obvious he'd immersed himself more than once in the debris to collect as many iron rods as possible, presumably to sell them to buy bread.

The man sitting on the pavement lit a cigarette and watched the crane, flicking the dust from his eyelashes. His daughter was still buried under the rubble, but the men told him that she was definitely dead – and may God give him the strength to endure his pain.

We arrived at the mosque in the village of al-Mashrafiyah where we were going to shelter. Here, the locals were Bedouins. The mosque was spacious and divided into several sections using bed sheets. We would be staying here for some time, maybe several days. Many families had sheltered here before us and had left blankets, plastic sheets and simple kitchen utensils. We had brought some soft drinks, bread, cheese and water with us. There was no electricity here, and no water, but there were also no bombs.

We had only just finished cleaning the place up when the two old ladies of the house arrived, helped by Maysara and Suhaib, a nephew who had returned from his studies in Europe to work with the rebels, and to help out with the radio broadcasts and other technical work at the media centre. This was my chance to return to Saraqeb. And this time I was determined.

'I didn't come here to hide away from what's happening! You have to let me come with you,' I insisted. And to my surprise, they agreed.

The old women were carried from the car in the arms of the young men. It occurred to me that, between one displacement and another, there was something that weighed down on the soul yet made the body feel lighter. Sons placed their elders in safe places, and then headed to their own deaths. They exchanged roles with their parents. The elderly grandmother was angry and hadn't wanted to leave her home. The aunt was silent. There were tears in Ayouche's eyes. She told me that she hadn't wanted to leave her home either, to become a refugee. She would have preferred to die with dignity. Displacement stripped us of dignity. Better to die in our homes. But the men paid no heed to the women. They left them there in the mosque, while I went back to the media office with Maysara and Suhaib.

People were starting to emerge from their homes when we arrived back in Saraqeb at around five o'clock. Approximately seventeen barrel bombs had been dropped over the town, all of them on civilian houses and the marketplace. We didn't know how many rockets and cluster bombs had been dropped, but when we arrived at the office the young men said they'd soon find out. Maysara and Suhaib left me in the centre, which had been relocated from the marketplace to another part of town since my first visit. Marcin Suder was waiting for me along with the English journalist and the two young Syrian journalists, one of whom had a broken leg that was being seen to. Marcin was working on some of the photographs he'd taken and in the next room they were discussing which families had fallen victim to the day's bombing. Some victims had lost arms or legs. They'd lifted the dismembered body of one young girl from beneath the rubble.

Finding yourself on the ground in a revolution doesn't require any observation or analysis; you don't need to know how each day will end. All you need are calm nerves and the ability to stay on top of things minute by minute, quickly pinpointing the safest exits, staying as far away as possible from the bombing – which is actually impossible – and ensuring there are doctors and paramedics on hand, as well as activists to document the latest casualties of Assad's warplanes and missiles. You have to keep an eye on the Internet in the hope that it won't be cut off, leaving this small patch of land isolated from the rest of the world as it faces utter annihilation. You also need to be aware of the most minute details and, most importantly, you must hold yourself together and stand strong when confronted by mutilated human body parts and the colossal destruction of homes, never forgetting, even for a moment, that your own collapse makes life harder for everyone around you.

You simply have to walk up to tiny fingers and gather them up from under the rubble. Just pull out the body of another child, her clothes still warm from her urine. And then move on to the next site and carry on searching for more victims. You must forget the faces of the victims so that you can write about them later, so you can tell their stories and narrate to the outside world how their eyes shine as they watch the sky that showers us with barrel bombs and deadly gifts. It makes no difference if you are capable of analysing what is happening; you don't have time to wonder why civilian houses are bombed to smithereens – is it to undermine the popular support for the rebels? – or why the humanitarian projects that activists come back to work on in areas liberated from the regime's control are also targeted. Is it because the regime is targeting military supply lines? None of this matters on the ground. What matters is that you stand up proud and strong as the sky hails down barrel and cluster bombs, nailing you to the spot in fear. This is what I was thinking when the sky lit up again.

Three barrel bombs fell consecutively, along with cluster bombs. We raced down the stairs of the office building, with Marcin and the English journalist carrying the young man whose leg was broken. Then we stood in front of the building's entrance, where a group of young people I didn't know gathered beside us. We didn't know where to go because the helicopter was still circling above us. It had started to get dark outside and it looked like another cluster bomb had landed nearby. The strangers invited us to go with them, but I said no. I told Marcin that it was best for us to go back in since I didn't know who they were and I had been warned about cases of abduction. We wouldn't gain anything by going with them and we really needed to go down into the shelter. The strangers objected, arguing that shelters were no protection from the barrel bombs.

Marcin said he was going to take some photos of the helicopter from the roof, which meant the others would have to carry the wounded man back upstairs. I said I'd go up and wait for him. Marcin looked at me in astonishment. His idea of filming the plane at that moment was crazy. So many people had been killed by exploding shrapnel. In the end, we both went up to the second floor and then out onto the roof. It was the first time I'd got so close to a military aircraft, and it was strange and terrifying.

The sky was a sheet of red. Night hadn't quite fallen. Houses were silhouetted against the sky while lights glittered in the distance and closer by were the residual sparks of explosions. Right there, within the dark-red streak of the dusk sky, a helicopter circled. The houses seemed eerily quiet and calm. For a moment, it all looked like a painting, except for the crowds of people gathered to assess the damage caused by the last three barrel bombs. The aircraft was approaching.

'Let's go down right away,' I said to Marcin, who grabbed hold of me and dragged me towards the stairs. I lost my balance. The sound of the explosion forced us to crouch near the door. Another explosion followed, then a third.

During the moments that precede death, the body is reduced to millions of sensors that are desperate to touch something, the body's only aim being to cling on to anything that can prove it's still alive. It's an instinctive reaction ranging somewhere between delirium and an animal instinct that fights fiercely against the threat of annihilation. My fingers clawed at the air in search of any live organism. I was temporarily blinded. I could see only shadows. Marcin and the English journalist were suddenly in front of me. We collided, then, after a loud bang, separated again during the following moment of silence. We ran as if nothing else mattered. No one wanted to die. Bravery meant nothing now; we were just terrified mortals, running from the threat of oblivion. We sprinted out of the media centre, down the street, and kept running until the bombing stopped.

Mohammed's car pulled up. He had been travelling between bomb sites to help the wounded and document the cases. A young man in the car with him explained that they were now on their way to take food to families at a bakery on the edge of the town. We got in and drove away from the area under attack. Anti-aircraft machine guns could be heard from several districts of Saraqeb, which meant that a plane had been spotted; then explosions echoed nearby so we drove faster. Men were running along the roadside and through the windows on the right-hand side of the car we could see a mass of dust and flames rising. But we didn't stop and we stayed silent. It was pitch-black. When we arrived at the edge of the town, we parked in front of the bakery, which was essentially a large space with a concrete roof. A group of fighters and activists surrounded it, mainly young men with some older men too. The bombing continued, but we sat down and spread out the food we had brought on the ground.

The fighters here were from the Saraqeb Rebel Front, and as such part of the Free Army. With them were an old man and his family, and in a while other families came to join us. There was a machine gun right in front of me. As we ate, I felt embarrassed about reaching my hand out between theirs. Was it possible to think of these young men without associating them with death? Their fingers dipped bread into olive oil. Their faces were tired and their hunger, fatigue and exhaustion remained obvious during that moment of respite, while we ate in peace. Then that sound again. That sound, which still echoes in my ears – the sound of another missile, and the tremors.

I didn't eat much. I smoked; I was smoking constantly. I'd been saying for years that the day would come when I would stop burning my lungs, but I hadn't yet found any compelling reason to give up. Especially now, as I gazed at my cigarette, savouring it as one of the most enjoyable pleasures to be had in life with a hot cup of tea, beneath the bombardment, in such an odd building as this, sitting next to a machine gun and surrounded by combatants cheating death. I was worried about Noura and Ayouche and the old women, even though I knew they were safe while they were sheltering at the mosque. Ahmed brought me to my senses.

'What is it, ma'am? Are you scared of the machine gun?'

Mohammed glanced at him disapprovingly, but I replied, 'Yes, I'm scared. Look: I'm trembling.' We laughed.

Ahmed was a twenty-nine-year-old fighter from Saraqeb. A Damascus rose had been tattooed on his hand. He'd studied at a business college and completed his compulsory military service. When he laughed, he bared his teeth and his cheeks bulged. He was tall, portly and could just about sit cross-legged. Now he raised his hands to the sky.

'O God! I finished military service in January 2011,' he told me. 'I didn't even have a chance to enjoy myself before the revolution began. We went out to protest like everyone else: it was peaceful and all we demanded was reform. Yes, I swear,' he said with a smile, and added, 'but they killed us and arrested us and burnt our homes in Saraqeb. We didn't carry weapons; we just took turns guarding our homes. We had one gun between us – three friends protecting our women and our children from the *shabiha* and the secret police. They killed our friend, and so there were two of us left. I joined the Martyr Asaad Hilal Brigade after that.'

'What made you think about arming yourselves?' I asked him.

This time he didn't laugh. He stopped eating and lit a cigarette.

'A member of the *shabiha* shot at us and our guys here fired back in response. We decided to protect ourselves because they then started shooting at us indiscriminately. We formed vigilante groups of between fifteen to twenty people to protect the town, and in turn they erected five checkpoints around Saraqeb for the army and the secret services.'

Everyone was listening to him. They'd almost all stopped eating, the bombing had subsided and Ahmed's was the only voice to break the silence.

'I didn't intend to kill anyone when I joined the battalion. Whenever we'd enter a battle we'd make sure not to aim our guns at a lethal part of the body. We all agreed to point them at the feet but then things changed. You know . . . they bombed us, arrested us and killed our boys, and things got out of control. They were brutal and we stopped caring where we pointed our bullets. I live with my mother, father and brother now, and I'll never stop fighting Bashar al-Assad, for the sake of the friends who I saw killed in front of my eyes.'

I asked him about the religious extremist battalions that had diverted the revolution's original path.

'I don't understand who you mean exactly; there are different groups. There's a big difference between ISIS and the Nusra Front. A big difference,' Ahmed replied.

'But the Nusra Front are some of the best people; they don't steal, they don't kill. They protect the people,' said another man.

'Not true!' another fighter interjected.

'I'm not insulting the Nusra Front,' Ahmed continued, interrupting the two young men. 'They aren't harming anyone, whereas ISIS has insulted both Islam and Syria. They're strangers who're not related to us in any way. And all Muslims have the right to decide how they interpret their religious law, even when it comes to whether a woman wears the hijab or not.'

I didn't respond to his last comment because I didn't want to engage in that debate, but he was waiting for me to say something. 'Honestly, I can only respect the Nusra Front after they liberated many areas,' he continued.

'But what about their political aims?' I asked.

'This, I don't know!' Ahmed answered. 'But I'll tell you something. Right now we're in a phase of chaos and filth. Everything is grimy. From the regime to the jihadist battalions and the intelligence services, to the police and the rebels. The whole world. We're all mired in filth right now. There's a difference between fighters who have left their families and livelihoods to come and fight in Syria for the sake of their faith, and their leadership, which has associated itself with the secret intelligence services, selling itself to the regime and others. Yes, the leadership of some of the battalions has been infiltrated.'

Ahmed received a modest monthly salary of 1500 liras from his battalion which, according to him, was only enough to cover the cost of his cigarettes. He said he wanted to get married because it was likely that the fighting would carry on for a long time.

'And what about you, ma'am, did God bring you here as some sort of punishment?' he joked. But I didn't laugh, asking him instead how he felt during a battle. I kept a sober expression on my face and he replied with the same degree of solemnity.

'During battle, we're not human, we're animals. It's either kill or be killed.' He gave an ironic laugh and continued, 'The problem is that whereas only some Sunni fighters support the rebels, all the Alawites are behind Assad. So why should all of us Sunnis die while the minorities survive? If they're Syrians like us then why are they keeping so quiet? I don't understand it at all, I swear.

'I'm a fighter but I'm from a good family, I'm educated and I hate killing. I want to get married and have children – which is why I fight, so I can live. But I know the revolution has been infiltrated and we're surrounded by enemies.

'Sometimes I feel like I'm a chesspiece, a pawn, but what should I do? I know they're moving me about as they please. All I know is that I'll never stop fighting Bashar al-Assad. And I realise this is absolute madness and we're heading towards death. But should we die without defending ourselves?

'I've been to Turkey twice. I walked around the streets there and it felt very odd. There was no bombing! There were no planes! And no rockets killing people. Do you know what else? I felt alienated. Because all there is here is death and dying!' He stopped talking.

'Give me a cigarette would you, boss?' I said after a moment's silence. Ahmed's last outburst had left him seething, but now he laughed.

'Nothing's worth it,' he said. 'We're all going to die, perhaps any minute now.' He lit my cigarette and smiled to himself.

'Why don't you write about Abu Nasser?' he suggested, pointing to a thin, young man with a pale complexion and anxious eyes, whom I hadn't really noticed before. He'd been sitting slightly to one side and seemed unconcerned by what was around him. I learned that Abu Nasser was born in 1991 and he'd tried three times to pass his final school exams, the Baccalaureate, but never managed it. He seemed shy and didn't want to speak, looking at me from the corner of his eye.

'Don't be shy, Abu Nasser,' I said. 'You're like my little brother.'

'You are dearer than a sister to me, ma'am, I swear,' he replied quietly and then began his story.

'I took up arms as part of my jihad, my struggle for the sake of God, with the Hassan bin Thabit Battalion that's linked to Ahrar al-Sham. I stopped smoking and went to the front line with them. After we'd stayed in Aleppo for several months, we moved to Menagh airbase at Azaz, where I was given a rifle. I've never fired a single bullet, other than to avenge a friend who was killed in front of me.'

I asked him to tell me about the battalion he belonged to.

'They're an independent group – there were many groups working autonomously. We were at the airbase for three months without striking a single blow. Instead, the Syrian Army attacked us and executed some of our men by shooting them in the head. And then the battalion commander turned out to be a liar. He abandoned us during a battle and just disappeared. I was furious – he was supposed to be our emir! How could he just run away? He even took my rifle with him, even though it'd been given to me as a gift. I found out he'd been taking drugs, smoking and committing all kinds of other sins.

'So I joined up with Abu Tarad, the commander of the Saraqeb Revolutionaries Brigade, and stayed with them for four months. But I can't afford a new rifle – a gun like that costs more than a hundred and thirty thousand liras.'

Abu Nasser said he wanted to continue fighting even though he hoped to finish his studies. He had studied various musical instruments and could play the violin and oud.

Ahmed laughed and interrupted him, saying, 'He's an excellent oud player.'

But Abu Nasser shook his head. 'I really can't play any more!' he insisted.

'Don't lie!' Ahmed shouted back.

'I swear to God, I love the oud but I don't know how to play any more. I have no idea why! I used to think I was fighting against infidels who were killing Muslims. Now I say I'm fighting injustice. If Bashar falls and I'm still alive then I'll go to America where my brother lives, and study music. Before, I was scared I wouldn't die a martyr because I wanted to go to paradise, but then I saw the deceit and the contradictions between what the emir says and does . . .' Appearing older than his age, Abu Nasser straightened up, agitated and morose, his voice filled with despair. 'Now I don't even think about getting married. How can I get married when I might die at any moment? As you can see, we're living under permanent bombardment. And I can tell you that the situation is becoming worse. In Aleppo, if we found a man drinking alcohol, they'd whip him in full view of everyone. There are jihadist battalions who are whipping, burning and slaughtering people.'

'Who are these people?' I asked.

'That's not important,' Abu Nasser concluded, 'but I've seen them slaughtering people because they were Alawites. And whipping people for not following sharia law.'

It was six o'clock in the morning and I was staying at the media centre. The planes had taken to the air early to bomb Saraqeb. The bombers made no effort to hide and we could easily distinguish their unmistakable sound. Through the window facing the battalion headquarters, I watched while a young combatant took up his position behind a 14.5mm machine gun, in the boot of a minivan, and directed the gun towards the sky, aiming it at the plane. I knew the young fighter so I waved at him and started monitoring the sky too. He was soon in another world, concentrating with his body wedged against the machine gun as he fired.

Then I heard the radio screech, 'The plane's gone, guys. God give you strength. Keep your eyes peeled.' The men in the media centre explained that the plane had been deterred by the machine gun.

I went back to the window. The young man was still in the same position, but now he lit a cigarette as he watched the sky. He looked relaxed for the moment as he listened to the transceiver he held in his other hand.

There was a large group of us in the office, including a young man from Damascus with a PhD in law who'd left the capital to join the struggle and help out with the centre's technology and software. He was thin, fiery and enthusiastic, but also anxious. He would end up staying for a few days, working continuously, and then leave – like several other activists who came and went. 'Just like you!' he pointed out to me.

Suhaib, the nephew of the family I was staying with, was also there. A brave fighter, he refused to leave Saraqeb until he died, even though his leg had been crippled during a battle. 'We'll either win or die,' he'd always say. I argued with him often, especially on longer journeys when he drove us up into the mountains to visit the women in the villages, as I was worried that he took too many risks and spent too much time at the front line. But he had a pure heart and was exceptionally brave.

The group included Ayham, a maths tutor, who at the time of my visit was still teaching children. He lived with his brother, who was a teaching supervisor for groups of students and raised pigeons; and he told me he had no plans to leave for the foreseeable period. However, he did end up leaving the area soon after, and months later I learned he had been killed by a missile fired from a plane. My permanent travel companion Mohammed, Manhal, the journalist Marcin Suder, some men from the Ahrar al-Sham group and a bunch of media professionals were all there. In these two modest-sized rooms, they still dreamed that the revolution would continue.

'A miracle will have to happen soon,' said one of them.

Two young men were talking in the corner of the room about how the Islamic battalions had started claiming spoils of war – a principle that paved the way for abuses, looting and the emergence of thieves. The Free Army battalions, on the other hand, had fought against it, deeming it robbery.

'But in the end the Islamists have won,' added the young man who edited and published *Zaytoun and Zaytouna*.

The work in the centre wasn't always very professional but they were learning. Sometimes the relief workers would be required to fight too, and everyone's roles would be turned on their heads, as those documenting events and taking photos were entrusted with tasks related to communications, combat or humanitarian relief.

The office itself, a constant hub of activity, was looking pretty neglected. I felt a bit uncomfortable but I asked Ayham, the maths teacher, and a sixteen-year-old called Badee, who had given me a hand before, to help me clean the room. It was a bit strange for them at first but they did eventually help me.

In the early evening the plane appeared again, making us leap up and head to the window overlooking the machine gun. The young man was still sitting there, aiming the gun and firing successive shots. I covered my ears with my hands and moved away from the window. But three of the young men went to stand next to the machine gun, watching the sky as if they were looking at a paper plane. As usual, it was over within minutes. Then the door opened and Shaher appeared. He was a quiet yet friendly and energetic young man from the Saraqeb Revolutionaries Brigade, part of the Free Army.

'There are two dead bodies in the wadi,' he said. 'Come and help us to identify and bury them.'

'I'm coming too,' I said, covering my head. He gave me an odd look but didn't say anything, and so I followed them.

The sun was scorching and there were sounds of distant shelling on the other side of town. We stopped on the highway. Cypress trees enveloped the road, and on our right was the deep wadi, a dry riverbed, where the two corpses lay, decayed beyond recognition.

The place reeked. I wasn't allowed to move any closer but I caught a glimpse of the colour of the corpses' clothes – one wore tattered red, the other was in black. The heads were missing from the bodies, although one lay not far away. Flies formed a small cloud over them.

Shaher had been relatively cheerful, but now his mood turned sour. Nobody could identify the dead men and it was decided that they should be buried at once. The men started to climb down into the gully, but they wouldn't let me go any further. The cypress trees were slender, their colour tending to a pale green. All around us in the distance we could hear the sounds of aircraft and bombing. The men put masks on and began digging. For a moment I thought I might fall to the ground, overcome by all this death.

I looked across at Shaher, who was a native of this country and who defended it by simply carrying a weapon and fighting. Yet on the other side there were foreign fighters who were more like mercenaries, decapitating people in the name of religion, rewriting the rulebook and stopping us at checkpoints as if they were occupiers of our country. Only the other day, in al-Mashrafiyah, I'd noticed the large number of ISIS fighters at the bomb sites and among the crowds, openly wielding their weapons. They didn't blend in with everyone else but stood out immediately as foreigners. Their skin tone was a slightly bluish dark brown, a different hue from the Syrian tanned complexion. At one of the checkpoints, the men who'd stood in front of our car included three from Mauritania, a Yemeni, a Saudi and an Egyptian. All this chaos, while the rebels desperately struggled to defend the revolution that was slipping away from them. Their fight was on two fronts: against both the Assad regime and the jihadist groups that had started to make their lives hell.

I sat down by the trunk of a cypress tree and watched. 'How can I write about all this ruin?' I muttered to myself.

The stench was overpowering. One of the young men behind me had heard me and leaned over gently. 'Ma'am, I swear, you don't need to see all this,' he said. 'Let's go back.'

My eyes had begun to glaze over. Shaher and the young men were heading towards me, signalling for me to leave. I got up with difficulty. The smell was lodged in my throat and the image of the decapitated head filled my mind. The murderer and the murdered. Nameless. The chaos of absurdity and destruction.

'I don't think they were from our group,' Shaher said in the car on the way back. 'Maybe they're from one of the regime's gangs!'

'And how would you know?' somebody else replied. 'Anyway, may God have mercy on them, whoever they are.'

Another young man interjected, 'No, may God *not* have mercy on them if they're from one of Bashar's groups! Let their carcasses rot in hell!'

There would be nothing left for us here when it was all over. At that moment, I realised that I had brought myself to a truly lethal place. Everything I saw seemed unbearable. I was too weak for this relentless killing, for this evil that kept reproducing itself every second, growing and multiplying until it would swallow the entire country. I no longer felt I had the strength to carry on as I had done before. Nothing meant anything any more. My head felt like a nest of scurrying ants. The sounds of the bombing were distant and so too was the buzzing of the flies over the two dead bodies, along with the image of the little girl's face underneath the rubble. I swam in the sweet temptation of surrendering to death.

Shaher's voice shook me from my waking nightmare, when he announced we'd arrived back at the media office. The local council of Saraqeb was meeting there that evening to discuss the bread crisis, as Saraqeb's supply had been cut off the day before. The council had started to lose its influence because of the emergence of the Sharia Authority, as well as the lack of funding and the rivalries between the townspeople. Most significantly, the Sharia Authority and the Sharia Court were under the protection of the Islamic battalions, and they enforced their laws by military force and in the name of God.

I left them to it and sat down with Mohammed to organise our visits to the women's homes. We needed to set up a literacy course, to decide on a location for the women's centre and to follow up on various small projects, but my mind was vacant. I robotically noted down what Mohammed was saying. A young man joined us and started telling me about the foreign fighters who were asking families to find them martyrs' wives to marry in return for money. Many families rejected this kind of offer, but some agreed to it. I'd heard about this before, the previous day in fact, when we had visited the house of a beautiful young woman, the wife of a martyr. She told me that a Yemeni fighter had proposed to her and she was inclined to accept because she had three children and, apart from the Al Ihsan Charity linked to the Ahrar al-Sham movement, she had no other source of income. But she said she wasn't happy about it. We agreed to help her set up a small project where she would sell cleaning products from her home as well as women's sanitary items. She understood that while the venture wouldn't earn her enough money to live on, at least it might save her from having to marry a foreign jihadist fighter. (Later, I learned that she was indeed managing to support herself and hadn't married.)

One of the men was busy turning the ceiling fan into a generator to produce electricity, as the regime had cut off the power in the rebel-held areas. Two other young men were following the news on a radio station set up by local youth. There really were strong indications that an independent state was being formed following the liberation of these regions, yet many of these features would subsequently be wiped out by the incessant shelling and the spread of religious extremist battalions. However, in these two, small and neglected rooms, the revolution was going strong. The men here were taking part in a unique programme of self-government in a civil society. They were clearly capable of such self-government, but there were those who didn't want their democratic revolution to succeed and they were only too aware of this.

'Everything you're seeing now is happening in order to transform the democratic revolution into a religious war,' said a twenty-one-year-old man who worked on a newspaper published in the north of Syria. 'These *takfiri* Muslims . . . they don't know what they're doing, but their leaders do.' He spat on the ground. Two of his brothers had been killed by bombs.

Mohammed and I began our round of women's homes. On our way to Montaha's house near the media centre, a plane appeared in the sky once again, but it was thwarted by the centre's machine guns: the 14.5mm and the 'Dushka', the DShK, a Russian heavy machine gun. Some children appeared in a side street, where they formed a circle and started playing and laughing. But I wasn't laughing. My mind was distracted by the plane looming overhead, which could rip them to shreds in seconds. Two of their mothers were standing in a doorway, looking downcast. A man carrying a sack of onions came out of an alleyway, while a fighter carrying his gun appeared from another alleyway ahead. This was life.

Walls, faces, everything was covered in so much dust, I had to wipe my face on my sleeve every other minute. I feared I'd lose my mind before long. How could people not go mad under these circumstances?


The following morning I woke up feeling tired. I missed Aala and her late night stories. Yet I also felt an overwhelming sense of contentment that she was safe outside Syria. Aside from missing my little storyteller, I was starting to feel a bit uncomfortable as I'd been wearing the same clothes I'd been sleeping in for the past two days. I didn't wear pyjamas, because I was worried about being dressed indecently in front of everyone if bombing forced me to go outside in the middle of the night, and I always went to bed with my black abaya robe nearby. However, for several nights it had been difficult to sleep because of the mosquitoes and the stifling heat, and I'd just about drift off before waking up again.

The shelling had stopped and I wanted to go to the house of my colleague Montaha and her sister Diaa, and then on to the temporary school Diaa had established, to follow up on various projects. First, Mohammed told me we needed to check the shelter near Saraqeb market that we were planning to turn into a women's centre. The shelter wasn't in an ideal location, but the space was available and the townspeople had offered to let us use it for free, so it was a good start. Although shelling was normally concentrated on the market itself, as though the objective of the bombing was to kill the largest number of civilians, this had stopped an hour ago and Mohammed and I felt relatively safe going there. However, when I began listing the names of the martyrs' wives I wanted to see, in Kafranbel as well as Saraqeb, Mohammed warned me that it would be difficult and that we'd need a few days to cover that much ground. All the same, I was keen to get as much done as quickly as possible, and get to Kafranbel soon to see Razan, the female activist based there, as well as visit the displaced children's school project.

The market was quiet with very little activity. A few shops were open but the majority of them had had their doors ripped off by bomb blasts; the remaining few were swinging in the breeze. Shopkeepers had started to place sandbags in front of their windows for the first time, giving the market the look of a front line. We drove down the alleyway that led to the centre. Despite the bombing, the killing and the siege, I felt a flicker of happiness. People here just wanted to carry on with life as usual and it seemed like they were all determined to – women, men and children – but then a voice shrieked from the portable transceiver.

'A helicopter!' There was some interference before it continued. 'Where are you, you idiots? Didn't anyone see it? For fuck's sake, why didn't anyone put out a warning?!'

I grabbed the transceiver while Mohammed drove.

'Man your machine guns!' the voice hollered. 'It's over Saraqeb right now!'

We heard the crashing shudder of helicopter blades and a haze of dust puffed up around us. Mohammed slowed the car down and started winding up the windows. I placed my hands over my ears and screamed. I wanted to hear that I was still alive. The sound of humans screaming is the same as that of animals howling. Then came the thunderous noise again. A cloud of dust. Our vision cleared slightly and I spotted a man dash by carrying his wounded child, crying and shouting as he ran. I couldn't hear his voice because the ringing in my ears had turned into a sharp pain. I could no longer grasp what was happening around me. Just then, I heard a terrifying sound. I don't remember what it sounded like but it felt like my eardrums were about to burst and my head shuddered violently. The car was also shaking. Every cell in my body seemed to shake with the vibrating ground before everything blended together in front of my eyes. Mohammed tried to drive slowly through an alley that would take us out of the market. We stopped because strings of white smoke were falling onto the car, sliding over the side windows. Falling smoke and detritus and shards of metal. My head dropped down to my ribs; I heard the crash of flying objects scraping against the car. One fragment smashed through the glass of Mohammed's window and then another shattered my window inches from my neck. It was two or three minutes before I opened my eyes – I thought I was dying, I thought I'd see my final moments flash before me. But I wasn't thinking about life or anything of any grandeur. I thought death would be easy and I was only filled with panic because I didn't know which side the bomb would strike from and which side of my body it would hit.

What Mohammed and I didn't know was that the third barrel bomb, which the helicopter had circled with then flung down onto the market, had been directly above us and yet it hadn't exploded upon impact with the ground, but in the air. And what caused this incredible lucky escape? The helicopter had been pushed to a higher altitude because the rebels had acquired some anti-aircraft weapons that could hit aircraft at a height of six kilometres and they'd managed to take down several planes this way. So Assad's helicopters had been forced to fly higher than usual. And because the barrels were crude weapons, hand-made from primitive raw materials, and dropped from a high altitude, a fuse needed to be attached to them and lit before they were released from the plane. The length of this fuse hadn't been set accurately enough to allow the barrel to reach the ground before exploding. The reason we were still alive that afternoon was due to a combination of the time it took the barrel to reach the ground and the imprecise length of the fuse, which had burnt out while the barrel was still in the air.

We sped to Montaha's house. As Mohammed was about to drop me off, I asked him to take me out with him later to examine the damage that had been caused by the barrel bombs.

'Why, so that you can die with me?' he asked. Then he smiled and waved before driving off.

Dust continued to blanket the sky as I went into Montaha's house. The women were waiting for me: a group of martyrs' wives, neighbours and their children. As usual, the large house was buzzing with activity. A wall had been broken open to our left. I asked what had happened, while they set dishes of various types of food on the floor, all the while laughing and telling their stories of the blasts. A woman with oval eyes was hugging a child to her chest. She was the wife of a martyr and wanted to start a knitting project. Another woman was a doctor, single, and interested in literature. A woman with two children wanted a sewing machine. As I started telling them my story, I felt strangely disconnected now that I was plunged back into the flow of life after a barrel bomb had just been dropped above my head. My mind was completely blank and my lips were still trembling. They all surrounded me and a woman held my hand while another recited verses from the Quran. I didn't know whether my eyes were crazed or if my complexion was sallow, pale with fear, but I was truly grateful that I was still alive. I wanted to find out what the women did to keep up their strength. They were beautiful, clean and their food was delicious. Despite the poverty, it was obvious that their children were well looked after. One of the women had brought along some clothes she'd made.

Montaha's sister Diaa, who managed the temporary school she had set up, explained to me the importance of establishing networks of women who were able to educate children in their homes: we couldn't risk children gathering in old-fashioned school buildings where bombing might result in many more casualties than if they were taught elsewhere. Communities were already beginning to establish these privately run schools as local initiatives; where lessons took place depended on the intensity of the shelling. While this meant there were no set school days, at least the children were receiving a little education.

We spread out our paperwork in front of us and started making notes, examining the women's case studies. Even though I'd started to lose concentration, and my head was still completely muddled, I felt I couldn't stop. I felt embarrassed in the face of their strength. The sounds of a plane and ambulances outside were continuous, so too was the noise the children were making and the clacking of the plates of food being brought in and out.

Then suddenly everyone lost focus on work and the conversation started up again, as if their appetite for talking had returned in one sudden surge. A twenty-year-old girl said she was against what the Islamist battalions were doing and described how one day they'd cut off a soldier's head, stuck it on a pole and paraded it round Saraqeb market.

'Yes, but do you know what he'd done?' another woman interrupted. 'He was in a tank and they'd asked him to surrender. They didn't want to shoot him; they didn't want to kill him. My cousin was there and saw what happened. But he fired at them; he wanted to kill all of them. He killed two of the men before one of them turned around and killed him. They were livid.'

'We didn't go out against Bashar so we'd have our children witness these barbaric scenes,' said another of the women. 'It's criminal, despicable. Why did they have to display his head in front of everyone? We wanted to send a petition to the Sharia Court, but we're helpless now, you know.'

'It's unacceptable,' agreed another woman. 'We don't want our children to be raised in this savage way!'

'What's coming will be even more monstrous, I swear,' one of the women whispered.

The children were running in and out and jumping into our arms.

'But what should we do?' a young woman replied. 'I can't just let my son turn into a murderer and a monster because he's seen something like that.'

I was writing down my observations on each woman's background, still astonished at how they were fuelled by this determination to live, this resilience that I could almost touch with my fingers and inhale deeply. They were the ones who had no choice but to stay, whereas I had the opportunity to leave this hell and live abroad.

When the roar of aircraft returned again, one of the young women, the daughter of a martyr, screamed out, 'This one's a MiG!'

We heard the boom of an explosion.

'And that's a cluster bomb,' a woman said.

We quickly gathered our papers, and hurried to seek shelter. Montaha asked me to stay with them but I knew Mohammed would be waiting for me outside, under the shelling, and I became even more flustered as I rushed out to the car.

Back at the family's house, Abu Ibrahim, Noura and Ayouche had already gone down to the shelter and were waiting for me. The family had returned from the mosque in al-Mashrafiyah, where the displaced people were sheltering. Noura was angry. Ayouche wanted to go upstairs to be with the two old women, so I went up with her. Then we took a plate of food to the steps of the shelter and ate in silence. Bombs were once again falling incessantly; it seemed insane to consider doing anything between each festival of death we were experiencing here. Even so, my mind was preoccupied with calculating how much time remained for me to complete my work with the women, and ideas for how Diaa could teach the children amid the bombing. The violent bombardment might render it impossible.

Later that evening, Mohammed, Montaha and I managed to get to the home of a woman who wanted to open a hair and beauty salon, which surprised me as I couldn't see who would care about such things now. The woman, Fadia, was dark-skinned, slim and no older than twenty-five. She had three children. No one knew at that point what had happened to her husband. The beauty salon would be in her house, much the same as the other projects since tradition in this rural community didn't allow women to go out very much on their own without a male chaperone such as a husband or relative. Before the revolution the economic situation had been better and most women didn't need to work. But things were different now. Earlier, the female doctor from Saraqeb had told me that a large proportion of women in the town were university graduates. But the influence of customs and traditions prevailed. Religion wasn't the only factor; they were also scared of what people would say.

During our tours of the women's houses over the next few days, Mohammed and I had to make regular stops because of the bombing, which allowed me to meet a large number of people, mostly middle class, whose financial situations had deteriorated since the start of the revolution. They were kind and generous and whenever I went into one of their homes, they would try to start up a discussion with me about the sectarian war, how they weren't involved in it and didn't agree with it. They said they didn't want these extremist battalions among them, but that it wasn't up to them and they felt powerless. From their efforts to dissociate themselves from sectarianism, I understood that they must have known who I was. I didn't feel like my life was at risk when I was with them. But what happened shortly afterwards made me leave Saraqeb for good.

When I glimpsed the shadows of feet beneath the door at the media centre, I thought it must be the men doing some repairs to the power cables or the satellite Internet device, and even though their movements were suspiciously silent I felt safe because the iron door downstairs at the entrance to the building was locked. I ignored the shadows and didn't feel scared or worried. I was completely calm. My bones and head ached, and my ears were ringing; every movement I made felt heavy. I closed the door of the room and opened the window, recalling the scenes from the night before.

It had been another challenging twenty-four hours. The previous night, the bombing had been far enough away for a number of us to stay working to the small hours in the media centre. With me, Mohammed and Manhal were the journalist Marcin Suder and sixteen-year-old Badee, along with Abu Hassan, a former leftist. Four activists were also getting on with their work on the Internet. At some time after midnight, the media centre received a call for help and some of the men had needed to go to hospital, so I had gone with them. Marcin came too, photographing every detail of the impact of the bombing: the bloodstains, the burnt-out buildings across the road, the bodies of the wounded, the faces of people passing. The people waiting. The colour of the sky. The trees.

We stopped outside the room of an injured child. I was quite steady until that moment. The boy was probably no older than four, very thin, and appeared as if he'd just woken up. He was beautiful. He wasn't crying but just sat there looking up at the ceiling, unblinking. There were no obvious wounds on his body apart from a deep puncture in his chest, the mark of a piece of shrapnel from a cluster bomb that settles in the body before it crumbles and kills its victim from the inside. The doctor told us that he would have to open up the child's chest to remove the shrapnel.

As I looked at the little boy, I don't know why, I gasped and started muttering, 'O God, O God . . .' I had to leave the room. I couldn't fathom the depth of the horror. A forlorn child like a little bird. Quiet and uncomplaining. In pain. His wide eyes full of the whole world's hope. He was oblivious to what was happening around him. Then I noticed I was standing on a large bloodstain and I suddenly felt like I was standing on a corpse. I screamed and moved away quickly.

While Marcin took photos of the child, I wandered around the rooms of the hospital, which was shabby and lacked all sorts of medical equipment. Even though it was almost one thirty in the morning, people were still streaming in with casualties. I went back to the child, who was still staring at the ceiling although tears had now started to flow from his eyes. The doctor was preparing for the operation to cut open his chest. We left.

I walked slowly while Marcin comforted me and Manhal went off ahead.

'Everything will be OK,' Marcin said calmly, in English. 'He will survive.'

It was a long journey back to the office and we had to stop several times because of the bombs raining down ahead of us. Marcin continued to take photos of everything. He didn't bat an eyelid. He didn't tremble. He carried on taking photos as if the shells pouring down over our heads meant nothing.

It was unfortunate that our trip to the hospital had taken place so late at night, and while the area was being bombarded with cluster bombs, as it would be the last time I'd see Marcin. I never imagined I'd be a witness to his abduction.

At ten o'clock the next morning, I was leaning against the window, lost in my thoughts, when shouts echoed, followed by the sound of shots being fired and a lot of noise. I checked that the door to the office I was in was closed and held my breath tightly. Shouts and gunfire, then a loud banging on my door and more bullets being fired. Manhal was talking, trying to find out what the intruders wanted. My ears were ringing and I didn't know if the sky was showering us with bombs or rockets. But I now realised there were armed men inside the office and it was their shadows I'd just seen under the door. It must have been as they were preparing to conduct their raid.

Manhal was yelling, 'The computer, Samar! Give me the computer!'

I managed to put on my abaya and a veil and opened the door slightly, gripping the computer. Manhal was standing outside my door, his face streaming with blood as he blocked a man from forcing his way in. I could barely be seen through the cracked open door. Manhal immediately shut the door and I went back to where I had been sitting. After one or two minutes, I opened the door. I couldn't just sit on the sidelines. The stranger was still in front of my door, and Manhal was standing there with his face covered in blood. Manhal told me later that the man had smashed his head with the butt of the gun. I thought we were going to die.

One single thought occupied me: that these were ISIS fighters who had come to either kidnap me after finding out who I was, or to kill us because they had recently been rounding up the revolution's activists to arrest or murder them, the same way Assad's regime did. ISIS was targeting secular civil activists and media professionals such as myself and, in terms of my family's Alawite religious identity at least, I belonged to a sect they believed to be infidels. People they killed under the charge of apostasy and heresy.

Manhal's face was dripping with blood and my eyes slowly blinked open and shut. He was bleeding so profusely, I thought he was dying.

'Are you OK?' I asked.

I had almost forgotten that the masked gunman was still there until he hollered terrifyingly, 'Get inside, will you!' He pointed the pistol at my face. I heard my heart drop like a bomb, but I looked at him steadily.

'I'm sorry, excuse me,' I said calmly, then closed the door and sat back on the bed. I couldn't stop thinking that Manhal would collapse at any moment, and the gunman would open the door and fire a shot at my head, or I would disappear into the darkness of abduction. I sat in silence, my lips trembling.

The masked armed militant wasn't Syrian; he was one of the foreign fighters. He had hazel-coloured eyes. I clung to the image of him staring at me; his weren't like the eyes of a conventional murderer. He was young and handsome, his cheeks pink and his eyes flickered – yet he was a killer. Probably no older than twenty. I was shaking and could not stay there a moment longer. I opened the door and they had gone. The whole episode was over in less than ten minutes.

I heard later there had been nine armed and masked men. They'd tied Mohammed up with a sharp plastic strap, the same type of strap that the secret police and the *shabiha* used to tie up detainees and anyone they fancied laying into. This sort of restraint was used as handcuffs and tightened around the wrists until it sliced into the flesh so that any movement would cause more friction to the skin. Abu Hassan was tied up and so was Badee. They had been beaten with the butts of rifles. All the office equipment had been stolen. The intruders hadn't left anything, not even the cables that were used to connect the equipment. They had stolen the papers and files – everything that was there to steal. Methodically the place was cleared within minutes. But the biggest shock was that they'd taken Marcin too. Besides the daylight robbery, it had been an organised operation to abduct a foreign journalist for ransom.

And it didn't end there. Manhal and a few men had chased after the car, but it had disappeared. When they tried to complain to the Sharia Court, their petitions were in vain. Manhal refused to clean up his wound until he got some commitment from the Sharia Court that they'd do something about the kidnap. But the Sharia Court wanted proof that it was definitely ISIS who had kidnapped Marcin.

After stopping by quickly at Abu Ibrahim's house, we returned to the town centre to speak with the battalion of the Free Army whose headquarters were next door to the media office. They called their commander Abu Diab to come and join us, and we sat down with a group of the fighters and townspeople. As I talked to the men, I was adamant that the masked attackers must have been tipped off by someone who knew the office and the people passing through. They'd only started to rush when they realised there was a woman there, and they must have worried that the noise of gunfire would attract fighters from the nearby battalion. But still, no one could stop them.

It was clear that the operation had been intended to intimidate the secular, civilian activists, since many similar incidents followed where secular activists were abducted and killed. It seemed they were being deliberately pursued. Chaos was rampant and abductions of foreign journalists were also on the increase, either for ransom or to prevent them publishing the truth about what was going on.

We were depressed. Marcin was an exceptional person. With his fair complexion and dimpled cheeks, he was always cheerful, calm and courteous. Even though he was always busy taking photos as we went about under aerial bombardment, he'd never forget to get out of the car first so he could open my door. He had been running a photography training course in the centre, and would pat the men on the back encouragingly after surviving another bombardment. He used to smile kindly when he talked to me about his experiences of campaigning.

'I support your people's cause,' he would say. 'I understand it, but I'm afraid it's difficult and complex out there.'

Now Marcin had disappeared and news of my presence among the activists in the office started to spread, despite our best efforts to keep it quiet so that the gunmen wouldn't return for me. It became vital to leave Saraqeb. Although my friends from Kafranbel came to pick me up as soon as they heard the news, I preferred to stay for a few days to make sure everything would be all right for those I knew and cared for in Saraqeb once I'd left, and to help the young people with their testimony to the Sharia

Court. It didn't occur to me that the Sharia Court would consider my presence a crime in itself.

I went back to the family home.

Noura screamed when she saw me. 'Oh, my God, what would I have done if they'd kidnapped you!' She clasped her palms to her face and then hugged me.

Ayouche showered me with affection and attention. She had been on her way out to buy vegetables and meat, but came and sat with me for a while.

'Before the revolution, the men would buy everything we needed,' she said. 'Do you think the revolution has marginalised women? I don't think so. Since the revolution we've been going out doing our shopping and moving around without male chaperones. The problem with the foreign *takfiri* battalions that have taken control of our lives is that we want to get on with life. They won't find a place for us. The men are fighting on several fronts: Bashar al-Assad, the armed extremists, the kidnappers and the mercenaries. They can't do all these things at once – and we're working too. It will be a disaster if things go on the way they are. This country will never be the same again.'

Securing food for a single day required an unbelievable amount of effort, despite the fact that Ayouche's family was relatively well-off. Having to survive under bombardment, with the lack of food, the high prices and the loss of electricity and water, made life a living hell. The women in the house ensured the basics for day-to-day life were secured, organising everything related to food, hygiene and what they needed for the survival of the children and the men. Very few shops were still open, and most people ate only one meal a day – if they ate much at all. A lucky few were able to grow produce on their own plots of land.

Earlier in the week, Mohammed, Montaha and I had visited the women's Grocery Store project in Saraqeb. They were making food as well as packaging products, which they sold to people at a fair price, and this gave them financial independence. Our visit had taken place in the evening, after *iftar* – the daily breaking of the fast during Ramadan, and we had sat in the courtyard of the house, with the mother at the centre, surrounded by her seven daughters and three other families. Even in the fading light, the courtyard was alive with colour, with purples and reds, and with different varieties of flowers in pots. An olive tree stood in the middle. The tranquil scene seemed at odds with the look of the house from the outside, battered by a shell that had struck the front. The workplace was a spacious kitchen with a refrigerator, stove and shelves lined with glass containers filled with different kinds of foods and sweets. The project needed a big fridge to store the food and keep it from going off and a generator to keep it running. As we sat there, it became very dark despite the candlelight.

'We're rationing the use of the generator because mazut is so expensive,' the son had told me. He was in charge of delivering the orders to people's houses. 'Our business is based on profitable home-made products, but how can we carry on in these circumstances?'

Ayouche left for the market without me this time. The others begged me to stay at home. The whole family started spoiling me. Everyone in the household gathered round and started making plans for the following days. How could people live here with the constant bombardment on the one hand and all the profound changes society was facing on the other?

The nephew Suhaib was an educated and pleasant young man. 'How can we carry on living here?' he asked. 'The situation seems impossible. All we can think about is getting hold of the essentials. The land has been scorched, trade has come to a standstill, the young people have gone to fight and will only come home as martyrs. We can probably tolerate this situation for another year but not for several years. We're going back in time to the dark ages, and if the Sharia Courts carry on like this, and the jihadist military battalions oppress us with their foreign fighters, we'll become a country governed by the military and religious extremists. Islam is a religion that should spread prosperity not poverty.'

Later that day, I listened to the discussion develop on the theme of ISIS, wondering what they might do to Marcin.

'They won't kill him, right?' I asked.

'No, they'll keep him for the money,' said one of the men. 'The problem is that they aren't admitting it was them who kidnapped him.'

ISIS's kidnapping operations and killing of activists hadn't yet taken the brutal form it would do after my departure from Syria. At the time Marcin was taken, kidnappings were mainly carried out in a haphazard fashion for ransom money, especially when it came to foreign journalists. The days were yet to come when they would develop a strategy for terror that combined kidnappings with killings, and which involved releasing videos of beheadings.

The others told me that a member of the Sharia Court, a certain Abu al-Baraa who was also with the Nusra Front, had said to Manhal that he intended to uproot all the secularists in the country, and he had even referred to cutting off their heads. I tried to focus on what everyone was saying, but Abu al-Baraa's threat to the activists lingered in my mind. The women repeated what he'd said, clearly shaken by his words, as they chopped the vegetables for the evening meal, coming and going between the kitchen, which overlooked the courtyard, and the room where we now hovered around the transceiver.

While we prepared dinner, I learned that another man who'd been seen at the Sharia Court that day had been Abu Akrama. One of the leaders of the Nusra Front, Abu Akrama was a member of the Saraqeb security committee whose role was to act as a kind of safety valve, releasing tension in the community. He was aged about forty and was a plump, intelligent man with a soft, deep voice, who wore civilian clothes instead of the Islamic attire popular among al-Qaeda members. When he'd first arrived in Saraqeb, people had mistakenly thought he was from the Houran region in the south. However, he was Palestinian-Jordanian in origin, and had come to Syria after living in Afghanistan, Iraq and Pakistan. Although he was a quiet man and never talked about himself much, people gradually found out that he had trained as a mechanical engineer and could speak English and French as well as the Afghan languages. It was said that he came to the Levant to fight the tyrants and the Shiites, whom he referred to pejoratively as the Rawafids.

'How are we supposed to live if they keep allowing all the mercenaries of the world to enter Syria?' asked Ayouche, who had returned from her chores.

One of the women of the family spoke up: 'And you, you men of Saraqeb, why have you handed our city over to foreigners?'

But by now only one thought occupied my mind: how could I possibly remain here if it was difficult for me to go anywhere alone, or to even travel a few metres outside the house without needing protection? Would I be able to stay here as I'd planned? And how could that happen without my becoming a burden on these wonderful people, without being an added source of misery for them?

'The women will come here to you tomorrow. It's safer for you that way,' said Mohammed.

I looked at him and then at Noura, who had settled on the floor to cut some fabric on the rug. Mohammed had read my mind.

'We're not worried about what ordinary people might do to you, I swear,' said Noura, looking at me sadly. 'It's the mercenaries and thieves we're worried about . . . the bandits and crooks.' I stayed silent but decided it was time for me to move on to Kafranbel, which would be the best way to make everyone feel safe. My presence among my adoptive family had become a threat to their lives.

The media centre in Kafranbel had completely changed. It was now situated in a large house consisting of several rooms, which were used by Arab and foreign journalists, as well as activists who'd been forced to leave the regime-controlled areas after being pursued by *mukhabarat* intelligence agents, and who had come to the north to take part in the revolution. The house overlooked a large road and had previously been occupied by the regime's army; this was obvious from the bullet-shaped holes that littered the place, and also from the holes in the kitchen wall through which snipers had targeted their victims. When the army left, the owner had donated it to the rebels, who'd cleaned it up, but the damage remained.

There was a spacious roof terrace overlooking an olive grove, where we gathered now as my companions told me how worried they had been about me remaining in Saraqeb after Marcin had been kidnapped, and that they wanted me to stay with them until I left Syria. They also told me about a youth programme they'd set up to offer training in running a radio station for Idlib province.

'The aim is to launch a public space for debate and discussion, and to talk about our problems in a responsible and transparent way,' said Raed Fares. He saw this as a necessary component of the nascent democracy.

All the work that took place in the centre pivoted around Raed, who spoke constantly of his hopes for the future. He hadn't lost faith in the success of the revolution, no matter how far it had deviated from its original path, and even though Syria had become the battlefield of a proxy war where international parties settled their scores with one another. He often seemed tireless and I would try to draw energy from him.

Working alongside him were Khaled al-Eissa – who I had met before, a young man called Abdullah, an engineer in his early thirties called Osama who was in charge of the radio broadcasts from the basement, and Hammoud who was totally dedicated to his work, as well as a group of young men who had initiated the peaceful demonstrations in the area and who were all involved in running protest-related activities. Razan, my female activist friend, was also there. I learned that Ahmed Jallal the painter would still call in from time to time, calm and quiet as usual, just as he had been the first time I met him.

'We'll either die or the revolution will succeed, or we will die and the revolution will fail,' said Abdullah, laughing. He was twenty years old and had devoted the last three years of his life to the revolution.

It being the month of Ramadan, it was approaching the time to break the fast, and everyone started busily preparing the food. Raed put together a green salad and said he tended to buy vegetables from Maarat al-Numan, braving the bombardment on the front line, because they were cheaper and better quality there. We talked and laughed, as Razan shuttled back and forth, in and out of the kitchen. In Kafranbel we could sit out in the open, cross-legged on the terrace, and gaze at the olive trees. As we prepared the meal, we were joined by a few others, including four Syrians who were deeply involved in civil society activism. Among them was Ibrahim al-Aseel, a volunteer who had come to give the rebels management training, which entailed guidance on how to run a small business, along with training in providing psychological support, and human resources workshops for developing skills and increasing manpower. A brave and dedicated young man, he travelled through the rural provinces, guiding media professionals and local activists.

While we talked, I leaned my head against a pillar on the terrace and, for a fleeting second, wondered whether one of the regime's soldiers might have rested his head there in the past, and whether a bullet penetrated his forehead. The young men were starting to hand out glasses of water with which to break the fast.

Suddenly the transceiver shrieked, 'There's a chopper above the market. A chopper at the square, guys.'

The warning blared out at the same moment as the call to the sunset prayer signalled the time to break the fast. We stared at each other.

'Come on, everyone, tuck in. May God accept our fast.'

I took my plate and served myself, as the young men did. Hammoud was just coming to sit down with us when the bombardment began. We abandoned our dinner. I dashed to hide behind one of the pillars indoors and screamed at the others to do the same since they were almost completely exposed – it was a helicopter, which meant it was barrel bombs they were dropping. Then, when we heard the helicopter fly over, I ran behind Hammoud up the stairs to the roof so that we could see in what direction it was heading. Some of the men followed us. The helicopter tossed the barrel down nearby and we could still see the enormous cloud of dust.

'Get down!' Hammoud shouted, as he stood watching. Raed stayed on the roof for a moment, then sprinted off into town and the others followed him. They wanted to document what was happening, just like the men in Saraqeb did, and to help the wounded. We headed back downstairs.

One of the fighters sat down on the terrace and placed the transceiver on his lap. 'That's it: our daily dose,' he said. 'This happens every day – either before we break the fast, or just as we start eating.'

The rest of us gathered around the dinner. But we only smoked; nobody touched the food.

'Since the beginning of Ramadan they've taken to waiting until the sunset prayer to start the bombardment, whether it's aircraft or rockets. I've heard them talking on the radio,' said Abu Mahmoud, a forty-year-old fighter.

'How did you hear them?' I asked him.

'I heard them with this ear of mine,' he said, with a sarcastic smile.

'What were they saying?'

'I've heard them saying they were preparing us a tasty meal of barrels to break our fast on. And they were laughing.' I looked at him incredulously.

'I swear, ma'am, it's true. We can pick up what they say to each other as they throw down the barrels. One of them said to his friend, right before they hurled a barrel down: "Go on, it's time to feed the dogs!"'

'Is that really how they talk when they're throwing down the barrels?' I asked.

'Not always. Sometimes. It's my bad luck that I have to listen to them. It's one of my duties.'

Abu Mahmoud, this angry fighter who intercepted the pilots' conversations, was dark-skinned, blue-eyed and looked depressed. He said he had worked in construction in Saudi Arabia for six years before returning to Syria, where he had bought a car, got a job as a driver and built a house in Kafranbel. When the peaceful demonstrations began, he decided to leave his driving job and turn his energies instead to revolutionary civil activism. But when

Assad's army entered Kafranbel on 4 July 2011, the nature of his work changed and he started targeting pro-regime informants.

In the early days, all he had was a basic Russian rifle when he and his comrades fought against the army. It was a useless weapon, he said, so he'd replaced it with a sniper rifle, which meant he wouldn't be recognised as he fought Assad's army with the Fursan al-Haqq Brigade. (I remembered meeting one of the Fursan al-Haqq commanders at the media centre before, the genial Abu al-Majd.) Abu Mahmoud explained that, when Assad's aircraft began bombing, he had abandoned the sniper rifle for a 12.7mm heavy machine gun, and he now manned anti-aircraft weapons. He said he was protecting his people and his family from the bombing, even though his weapon was relatively futile. As he looked towards the sky with one eye still fixed on the transceiver, I asked him what he would do once the fighting ended. He gave a bitter smile and nodded.

'I'll go back to my work as a driver. I'll throw all this away,' he replied, pointing at his rifle, his voice filled with disgust and sorrow.

'I didn't intend to carry a weapon,' he added. 'This is a tool of death and I want to live. Hafez al-Assad's regime killed my father when he was in Palmyra prison, where they jailed him for eleven years. When they detained me in the Political Security branch, the brigadier general said to me, "Don't abandon your children the way your father did to you." You know, I grew up without a father. The regime robbed me of him and stole my civil rights, and still I didn't object. But then we went out to demonstrate peacefully, and they started killing us. I don't want an Islamic regime, I want a democratic, civil state . . .'

While he was talking, the young people had returned and now they told us what had happened during the bombing, where the bombs had landed, and the names of the casualties.

'The important thing is that no one died today. Let's eat,' said Raed.

I took the opportunity to watch everyone as we dined together. People were still coming and going. We were joined by some university students in their early twenties, young men who helped Razan run the Karama Bus project, which was a sort of mobile school for displaced people. The project was aimed at offering a temporary replacement for school so that children's education wouldn't be too neglected during the bombing. There was the risk of a whole generation growing up who wouldn't know how to read or write, and there had been attempts to recruit children to fight; ISIS had already succeeded in doing so in the city of Raqqa and the militant Nusra Front was also known to be recruiting children.

Of the young men involved in the Karama Bus project, Hassan was an economics student, and Youssef, Ezzat and Firas studied English literature. They were stressed and tired, and although much of the conversation centred on that evening's bombing, they told me about the work being carried out in the three schools in Kafranbel and two nearby villages, which included screening movies and organising sports and music activities for refugee children who had had to flee their home villages. I realised that Kafranbel deserved considerable praise in the short history of the Syrian revolution. The Free Army battalions still controlled the town and the extremist jihadist battalions and brigades hadn't yet proliferated there.

Over the next couple of days, we would be going with the Karama Bus team to nearby schools in rural villages. The young men buzzed in and out like bees in a hive, gathering up the equipment they needed for a film screening for the kids. Seeing their determination to pursue ordinary life under bombardment meant a great deal to me. These young men had no prior experience of civil society activism. They had had to invent all these forms of resistance work from scratch. I observed them all that evening, a lump in my throat, and I couldn't utter a word as I chewed my food. There was Hassan, the dark-skinned, sarcastic one; Ezzat, the nice and polite, but angry one; Firas, whose soft voice we could barely hear; and Abdullah, who was dubbed 'the crocodile' – the energetic, handsome one who looked like a Victorian portrait of a knight.

Now, as I watched them and got to know them, I found I was starting to discover myself. The permanent roots that I'd thought I'd be able to tear up: my family roots and ties to loved ones, my religious and professional identities, my concept of nationhood – all those roots remained a part of me, they hadn't been destroyed. I had tried to pull them up in an attempt to replant whatever remained of myself in fresh soil, ever-faithful to my lifelong devotion to truth and freedom. My own choices suddenly made sense and blossomed in that quiet moment, as I chewed my food and watched these courageous and lively young men.

The following day I cooked for them and we talked about what we could do for the women and children of Kafranbel and the surrounding villages. They praised the buffet I'd prepared as if they'd received an elaborate gift. Their eyes were full of gratitude, and I was aware of their ingrained and urgent need to feel that at least some of the ambitions they'd had for the revolution when they'd gone out marching two years ago had been achieved. They didn't want to believe that what was happening was a sectarian war, and their proof was my presence, this Alawite woman among them. But they never mentioned my background except jokingly, as they did a few days later, when, as usual, a plane began bombing the moment we heard the sunset call to prayer, and Raed started humming a song called 'We're Coming to Slaughter You'. Another young man responded by humming the tune of 'The Fourth Brigade'. Then the laughter and singing began as they launched into the two songs in earnest, adapting them with their own lyrics. The first song was about the presence of the Nusra Front in the city of Binnish and a small child threatening to slaughter Alawites; in response, the 'Fourth Brigade' song was about an Alawite child obscenely glorifying the killing taking place in rebel-held Sunni areas. In these gruesome ballads, children were being used as weapons of hate. The guys in Kafranbel sang with sarcastic laughter, as if they were erasing the meaning of death from the songs.

'Victory is ours, you dictator,' I said to myself. 'It may not last, and maybe we'll die after this, but right now we have defeated you. You might win because you're a criminal and we're the children of a Syria that's gone, but right now, we've defeated you.' But this feeling lasted only a moment, a fleeting moment, and soon the bombing increased and we sank into complete silence.

Once the bombing had subsided again, and we'd had several cups of tea, we headed off to the school. The electricity had been cut off in the area, but in the distance lights sparkled in the sky. The bombing was ongoing in Maarat al-Numan behind us as we travelled in the opposite direction – Razan, Firas, Ezzat, Hassan and I. With us was a young man called Hossam, who had been driving me round in his car while I stayed in Kafranbel, and who worked at the media centre.

The sky was clear and there was a full moon as we passed through the olive and fig groves. What was happening now in the country seemed closer to fiction than reality, and I took a moment to concentrate on the surrounding silence and stillness, which was nothing short of pure magic – no fear of death for the moment. Yet this tiny bubble of delight was quickly punctured by the distant missiles, confirming my suspicions that my own death wish was what kept pushing me towards returning here. No, it wasn't so much a death wish, as a wish to release myself from its grip and then master it. This was what prompted me to laugh now, and to take a deep breath, open the window and stick my head outside, stretching my neck in the cool evening air.

'We're here,' Ezzat announced.

The school was situated on a hill in the village of al-Dar al-Kabira, only a ten-minute drive from Kafranbel. At first sight, the building appeared to be submerged in total darkness, just like the surrounding villages, but inside the occasional dim light bulb hung from the ceiling, as the school was now a shelter for displaced families. A man came over to welcome us while another looked at us with disdain then walked off. Standing to the side, by a fence, a group of young bearded men were watching the goings-on curiously.

The team rigged up the lighting, the screen, the projector and the audio equipment: we were ready to roll. A group of children filtered out of the school building to join us. I couldn't distinguish their faces in the dark as they jumped about, but the girls kept apart from the boys. That seemed odd to me. There was a crescendo of shouts, screams and laughter, and then the children's mothers came out.

Some of the mothers came up to speak to me, curious at the sight of a stranger. One of them lived with three of her children. Her house in Maarat al-Numan had been devastated. Another woman had left Aleppo and gone to live with some of her relatives in Haish, but then the relatives had been killed and so she was staying here with her five children, all leaping around her excitedly.

Suddenly a ten-year-old girl stepped forward and started to sing, her voice loud and clear. She was holding hands with her twin sister, who had become mute since the bombardment, but she was trying to involve her in the song. Both girls were just skin and bone. The women from Maarat al-Numan started to explain that they'd been orphaned, but she was interrupted by a woman in her sixties who whispered to me, 'Can't you see what's happening to people? How long are we going to have to live like this?' My whole body stiffened.

This was the same thing I kept hearing whenever I visited the houses in the villages surrounding Kafranbel and in the town centre too. These were the people who believed in the revolution but didn't participate in it. They were losing hope after having been starved, besieged, bombed, and seeing their children killed. The older woman grabbed my wrist and moved closer.

'I lost three of my children and my house in the bombing,' she said. 'My fourth son is fighting and I'm here with six of my grandchildren and them' – she pointed at three young women – 'they're my daughters-in-law.'

The cinema projector started up and flickering light washed over the crowd. The Karama Bus team were addressing groups of children who were sitting in orderly rows. The show began and I went over to sit with the little ones. The film was educational, informative and entertaining, and it was followed by a discussion with the children. Adults were coming forward and contributing too, including some of the locals. There were no phones here or electricity, so there wasn't a lot to do in the evening.

The group of bearded young men remained nearby, watching what was going on with distaste. The Karama Bus team told me some people weren't happy with their work, especially with regards to the cinema, or the drawing lessons and a handful of other subjects they were teaching the children, which these people deemed blasphemous and sinful. But this bunch by the fence were only observing passively without trying to stop any of the activity.

'Who are they?' I asked, nodding towards the gang.

'The Nusra Front. And supporters of ISIS . . . and various other fundamentalists,' came the reply.

I couldn't understand how all this confusion had come about or how the rural provinces were being converted like this. If the situation continued, all forms of civic life would come to an end. Nevertheless, many people were resisting. Nature always changes and evolves towards the future, not the past, and there was a great fear of the jihadist battalions and their goal of establishing an Islamic state.

Halfway through the next film, we heard the sound of a huge explosion, then there was a flash and the sky lit up. I glimpsed the panic in the children's eyes. A rocket passed over our heads towards the next village. A missile landed near us. Yet no one screamed. The mothers ran, hugging their children close.

The organisers started shouting instructions, and one of them addressed everyone through a loudspeaker: 'What did we say we should do when a plane starts bombing or a missile drops? What should we do? What did we say about precautions?'

But no one was listening, although a set of precautions had been drilled into the children for situations like these – to prevent them from hurting each other by stampeding. There was a risk of them trampling over one another and the smaller ones ending up crushed beneath people's feet. Crowds would often impede their own movement this way.

'Switch off the projector! You're spreading light and attracting the bombers!' a man shouted. They turned it off and a woman came over to us.

'Hey, my dear,' she said to me. 'Just what do you think you're doing? You want to teach the children and help them cope with these disasters . . . Listen, they want to eat and they want this goddamned Assad to stop bombing. Go and stop him from bombing and then we'll be fine. May God not bless you, Bashar, and damn you and your criminal family!'

'I swear, auntie, if we could stop him we would,' I replied. 'This is all we can do.'

The team started packing up the generator and the rest of the equipment. Darkness returned to the area gradually, and the space emptied of children and adults, although we could see their faces peeking out of the windows of the schoolroom.

'If a missile landed when they're gathered together like this, oh, my God, so many would die!' said Razan.

'Then it would be God's will, his judgement and his decree,' one of the group of young bearded men who'd been monitoring the event responded scathingly.

Silence prevailed and the sky darkened. There was not even the tiniest speck of light. We got back into the car.

The next day, I travelled with the Karama Bus team to another school outside Kafranbel and this time they managed to complete both the screening and the talk. This school was inhabited by around fifteen families, with more than seventy children whose ages ranged between two and thirteen. Most of those participating were girls and they were very enthusiastic. The boys were more cautious, calling themselves men and claiming that it wasn't suitable for them. I asked a nine-year-old boy to join in.

'What! Do you think I'm a child?' he said indignantly. 'It won't be long before I run away and join the Nusra Front. I know how to shoot.'

His sister smiled. 'Liar. He doesn't know how to shoot.'

She was ten and lovely. Her little brother shouted at her, ordering her to shut up because she shouldn't be talking in the presence of men. And this nine-year-old boy wasn't the only one who thought like this. One of the fighters had apparently tied his twelve-year-old nephew by a rope to a pole outside their house because the boy had tried to run away and join the Nusra Front, hoping to fight. When his family brought him back home, he'd cursed them, sworn at them and declared that he disowned them because they were infidels.

I felt despondent because no matter how well intentioned all these psychological, developmental, cultural and economic projects were, or how they tried to support the refugee schools and the populations living out in the open, they were helpless in the face of the extent and horror of the daily tragedies. These children barely ate and were living in a constant state of displacement, and it wasn't enough to have the Karama Bus team drop by to try to give them some education for a few days here and there. The scale of the humanitarian disaster was enormous and these efforts were a drop in the ocean.

Back at the office, the battery-charged lights were on, and the others were waiting for us. Raed turned on the generator when we arrived. Hossam was there too, and gently poured tea for us. He was extremely civil and good natured in everything he did. While he had been driving me around town, he'd told me he had finished his university degree in Arabic literature and had dreamed of becoming a university professor, but they had appointed the daughter of an officer instead of him, even though she was lazy and made no pretence of working hard. He had defected from military service in July 2012 and fled Damascus via the Latakia mountains to the Idlib countryside, and participated in the liberation of the first checkpoint in Kafranbel. But after a week he had thrown down his weapon and returned to civil activism. He wasn't impressed with the actions of the Free Army and the military battalions, who he claimed were dishonest and given to stealing, and said he couldn't carry on in the light of all the murders and the brutality.

Hossam was one of the many young people I met who had struggled to find work because of the economic situation and widespread corruption, and who had a story to tell, which he recounted angrily to me one day in the car. At the time, we were passing through the villages surrounding Kafranbel, witnessing the aftermath of the bombardments – the fallen trees, demolished antiquities and crowds of displaced people wandering out in the open, their faces sunburnt. Children were sleeping under trees. A fire blazed between some huge stones. The scene looked like something out of the dark ages – as if time had suddenly been turned on its head.

During his compulsory military service for the regime, Hossam had been serving in the 4th Armoured Division when the colonel in charge of the engineering department had ordered him to blow up a silver Saba car. When he asked about it, he was told the colonel had bought the vehicle so it could be used to fight terrorist groups. The colonel had been on an explosives training course run by Russian experts, Hossam explained.

He continued, 'After the course, he trained us himself and I flew with him to Tal Rahal, where the whole area was surrounded by rebels. The battalion commander there gave us some IEDs, improvised explosive devices. I presumed we'd be detonating the car in a war zone, and I believed the story about the armed terrorist gangs.'

He shook his head sadly. 'The colonel told me the car was ready for the operation and that the only thing left to do was to attach the detonator. Once it'd been attached, anyone who switched on the car's engine would be blown up with it.' Hossam paused to wipe his forehead. Sweat was pouring from him in the oppressive heat, as we wound our way through the endless plains, the forests of torn-down trees.

'That night, the colonel woke me up at midnight,' he said. 'He told me two lads would accompany me to attach the detonator, so I went with them. They were silent, not uttering a single word, and they didn't answer any of my questions. I was worried about entering a war zone, but, as I was doing my compulsory service, I wasn't allowed to disobey orders.

'On the way, I discovered the men were from air-force intelligence. The next big surprise was when our car stopped at Qaboon Square in Damascus, not a war zone. We drove right onto the square, where two other cars were already parked. The men said that Major General Jamil Hassan had asked us to return in the two cars; they were both to travel in one of them and I was to go back in the other on my own.

'The whole situation came as a real surprise and a shock to me. I stalled for time so that I could disable the detonator. Then I attached the detonator the wrong way round so that it couldn't detonate – if I had attached it correctly, I'd have been responsible for detonating thirty-five kilograms of explosives in a square packed with people.

'When I'd finished attaching the thing the wrong way round, I was relieved. I finished up and we went our separate ways. And I defected first thing in the morning. Believe me, I really thought there were terrorists and I was wholeheartedly determined to defend my country from them, but what happened made me realise the truth. Assad's gang were the terrorists.'

As we sat together that evening on the terrace, singing and drinking tea at the end of another long day, I smiled across at Hossam. A gentle, soothing breeze came from the olive groves, and I recalled a conversation I'd had earlier in the day with another young man I'd met in a shop near the media office. The young man explained he was a university student who hadn't joined the military resistance.

'We're living under two occupations: the Assad occupation and the jihadist *takfiri* occupation it brought with it. We're tired,' he said.

In another shop, I'd had first-hand experience of how people were beginning to recoil from the media. There the shop owner shouted at me as I took photos with my iPad: 'Hey, miss, anything you take photos of, the regime will come and bomb. Two of my children have died and this pile of stones here . . . this used to be my house. Please leave, and may God bless you.'

'Thank you, uncle,' I said, before leaving.

After Hossam had gone home that evening, only Raed, Razan, Hassan, Ezzat, Hammoud, Osama and I remained. They were preparing to draw graffiti on the walls of Kafranbel the following morning. The caricature portraits they painted on the walls of their city, which they shared through photos with the whole world, were the strongest means they had at their disposal to publicise their suffering. Together Osama and I were working up a training programme on how to produce radio shows. While I didn't have experience of working in radio as such, I had been trained in television and radio broadcasting in Lebanon, and had gone on to produce and present a show on Syrian state television between 2005 and 2006. I had also worked as a TV critic during the same period.

Raed had promised to tell me the story of Kafranbel, about how the revolution began, and how far it had reached, but wanted to wait until everyone else had left for the day. I reminded him that Razan and I had to get back to her house before midnight. It was safer that way – although it was like being in a prison, as a female and a foreigner in these parts. Even the local women couldn't go out alone now since the spread of stories of abductions, robbery and murder.

'Shall we have some coffee?' I suggested. 'We have a long conversation ahead.'

'Your wish is my command,' Raed replied.

He completely understood what I wanted without needing much of a hint. He was clever and quick-witted, and well aware that he was the leader of the group here and at other centres in the region. I didn't know whether this awareness was a positive or a negative trait, but perhaps that would become clearer. My experience to date had proven that the revolution was in need of local leaders like Raed.

'Right, let's start. You talk and I'll write,' I said.

We sat indoors, cross-legged on a plastic rug, covered with a cluster of long cushions, sipping our coffee. Just as Raed was about to begin, two men in their early twenties came in. 'So, ma'am, is everything OK? There's no kidnapping or anything here. You're safe,' one of them reassured me.

I thanked him without asking who he was because by now I was used to young men coming to check that I was all right. After Marcin's abduction, I could tell they felt they had something precious on their hands that they needed to defend; they felt responsible for protecting whoever came to support them and were very worried that I might be in danger too. But they didn't sit down and for a moment there was an awkward silence. Then Raed relented and started to tell the story of Kafranbel and the revolution, while I wrote it down.

'The protests began in February 2011,' he said. 'Two groups started writing anti-regime slogans on the walls of Kafranbel. In March, we began to meet up very cautiously and started coordinating our approach. At that point, we didn't have any contact with other groups in Syria and communicated with each other in total secrecy, in order to initiate a local revolution against the Assad regime.

'It was agreed we'd hold the first demonstration in Kafranbel on the 25th of March. But the demonstration failed because too many people were afraid to protest and, to intimidate them further, a member of the Ba'ath Party local branch immediately arranged a pro-regime rally on the same day – ever loyal to their party leader, Assad. This only spurred us into going out on the streets the following Friday. There were about two or three hundred of us and it was a powerful demonstration, although half of the protestors were undercover security agents who wanted to find out what was going on. There are many informants everywhere in Syria and Kafranbel is no different from any other city, town or village.

'We filmed the protest and shared the video online. But then some of the powerful local families met us and insisted that we stop demonstrating, so we didn't go out the following week. They also formed "popular committees" of vigilantes who stood at the doors of the mosques to prevent any demonstrations. All the same, we went back out on the 15th of April, with "Kafranbel" written on our banners, along with the date. We held up the flags of the regime and signs with slogans such as "Only God, Syria and freedom".

'On the 17th of April, it was Independence Day and a public holiday, so we protested in the afternoon, calling for the downfall of the Assad regime. Security cars turned up, along with around two hundred intelligence officers, the *mukhabarat*, while we stood in peaceful confrontation. They opened fire. They pointed their machine guns at our chests and we stood, unarmed, and raised the victory sign. And they withdrew.

'After that, I went into hiding, as did many others. We'd go and see our families during the day, then at night we'd sleep in tents out in the forests and orchards. But we started to stage demonstrations on a daily basis. Still, popular support remained weak because the people of Kafranbel were afraid. For them, the memory was still fresh of the 1982 Hama massacre that'd claimed the lives of more than thirty thousand people in one week at the hands of Hafez al-Assad's forces and intelligence services.

'We didn't stop at Kafranbel; we'd go to the neighbouring villages and urge them to go out and march against the regime. The villages of Huzeiran, Jibala, Maarzita, Hass, al-Habeet, Kafr Oweid. We moved from village to village every day. We marched to the city of Maarat al-Numan and the people there came out with us. On the 22nd of April, we produced Kafranbel posters for the first time. We've been making them every Friday since, with fresh slogans on them each time, and we publish them online. People who'd originally been frightened also started to join us, and the numbers of demonstrators began to range between four and seven thousand people. Even so, people were still terrified of confronting the *mukhabarat*, the security services. But I'll never forget the women who showered us with flowers and rice as we marched and called out for freedom.'

Raed was so emotional that he had to stop talking. He traced a line on the mat with his finger, then lit a cigarette. I felt numb with exhaustion. Even though they'd taken part in all the events themselves, the other men listened to him with admiration.

Raed continued, 'We were wanted by the security services, and that in itself made people afraid of coming out with us. On the 2nd of May, *mukhabarat* officers raided houses in town. They broke into activists' homes, storming in and arresting around fifty of them. This prompted supporters to hold a sit-in outside the police station, which they then entered. Other people joined us as we barricaded the exits of the village with stones and car tyres that we set fire to. We also threatened to set the police station alight if the detainees weren't released. A delegation from Kafranbel went to negotiate the release of the detainees with the regime, but returned without success.

'The next day, the Ba'ath Party branch secretary came and asked what the people's demands were. We told him that our demands were to dismantle the security services, to end their stranglehold on everyday life, and to replace the president. We discussed it calmly, but when I said, "I want a different president for Syria than the one we've had for the last forty years", the branch secretary went quiet. He said the only way to achieve the release of the detainees would be if we stopped using slogans that were anti Bashar al-Assad, and if we refrained from cursing the spirit of his father Hafez al-Assad. But we hadn't cursed the spirit of Hafez al-Assad; we'd just chanted for Bashar al-Assad to be overthrown. On the 7th of May we held democratic elections for the rebel coordination committee.'

'How did the coordination committee begin, and how was it formed?' I interrupted.

He smiled and said, 'I swear, it happened on its own!'

We laughed, but then the sounds of bombing, which had been distant, seemed to get closer, making us instinctively turn towards the source of the sound.

'Don't worry,' Hammoud said to me. 'I don't think we'll be bombed today.'

'No,' Hassan interjected. 'Let her be afraid: there's always the chance we'll be bombed!' And they laughed again. They never stopped laughing, these men. It was as though they inhaled laughter like an antidote to death.

'The coordination committee started spontaneously,' Raed resumed. 'We began to see more higher-status people coming forward: well-qualified activists, important people. There were fifteen of us, including Yasser al-Salim the lawyer, Hassan al-Hamra and me. We didn't call it a coordination committee at the time; we were just a committee and we also didn't post our posters and banners on Facebook back then. This was back in February 2011. We achieved all of this in a spontaneous way, improvising as we went along, and what we wanted was to mobilise people. We elected seven people for political, military, media and administrative roles. When we felt that the people elected didn't have strong enough popular legitimacy, we met in the Cultural Centre and held further elections, announcing to everyone that the Kafranbel coordination committee had been formed.

'On the 1st of July 2011, we went out and held a major demonstration. But on the 4th of July the army cut the whole area off and we fled from Kafranbel. There were nine army checkpoints in Kafranbel, around one thousand seven hundred soldiers, one hundred tanks and one hundred military vehicles. We secretly re-entered the town, and made banners there despite the presence of snipers and troops. Then we marched from the Uqba mosque, until the army fired shots at us. It became a routine: we'd demonstrate then flee from the army, they'd fire at us and we'd flee. But we were peaceful and none of us was killed.'

He stopped and so did I. I sipped my coffee and lit a cigarette, while Raed contemplated the night and the olive trees surrounding the house.

'How did you end up carrying weapons, and how did the revolution suddenly transform from being peaceful to being an armed conflict?' I asked.

'We didn't think the regime would stay. We assumed we'd be able to topple them by striking and holding peaceful demonstrations. We didn't anticipate what happened next . . . but we did take up arms,' he replied.

'What else should we have done when they were killing and bombing us? What should we have done – die? Why do you think we needed weapons?' The interruption came from an angry-looking young man leaning next to the door.

Raed continued, 'There was a top-secret military fuel depot – it's now known as Wadi Deif, it's still there. Some of our men had dealings with a soldier at Wadi Deif and we got three rifles from there, which we brought back to Kafranbel. We managed to borrow another six rifles. We now had eighteen rifles buried under the soil of the fig orchards, which – following a decision by the coordination committee – we had agreed we would dig up only when we needed to defend our homes.

'These weapons remained buried and untouched until the army entered. On the 16th of August, we went out to demonstrate. The army attacked us and spread through the town, beginning a campaign of mass arrests. The mother of one young man tried to drag him out of their grasp after he was arrested, but they pushed her to the ground. When she fell, her hair was uncovered in front of everyone, which really provoked people. They were indignant, so they rallied round and we went to the al-Ayar checkpoint, having decided to respond to this insult to our honour. We were still only armed with one rifle and a sniper rifle, but we stayed for two hours, killing six soldiers at the checkpoint, including an army captain. And so the armed campaign began.

'The following day, the army retaliated heavily and arrested many more people at random. They converted the carpet factory into a detention centre and broke into people's houses.

'Our six armed groups became seven. Each group was formed of between ten and eleven people, led by a man who would be obeyed and respected. We would only mobilise to defend the town, and some expatriate Kafranbel families started sending us aid, which we would share out. We would give a married man six thousand Syrian liras and three thousand to an unmarried man. The money was meagre and so were the numbers of activists. Some people refused to take up arms and remained civilian activists.

'In November, we set up the first battalion – the Kafranbel Martyrs Battalion, which later became part of the Free Army. Our plan involved attacking army sites at night. Two people would ride a motorcycle, shoot at the checkpoint, then flee. After that, we'd be fired at all night long from the checkpoint. But we stopped them from moving around at night and harming civilians. We followed this same process with the nine checkpoints surrounding Kafranbel.'

Raed stressed this last sentence as if he wanted to offer some justification.

'Yes, we did it because they were tormenting our families and we wanted to end the suffering. They trashed our houses and arrested our men. We were only trying to scare them!

'During this period, Lieutenant Colonel Abu al-Majd – whom you've met – deserted from the army. He was the first officer to defect. Initially, we were nervous about it but he went on to become the commander of the Kafranbel Martyrs Battalion, which became the Fursan al-Haqq Brigade. We filmed ourselves and announced its formation in a video we shared online. Then people started to respect us and applauded our work, donating whatever they could to us and offering us all possible forms of assistance. Most of them supported the revolution, though the popular support for the revolution fluctuated from time to time.

'We planted mines made out of sugar, fertiliser and other substances, with a fuse attached, in front of the army vehicles, to protect the demonstrators by holding the military back. But the townspeople started to get angry about the destruction of the roads, and didn't support this new tactic. But what could we do? Our men were being tortured to death. We found their bodies after the liberation of Kafranbel in the grounds of a school the army had been using as a base.

'People were further incensed when their homes were caught in the constant crossfire between us and the army, and destroyed. The fighting intensified until the streets became a full-on war zone, which upset the families even more until they stopped giving us aid.

'When a ceasefire was scheduled between the regime forces and the Free Army for the 10th of April 2012, we hoped this would put some pressure on. If the fighting stopped – and the regime were to stop bombing and shooting – then the demonstrations would return to being peaceful, but the regime didn't want this. It wanted to justify the claim that it was killing people because they'd taken up arms. That's when we got aid from the military council, which is part of the Free Army, and at the end of April we received more weapons. We'd been buying RPG rockets that weren't fit for use; the arms traders had swindled us, and one of our guys died as a result. But with military council assistance, we received ten new RPG rockets. I think it was during this period that Assad's era in Kafranbel truly ended.

'We started attacking the checkpoints again. The al-Ayar checkpoint was the first, after which the regime's army began to shell us using tanks and Fozdika missiles. A missile could have landed on us at any moment. But we didn't stop fighting until we'd liberated five checkpoints.

'The real moment of liberation took place at three o'clock in the morning. We planted mines around a checkpoint in the village of Hazazin, where they had tanks, and detonated them. They started mortaring us and we ran in every direction. At that point, I stopped near to where the mortar bombs were falling and bit into an apple. I was waiting for death.

'We withdrew, deciding we'd return to liberate the army building the following day, but by then they'd pulled the checkpoint back to the district headquarters, and the other checkpoints back to the military base at Wadi Deif. There were only the headquarters and three checkpoints left in Kafranbel. That's when we started writing "Liberated Kafranbel" instead of what we used to write – "Occupied Kafranbel". That was in June 2012.'

Hammoud stood up. 'I'm afraid we need to bring this conversation to an end,' he said, shyly.

It was past midnight and I noticed that a sharp bolt of pain was shooting down from my lower back to my toes; my legs were stiff and I couldn't move.

Raed stood too. 'We'll carry on tomorrow,' he said.

I still couldn't move for stiffness, and for a moment I imagined we were emerging from somewhere deep underground, like one of the tombs in Rabia. It was this, the imagination, and nothing else that could transform life here into some sort of miracle. But as I stood up, it felt as if evil had escaped too; that it was surfacing from its burrows, spreading through the air and swallowing us up. As we headed back to Razan's house, only the night breeze could release me from my bewilderment.

The car's headlights ripped through the darkness on our way. Razan had been putting up a group of female activists who had come to carry out civil work in the liberated areas, although this kind of work was becoming more difficult as ISIS and some mercenary battalions were beginning to kidnap activists, male and female. These groups condemned the civilian activists as infidels for waging a secular campaign, and had been carrying out operations for months now to whittle them down. However, Kafranbel had enjoyed some immunity because the presence of the Islamists was limited there, although by this point in 2013 they were beginning to emerge.

The car stopped and we had to go on foot along the narrow pathway to Razan's house, where I was staying. In a large room in the basement lived a displaced family consisting of five separate households and countless children. The extended family had left their homes after shelling had killed three of the men in the family and left the survivors with nowhere to shelter. The women would huddle together under the window. Two of them were pregnant. All of them were very thin, even the pregnant ones. I had first come across their children playing outside in the shade of a pomegranate tree, where I told them stories. The children were barefoot and dressed in threadbare clothes, their faces dirty and their hair caked in dust. None of them had been to school for a year and a half. They and their families had moved from one place to the next, sometimes sleeping out in the open.

That night, the first floor of Razan's house was dark and we crept up the stairs quietly so that we wouldn't wake anybody. I found myself thinking about the children whose father and uncle had been killed, and whose mother was expecting another baby.

'They're asleep,' I whispered to Razan.

She nodded as she placed a small electric lamp on a shelf. The lamp had been charged up in the media centre since electricity was permanently cut off to the houses, as was the water supply, which meant we had to limit ourselves when we washed to mere drops of water.

'I want to smoke a cigarette in peace,' she said. The exhaustion was starting to show on her face.

The night was wrapped in a spellbinding silence. It was almost one in the morning, and I realised I could barely move my feet or stop my eyelids from closing. Yet I was suddenly filled with happiness, because it struck me that here I was, back within the Syrian border. I wanted to stay in this magical moment for the rest of my life and bask in it. It was a moment that would later become so ingrained in my mind that it has never left my sight.

In the distance, a powerful explosion echoed. The missiles had started to fall. Yet I managed to sleep deeply until 5 a.m.


In the morning, I opened my eyes to the sound of the missiles and felt a deep craving to return to the darkness. I wanted a lifetime of it, like a cave dweller. My feet were on fire from mosquito bites, although I'd learned to sleep covered in a sheet after waking one morning to find my face covered in bites.

I got out of bed and went to the window, which looked out over the house next door, now a bomb site, and towards the hill beyond it, where the shelling was focused. The whispering of two boys came from a corner in the rubble that had been transformed by bombing into a sort of tent. One child looked to be about six and the other one a bit older. Some weeds had grown along the walls and a patch of yellow flowers had popped up. Next to a pile of white plastic bags, the two boys were counting red, green and yellow marbles. The first boy pulled a piece of fabric out of his pocket, unfolded it and they started playing. They were from a neighbouring house. The sky was blue, and small soft clouds quietly drifted by. The sounds of the shelling grew louder. I moved away from the window. When an explosion boomed nearby, I shouted out to Razan to wake up and hide behind the pillar. But I couldn't stay still myself and after a moment I ran back to the window. The two children were still in the same place, still swapping marbles. Reassured that they were OK, I collapsed onto the bed.

A little later I joined Razan in the kitchen, where she had arranged her utensils in an organised manner. She sealed the packets of coffee and sugar using clothes pegs, and hung clothes over the doors and on the door handles. In one of the kitchen cupboards was a full-length mirror that we used instead of a bathroom mirror.

As we drank coffee together, I opened my small notebook and considered the tasks of the day. For every day I spent in the north of Syria, a month's worth of work needed to be completed. That's what I always said. So for me to stay a whole month, I'd need to achieve the work of several months. That was what was supposed to happen, but circumstances didn't always allow things to go according to plan. The constant bombing crippled life and transformed human beings into hungry and frightened creatures.

Today, my tasks included giving the men in the Kafranbel media centre a lesson in broadcasting and visiting the women's centre, then going to Maarat al-Numan and coming back that night to Kafranbel to continue recording Raed's story of the revolution.

I thought back to the boys playing outside in the shelling. No one was writing about the local people and their stories of everyday heroism, or about how they would transform the country. And even they were indifferent to the big slogans and buzzwords. These people whose lives I monitored here, I realised, were changing my own. Yes, even here on this small dusty road lined with houses that hadn't survived the shelling, with weeds growing around the edges. These people were the nameless and the ignored, the ones who rode their motorbikes to go about their daily affairs and who might be killed for the sake of buying three loaves of bread. They lived a bitter daily existence. The shells passed over their heads and planes destroyed their homes and set fire to their orchards and fields. And they woke up each morning grateful to still be alive. They lived between the stone alleyways and under the olive and fig trees. Simply, just as night and day rotate, they grew older and gave birth to children and died, without a murmur. Their lives passed in a flash. No one cared about them. And they weren't thinking about what they wanted as they sat on their terraces now. Most of the women slept on the ground with their husbands, if they still had a husband, and the children ran and played in small, confined spaces.

During the course of the morning, I passed a displaced family consisting of a man and his wife and five children living in a makeshift shelter. They were discussing how to get two extra litres of mazut. And the woman was asking her husband about where they could buy onions. Their twelve-year-old daughter, the eldest child, was sweeping the terrace and spraying some drops of water over it from a small plastic jug. The father, who was glancing between the sky and his wife and baby daughter, was muttering something I couldn't hear.

'Good morning,' I greeted them.

'Good morning,' they replied cheerfully, looking curious. Then I carried on my way.

Hossam was waiting for me in the car. I asked him if I could go and inspect the places that had been shelled and assess the damage to the town. In Kafranbel, as in most villages and towns in the area, there was usually a degree of destruction that people had come to regard as average, incomparable to Maarat al-Numan, where we would be going that afternoon. In the hour and a half we were in Kafranbel, I photographed the areas that had been destroyed: the school and some large water containers. Assad's aircraft deliberately targeted water containers in order to cut off the supply of drinkable water to the rebellious villages.

As in most cities and villages, the marketplace was a key target for shelling. One afternoon, planes had dropped three barrel bombs on Kafranbel marketplace and town centre, killing thirty-three people within minutes. An ancient mosque had been hit to the right of the square. The bombing was indiscriminate. We passed through the decimated market square, where the people of Kafranbel had erected a stone column decorated with marble and inscribed with the names of the martyrs who had died in the bombing. Yet the market was relatively busy. Hossam said that it was usually quite busy but that fewer people had been going to the market since the beginning of the revolution. Stores, vegetable shops and carts were still as they were. I watched a group of children in front of a vegetable cart. The eldest was fifteen years old. They were shouting and laughing, their voices loud, as they went from cart to cart.

Hossam dropped me off at the media centre, saying he would be gone for an hour but would come back to take me to the women's centre. In the meantime, Osama and I started our training session on producing radio programmes. The basement used for radio broadcasts consisted of three interlinked rooms, furnished with plastic rugs and some foam cushions. We entered the tiny room used for recording and transmission. It was so small it could barely fit a single person. The equipment and materials were basic. The men were putting together some pilot broadcasts and preparing the equipment they needed to communicate directly with the people. They didn't have any prior experience in broadcasting, but Osama was keen to produce a talk show with Ezzat and Ahmed that would deal with the daily issues facing families in Kafranbel: difficulties related to humanitarian aid, looting and the violations committed by the military brigades – the most sensitive topic that could be discussed. The young men wanted to open up a dialogue that would allow the general public to discuss their everyday problems freely. As one of them put it, 'We got rid of Assad's army and got the jihadist military instead.'

The basement became hot and some of the men went out to monitor the shelling that had started. Shelling by artillery generally caused less damage than barrel bombs, and there was a greater chance of survival. It was the destructive power of the barrel bombs that petrified us; even in the basement we wouldn't have been safe from them.

After the training session I went with Hossam to the women's centre. The place was basically another empty, poorly equipped basement that needed to be refurbished from scratch. Oum Khaled was the manager of the centre and her son was one of the activists. A significant portion of women from Idlib province aspired to achieve the revolution's initial goals of justice, freedom and dignity, through civil society and the local community, and Oum Khaled was one of them. She hadn't received her secondary school leaving certificate, but she liked to read and believed it would be women who made change happen. She prayed, fasted, drove a car, and ran a hair and beauty salon for women. She was waiting for me with a group of women who were taking a course in embroidery and beading.

Wearing the hijab was traditional here, but for over a year it had been made mandatory by law. In some parts of Aleppo, ISIS actively enforced it. After ISIS seized the city of Raqqa on the banks of the River Euphrates in the north-east, women had to cover their faces and bodies completely in black. The northern area of the country was impoverished just like most of rural Syria, but women here were educated to a certain degree, and capable of engaging in interesting discussion. And they were aware that profound changes were taking place that threatened to drag them into a dark tunnel with no exit, as the jihadist battalions were increasingly taking charge using the power of weapons and money. But, under the constant bombardment, talking about these issues seemed indulgent and a bit meaningless. That's what the women said as we sipped our coffee on the second floor after inspecting the basement. They wondered aloud what could be done in their difficult circumstances – how to carry on working without coming to harm, or causing harm to their husbands and families, and how to avoid contravening customs and traditions.

'It's all very difficult. We have to stick to teaching women sewing and beading work, cutting hair or nursing. No more and no less. And when this war ends we can think of other things,' one of them told me.

But Oum Khaled had a different opinion. 'We can teach English and French, and give literacy courses and computer courses,' she said.

I told them it was essential they had computers and Internet access, and training in psychological support. But most important of all were literacy courses for women. As we were chatting, suddenly a bomb fell nearby. We had been sitting beneath the window but, in the blink of an eye, we ended up piled on top of each other in the middle of the room. Minutes passed as we looked at each other in a daze, until we drowned in a fit of giggles. But I saw that the women's faces were pale and frightened. Mine must have been too.

It was already 1 p.m. and time to return to the office, in order to go to the front line with Abu Waheed, the commander of the Freedom Martyrs Brigade whom I had got to know during my previous visits. But Hossam was late coming to collect me, there were no phones, and I couldn't walk alone in the street; the women confirmed that they didn't go out by themselves these days unless absolutely necessary. Yet, in spite of the chaos that inevitably emerged in war – let alone during the bombing – the women believed it was best to carry on with life the way it was.

'Yes, I live in a state of war and bombardment, but I want to teach our girls how to live their lives well,' said Oum Khaled. 'We all want to get married and have children and build our lives. We don't want to surrender to death.'

I was amazed by the way she talked. To my mind, Oum Khaled was the living embodiment of the sort of partnerships that could be formed in a local civil society to foster development and knowledge. I had much more faith in this grass roots society than in the political and cultural elites.

The women were curious to know about my personal life and Oum Khaled managed to convince me that it was important for me to have my hair done, so I did. I went with her to a hairdresser who'd opened a salon in her home. The salon was modest and basically equipped, but good enough to produce the most radiant brides in town.

It was the 1st of August and, on the way back to the office with Hossam, I thought to myself that I mustn't lose hope, because the women around me had such courage and determination. Yet I felt suffocated by the combination of the scorching sun and my black clothes weighing heavily on me. I also felt anxious. Until that moment, I still shivered whenever I heard the sound of an explosion, but now ... now I was heading for the first time to the front line.

Abu Waheed was waiting for me and we set off in his car immediately. He hadn't changed much since I'd last seen him in February, but he was thinner, talked sparingly about battles and seemed in low spirits. He told me he wasn't receiving enough funds to finance his soldiers.

'Have we been defeated?' I asked him.

He looked at me intently. 'Oh, what can I say?' he replied. 'We've both succeeded and been defeated. Don't ever believe that we've been defeated. The whole world was against us ... everyone.' His fingers were trembling on the steering wheel though his arms remained rigid, strong and sunburnt.

I asked him about his wife and children.

'They're worth more than the world to me,' he answered.

'Can I smoke?'

'No,' he immediately replied. 'It's Ramadan and the Front or ISIS might be around and could suddenly turn up. It's safer if you don't.' I apologised to him for forgetting.

The air was hot and blasted our faces as we passed through the villages. When I'd met him before, Abu Waheed was still dreaming optimistically. 'Everything is fixable. We're still trying to realise our dream,' he'd said then. This time he was mostly silent, so I didn't try to engage him in a discussion about the outcome of the revolution or on why the jihadist *takfiri* battalions had come to the fore. I knew what he would say about the funding, and about the men who flowed into Syria every day from various corners of the world to fight under the pretext of defending Islam.

'We'll be picking up a fighter on our way,' he said.

We stopped in Maarzita to collect Abu Khaled. The fair-haired fighter no longer lived in his own home but had brought his wife and her sister's family to live with him near the front line in a deserted poultry barn, so he could be close to them. He said he couldn't leave them alone in the open. The poultry barn was situated on a plain completely bare except for some dry patches of grass. Inside the building, the only furnishings were an old plastic rug and a cushion just about wide enough for two people. Bare concrete and stone pillars sectioned off the interior of the barn.

While we were there, I asked Abu Waheed if I could meet Abu Khaled's wife and her sister. The wife, Oum Fadi, was hugging her two children.

'They bombed our house, and we spent the winter here. There's nowhere else to go,' she told me. 'When they bombed us, we left all our belongings behind and ran off into the street. There're eight of us living here, or eleven if you count the men. This poultry barn has been sheltering us for a year.'

The worn-out iron door shook and I started. They laughed.

'It's nothing; it's just a cat,' they said. I felt embarrassed because I'd thought a shell had exploded.

Oum Fadi's thirty-seven-year-old sister spoke confidently, but with sorrow. She was dark-skinned and her eyes were frightening: dark, sharp and bloodshot. She stretched out her bare feet and her heels were noticeably cracked. The children with the women were barely clothed, and stared solemnly at their surroundings, their eyes wide and unblinking like many of the other displaced children I'd seen.

When Abu Khaled called out, his wife got up to prepare his combat uniform.

'Are you going there, too?' the sister asked me.

'Yes,' I replied.

'Do you want similar clothes to the fighters?'

'Ma'am,' the husband called from inside, 'I swear, if you dressed like us it would be better because we're going to be exposed out there.'

But I declined. I asked her how they survived and she told me that her husband brought the food, they bathed once every two weeks, and they rotated the clothes they had with them. They had barely brought more than the clothes on their backs.

'In the winter, we use plastic bags to block up the draughts,' she said. 'The cold weather is shortening our lifespan. We can't get firewood any more, because there aren't enough trees left.'

Her sister Oum Fadi interrupted, 'We can't leave our husbands when they're fighting. We always follow them. I was a doctor's secretary and I'm good at reading and writing. Now we live like cave people. We move from village to village, dragging our children along. We just about have enough to eat, and our husbands fight. Can you imagine what that's like?'

She placed her hand in mine as she spoke and stared into my eyes, then squeezed my fingers in her palm. It was painful and her voice started to hiss.

'Do you really want to tell people what happened to us? Swear that you'll tell the whole world that the people of the other villages made us leave. The situation isn't as it seems to you. The people aren't united! There's a growing hatred between them now. You see over there?' She pointed towards the window, which was barely fifty centimetres wide, the metal frame worn and rusty. 'There's the front line. We see them and they see us. There're only three kilometres between them and us. We live here in isolation, penniless. You can hardly call it living. If it weren't for the fact that I fear God, I would've killed myself.

'We're dying slowly here, like animals that have been tied to a tree and left to starve to death. Our relatives who stayed behind have died in the bombing. The snakes creep around us day and night. Would you be able to spend one night with us? Impossible! Look at these bags.' There were three medium-sized bags hanging on a column. 'These are our clothes. We stuff them into bags so that we can leave quickly at any moment. We're lost and homeless. See my stomach?' She rubbed her swollen belly and continued. 'I'm going to get pregnant every nine months and keep having children so that we don't become extinct. Our children will regain our rights. We want them to be educated. We want them to fight so that we can return to our homes. We won't kneel down to Bashar al-Assad. We will never kneel. And we won't go back.'

She let go of my fingers, which were red from her grip. I could barely breathe. I didn't want to cry. I bit my lip and the tears fell silently down my face as she looked at me. No one smiled. Two of the children approached me as I moved to get up, and I asked if I could take photos of them. They didn't smile either.

As I left I waved and promised I'd be back, but I didn't keep my promise.

'You won't come back,' Oum Fadi said and she was right. I never saw her again.

Abu Waheed, Abu Khaled and I drove in the direction of the town of Haish, which was one of the first battle fronts in Idlib province. We left the small hill behind us with the wretched poultry barn at its summit. Another barn could be seen from afar across the bare plain. The sky started blending into a deep blue, not a cloud in sight. We were heading towards the front line, which at this point was only 700 metres away from the forces of the regime.

'Are they safe up there on their own?' I asked.

'Allah is our protector,' Abu Khaled replied.

Haish once had a population of 25,000, but it was an intensively bombed area, and had once been bombed continuously for fourteen days. Abu Khaled hadn't prepared us for the scale of the destruction I saw. The population had disappeared. Around 25,000 people had either fled or been killed or arrested. It was as if the town had never existed. There were no roads or streets, just broken, dusty paths, pitted with craters from bombs and shells, which meandered between the ruins of houses. Everywhere there were collapsed buildings tumbling onto the road. They hadn't just been destroyed, but pulverised into heaps of stones. Some of the pits and craters were staggeringly huge. Abu Khaled said some houses had been repeatedly pummelled by barrel bombs. Any remaining reinforced concrete pillars stood several storeys high, not crumbled, but twisted. The occasional chinaberry tree still stood, green and tall, shading some of the rubble.

As we entered the combat area from behind, I lowered my head. It was crucial I shouldn't be spotted from the other side: a woman among the rebels. It was so unusual for women to be on the front lines that, if they spotted me, the opposition would be bound to try to work out who I was, attracting more attention our way and putting us in even greater danger.

'Can they see us?' I asked Abu Waheed.

'We're trying to go around them,' he replied.

Only a street and some destroyed houses separated us from the enemy, who were positioned on elevated ground. We stood facing them and both the men lowered their heads too when we got out of the car. Abu Khaled used his body to conceal me, acting like a protective shield from bullets. Behind us was a street littered with huge mounds of rocks, and the small green branches of the chinaberry trees emerged from between the mounds. In every direction, there were heaps of rocks mixed with iron and charred, freshly burnt-out cars. They clearly hadn't finished bombing this town.

We entered a small and relatively unscathed room, where there was the usual plastic rug on the floor and a few cushions scattered about. Then the fighters streamed in. There were at least ten of them. And shooting began outside.

'They found out you're here,' one of the fighters said.

'But we were careful and we avoided the street; how did they know?' I asked.

There were some pictures on the wall. A still life. A photo of a fighter. Another painting of colourful flowers and some nails with a few shirts hanging off them. The room was just about big enough to hold us. Each fighter sat with his legs over his machine gun, entwined as though they were looped in a dance. The weapons were shiny and I could see their muzzles clearly – black muzzles forming a ring around my neck as bullets whistled over the roof above. The men looked at me with a mixture of curiosity and delight.

'Hey, ma'am, weren't you frightened? You should've dressed like us so that they couldn't spot you,' one of them said, a chubby young man of about twenty-six with a lightly tanned complexion and a jovial face, who was holding on to his machine gun.

I smiled at him and explained that I wanted to find out about him and his fellow fighters, who they were and why they'd stayed, whether it was true that the battalions here followed the Nusra Front and Ahrar al-Sham, and whether ISIS had arrived.

'Everyone you see now is from Haish and we haven't left our town,' the fighter replied. 'We're staying here because our houses are destroyed. My name is Fadi and I used to work in Lebanon. When things kicked off here, and I saw on television how people were being killed, I left my job and came back. This is my country and I have to stay. My speciality is mines and RPG grenades.

'I see this as a Sunni–Shiite war and nothing else. It wasn't like this at the start, but the Iranian Shiites started interfering and fighting against us – them and Hizbullah. We can hear them speaking Farsi on the radio. There are only a couple of hundred metres between us; they're now at the front line you passed by. As you can see, Haish has been completely devastated. And we don't have a media centre like the other towns. They've bombarded us with every kind of weapon going: surface-to-surface rockets, barrels, Scud missiles, bombs. There isn't a single building still standing.'

'This is a religious war and nothing else,' another young man added. 'I'm Sami. I'm twenty-two years old. I used to study at university. Do you see it as being about anything other than religion?'

'Yes, it's religious,' a third young man confirmed, as they took turns talking.

A thin, calm young man spoke next. He looked a bit pale and smiled curtly. 'I'm Anas,' he said. 'I'm twenty-five years old. We started going out on peaceful protests from here, the centre of Haish. We never broached the subject of religion. We just said: "Down with the regime!" but it turned out that the regime were infidels; that's why we took up arms. Do you know why they're infidels? We had fifty bombs drop on us in one minute. They've used every kind of aircraft but they haven't managed to enter the town. Eighty-five of their soldiers were killed and still they didn't manage to enter.

'Here in this battalion, we're all sons of Haish, but we aren't on our own. There's the Nusra Front and other battalions. But the international community has abandoned us. All we can say is, "There's no God but God and Mohammed is his Prophet." Death awaits us and we seek God's help to defeat the tyrant Bashar.'

The anger was spreading quickly on their faces. 'The Alawites have killed us and we will kill them,' another said.

Abu Khaled looked at me with a smile and intervened, saying, 'These young men are all from poor working families. The regime destroyed their homes and killed their families and made the rest of them here homeless. As you see, they have some feelings of sectarian persecution.'

One of them interrupted him. 'No, sir, the Alawites and Shiites don't know God and they're infidels.' The rest of the young men repeated similar statements.

The battalion whose fighters I was sitting with called themselves the Haish Commandos. The Nusra Front had refused to meet with us in several locations, and now Abu Waheed wouldn't even let them know I was here, for fear of reprisals if any of the Nusra fighters found out who I was. The shooting had intensified and Abu Waheed wanted us to leave immediately, but the Haish Commandos were wound up, keen to tell me their problems, about how they'd been neglected and how their city had been abandoned. They needed to start up a media centre but the constant bombing made it a challenge. Their civilian activists had also been killed; only Anas was left and he'd become a fighter.

'We once tried to ask for help from several villages and several well-known media offices here, but they haven't helped us. They've all deserted us!' one of them said.

The young men had a point as the town did seem to have been forgotten and neglected, as if it existed outside space and time. And they, with their young, angry faces, inhabited it like the living dead. I wanted to leave; my hands started trembling as they told me stories about how their friends were dying, one by one.

One of them joked, 'Today's my turn. I'm going up to the heavens.'

'No, I swear to God, you won't go before me,' another replied, and they laughed.

Abu Waheed became stern. 'We have to go, guys, the situation is dangerous for the woman.'

I wanted to stay and listen but it would have been dangerous to leave any later and the bombing could have started up at any moment. Snipers on both sides of the front line were still shooting. I didn't shake the young men's hands but I wished them well. The men in this area didn't shake hands with a woman. Most wouldn't even look into your eyes and would barely greet you.

We crossed the threshold to leave the house, keeping our heads low, with Abu Waheed leading the way. Four of the fighters followed me and Abu Khaled out. A young man I hadn't spotted clearly, as he'd been sitting in the shadows, spoke up now.

'But tell the world, ma'am, that we're dying alone and that the Alawites killed us, and that the day will come when they'll be killed. We will return the harm in kind, to them and the infidel Shiites, them and their prostitute wives.'

'Come on, man,' said Abu Khaled. 'That kind of talk is very offensive.'

'No, it's not,' the guy replied sharply.

I stared at him. 'May God protect all you young people, and compensate you,' I said.

'Amen, ma'am,' they responded. 'May God protect you. We swear it's been a pleasure having you here. You should've stayed to break the fast with us.'

'Blessed *iftar*,' I said, then bowed my head as I headed to the car. I glanced back at them. A bullet flew over our heads.

'My family are Alawites,' I said quickly and spontaneously. I got into the car and two of them ran after me and poked their heads through the open car window.

'Please don't take offence, ma'am. I swear we didn't mean you! I swear we don't hate all Alawites. We owe you and your family our respect.'

I was as silent as stone, listening to the beating of my heart and the sound of the bullets.

'Don't be upset. I swear they didn't mean it,' said Abu Khaled.

'I'm not upset,' I answered quietly. But then the stream of apologies kept coming. Anas, the twenty-five-year-old, leaned into the car, his eyes glistening with tears. 'I swear, ma'am, we would protect you with our souls. You're a daughter of this country.'

'You shouldn't have said that,' Abu Waheed whispered. Abu Waheed and Abu Khaled were both angry with me because of what I'd said – and I didn't know why I had, although someone had to break through this wall of hatred. I felt that keeping silent would have been a betrayal of every innocent Alawite and a betrayal of the soul of the revolution that we'd set out to honour two years earlier.

The young fighters were clearly embarrassed and now they wanted to compete in protecting us, advising us on safer routes we could take. Two of the young men walked ahead of us, beneath the crossfire, as our car crawled behind them. Every few seconds, one of them turned around and looked at me, his eyes apologetic and full of gratitude, and I'd smile back. I wasn't thinking about the number of bullets whizzing through the gaps between the dilapidated houses. My neck felt tight, or more accurately it felt as though it was being crushed; my throat clicked when I swallowed.

'No photography here; we don't allow it,' Abu Waheed said. The two young men who had been following us quickly overtook our slowly proceeding car and took up their positions with their machine guns. We were on the front line.

'Let's wait and see what happens,' I said, but Abu Waheed refused because the battle was fierce and we had to leave quickly.

Before the car turned round, I waved at them. The four stopped and waved back, still visibly embarrassed. We turned onto a dusty road and Abu Waheed set off at top speed. After a few minutes he looked over at me.

'I won't ever take you back to a place like that. What I did was risky, though it was good for you to see how these guys think. But you need to understand that other people might have reacted differently! And you could have been killed.' I nodded and glanced back through the rear window. Only one thought crossed my mind: were any of my relatives on the other side? My family whom I loved, whom I missed, with whom I'd spent my childhood, and whose beloved faces danced before me in the car window, full of happiness, as we crossed the thresholds of childhood and adolescence. I didn't wish death on them; I didn't want them to end up murdered.

I put on my sunglasses because my eyes were welling up. The sun was no longer a strain as it was starting to set, but the time had come for tears. Abu Waheed said that we had been only 300 metres away from the regime's soldiers. I nodded. I was crying noiselessly, hiding my face behind the headscarf and my wide glasses. It all felt unbearable, as if my heart would explode. I could hear it beating louder and louder, and then I forgot to ask if we could call in at the poultry barn so I could see the women again. I had broken my promise.

Abu Waheed said that the following day we'd go to Khan al-Assal in Aleppo. 'There was a battle yesterday. Within a few hours, five hundred men were killed on both sides.'

I didn't turn towards him or ask any more questions. I was just thinking about how so many people could die like that in such a short space of time. I was so lost in thought that I didn't even notice when Abu Khaled got out of the car until he approached my window to say goodbye. My ears were ringing as I watched the sun disappear beyond the vast plains that stretched into the distance and the hills topped with clusters of mostly burnt-out houses. When I reached the media centre in Kafranbel, I washed my face and sat on the terrace, leaning back against a pillar near an olive tree, totally spent.

The view from where I was sitting was of a small house. Two boys were feeding two lambs in a newly built enclosure. Piles of kindling were lined up against one side. The children came up to the olive tree and playfully threw a stick of firewood at me, which fell in my lap. Looking down I noticed the mat I was sitting on was brown, my favourite colour. The activists were all busy with different tasks: Raed was cooking dinner on the terrace and joking with everyone. He brought out chunks of meat, which he barbecued with some oil, vegetables and a few chili peppers. Hammoud washed the vegetables. Abdullah swept the floor and wiped the mat. Razan washed the dirty dishes she was given. Preparing the *iftar* was a celebratory ritual that preceded the deadly missiles. Time to rejoice that there were still vegetables and other food to eat, that there was still someone to chop and cook for, friends to eat with and celebrate these small details. The jug of water was washed several times and placed alongside several clean cups. Two fighters came in and joined the work force.

Raed laughed. 'In an hour we'll eat and in an hour we'll be bombed. But we can't die without eating a good meal first!'

I remained silent.

'We'll continue the Kafranbel story when you get back from the school this evening,' he said to me.

'Of course,' I replied, a little abruptly. I was still feeling bewildered after the trip to Haish. Yet I needed to keep a hold of myself until we came back from the school, and to save a batch of my strength and resilience. The next bomb strike would only last for a few minutes. If we didn't survive, I wouldn't need to carry on with my remaining tasks, and if we did survive, we'd go to the children's school and then continue with the final task: the story of the revolution in Kafranbel. It was as simple as that.

We ate, and we survived the bombing. The missiles dropped exactly five minutes after the sunset call to prayer in the western side of the town, and soon we could breathe again.

It was past ten thirty at night when we returned after finishing our work with the Karama Bus project and the displaced children. We had about two hours to go through the rest of Raed's story.

'We're back. Come on, Shahryar, back to the story,' I said to him. He laughed at my calling him the name of the king from *One Thousand and One Nights.*

'No – we've swapped roles: you're Scheherazade, the storyteller, and I'm the scribe,' I added. 'We'd got to June 2012, when the revolutionaries took control of Kafranbel – but the army checkpoints were still in place?'

Raed nodded. 'Yes, the checkpoints were still there, but the regime's soldiers couldn't move past them into the town unless they were in their tanks. On the spur of the moment, on the 6th of August, we decided to embark on a final battle of liberation. The group was led by Fouad al-Homsi, a brave fighter who'd gone out during Ramadan to ambush an army checkpoint on the road to Latakia. He hadn't succeeded and had returned to Kafranbel. But there'd been an exchange of gunfire between him and the soldiers at the checkpoint, and he'd sent a message saying he and his men were surrounded by army troops. At that point, some men set fire to a load of tyres and shouted, "We're here to help! We're here to help!" And so the battle of liberation began and young fighters streamed in to back us up.

'There were around a thousand of us armed rebels. We fought continuously for five days. We took up defensive positions around the town to barricade the roads. We managed to cut off the army's food and drink supplies. The fighting carried on non-stop. Then they started bombing us with aircraft. On the seventh day of our struggle for liberation, army helicopters turned up and started bombing us as well. They wanted to rescue the army troops. The aircraft bombing wasn't as barbaric as it is now. They were only bombing to provide cover for themselves, for military self-defence purposes.

'But the truly barbaric bombing began on the 8th of August 2012, which was the day that they dropped the first explosive barrel bomb of the Syrian revolution. I had my camera near the checkpoint and photographed everything that took place during the battle. Since then, we've been bombed continuously using barrels.

'On the 9th of August, they bombed us with MiG aircraft, and on the 10th MiGs circled over us intensively, constantly. But between the 8th and the 10th of August, Kafranbel was liberated from the regime. We made the liberation declaration in the mosque. We were proud because Kafranbel became known as "The Liberated". We thought that we were close to our victory over Assad.

'Other checkpoints began to be liberated, including those of the villages Hass and Kafrouma. But people started leaving after the army withdrew, because there was daily shelling; the battle was ongoing and the shooting hadn't stopped. Only the revolutionaries stayed during the liberation and there was at least one massacre in Kafranbel.

'On the 22nd of August, twenty-six people were martyred in the square where the demonstrations took place and on the 25th of September seventeen people were martyred. On the 17th of October, there were thirteen martyrs and at the end of the month eleven martyrs, and on the 5th of November thirty-two martyrs fell. After the liberation, they bombed us every day, and Kafranbel turned into a ghost town. Its population went down from thirty thousand to about fifteen thousand, and those who stayed would travel to the neighbouring villages during the day and come back at night. In October, Maarat al-Numan was liberated and the families of Haish – which was completely devastated – moved to Kafranbel. These displaced people were dying with us in the massacres.'

Raed fell quiet. I pushed aside my small notebook.

'Let's take a break for five minutes and have a cigarette,' I said.

He smiled. He knew he was being listened to but I'd noticed something strange about his expression. It was the same thing that had appeared in Abu Waheed's face: grief. Two and a half years of daily killing. First the peaceful civil struggle, then the armed military struggle. And now the religious extremist groups hijacking the revolution. But both of the men, despite their different paths, still had faith that nothing would be solved without the downfall of the Assad regime.

I picked up my notebook. 'Tell me, oh happy king . . .' I said, raising my voice.

Raed straightened up and stretched his legs. He'd been sitting cross-legged for hours. 'Of course, an important detail is that in June 2012 there were many defections in Kafranbel by officers and soldiers,' he explained. 'One thousand soldiers and thirty-five officers left in one mass desertion. The highest-ranking officer would take charge of the battalion – the liberation battle was led by Hassan al-Salloum.

'The problem was that after the liberation a competition for power emerged among the newly defected officers and the people who'd joined the revolution more recently. When the first military council was formed, made up of officers and five revolutionaries, it was dissolved after only a week. There were disagreements between the Kafranbel battalions and other battalions. One of the top officers, who was rich and had good supplies of weapons, withdrew. As you know, having met him, Lieutenant Colonel Abu al-Majd from the Fursan al-Haqq Battalion stayed. His was the first battalion to participate in the revolution and so it grew, taking on more members – its leaders liberated Kafranbel. Since then, the situation has fallen into chaos as more military battalions have been formed.'

'Why haven't the jihadist military battalions taken charge in Kafranbel, the way they have in so many villages?' I asked.

Raed shook his head. 'I knew you'd ask that,' he said cynically. 'You're afraid of them.'

'Yes, I'm scared, but not for me, for the future of the country.'

'Yes, yes. They did attempt to seize control. Ahrar al-Sham had offered to liberate the checkpoints in September 2011. We declined. We were afraid they would stay in Kafranbel after the liberation. In February 2013, the Nusra Front also offered to participate in the demonstrations but we kept saying no. In my opinion, the locals wanted the Islamists there because they thought they were the only ones who could free them of Assad, because the Islamists had money, weapons and faith. The Free Army had limited financial support and some of them resorted to theft in order to fund themselves. The locals also thought that if the Islamists came in, they would govern them fairly after decades of unjust rule during which they'd only reaped murder and injustice. After all, ever since the era of Assad senior, Hafez, the regime has presented itself as being secular.

'But after the Islamists entered the liberated areas and started to govern them, people realised that the Islamists weren't fair rulers either – that they were in fact a carbon copy of the regime. And by Islamists, I mean the al-Qaeda affiliates who want an Islamic caliphate and to impose the restrictive sharia law. Now there is widespread rejection of them and the locals want them to go.'

Once again, I invited Raed to take a short break. 'Here, have a glass of water, Shahryar,' I said.

Then I got up and made another pot of tea. I was suddenly full of energy and felt like I could stay up for another twenty-four hours. I was enticed by the idea of recording the testimonies of everyone in the country, from detainees and civil activists to fighters on the front line. I would in turn be the narrator of this tale. I was part of a fragile thread of truth that had been obscured by history.

But there was no absolute truth. The headlines claimed the Assad regime was committing crimes the likes of which had never been known in contemporary history. But then in other stories, we heard of a clandestine conspiracy to exploit the country's economic and social circumstances, its ethnic and religious make-up, to transform the liberated areas into regions controlled by the jihadist battalions. Facts on the ground were proof that this place was resisting on two fronts, and that the rebels, despite most of them being killed, detained, abducted, or fleeing the country, were still resisting. Their resistance was unique, it was ambiguous and complicated, and the situation was turning bit by bit into a religious war, not unlike many revolutions that have occurred in history.

'Civil war is part of the reality of war,' I said as I set out the glasses to pour the tea. 'Yes, we need time, but the situation is difficult.'

The others were moving inside from the terrace. 'Please don't leave until I've asked all my questions,' I said. Razan decided to go home ahead of me while I stayed with Raed and Hammoud.

'People don't want the jihadist battalions any more, but isn't the popular support for the revolution also in serious decline?' I asked.

'Yes,' Raed replied, and nodded in his usual way, gesturing at the same time with his hands. 'Some of the first activists made mistakes that angered people, but the main frustration was directed at the rebel soldiers, because they weren't able to respond to the constant bombing from Assad's aircraft. At the beginning of the revolution they had faith in the Free Army and glorified it, but their weapons were so limited. For example, the Free Army attempted many times to storm and liberate Wadi Deif early on. Ten failed attempts. Thousands of people have been martyred as the Free Army has tried to liberate the land, but our lack of anti-aircraft weapons has meant we've lost it. And there was a lot of talk of betrayals. This made people lose confidence in the Free Army.

'Then there's another reason: the regime has its cronies here, and they've done everything they can to tarnish the image of the Free Army and fabricate vicious rumours about the rebels, about everyone – the relief workers, the media activists, the armed fighters. The regime's used rumours as an essential weapon of war to spread terror and division among the people.

'We are also just entering the third year of the revolution; people are tired and they're searching for someone to blame for what's gone wrong. The futility of this unbelievably tough struggle that's dragged on so long, along with the brutal violence of the regime, and the departure of so many activists and people from Syria . . . these are all important reasons. The Free Army battalions are fighting day and night without making any gains, families see their children are dying for nothing, the media shows all this footage in vain, and we get barely a quarter of the aid we need, and there's no water, no electricity, no food . . . In short, people are exhausted. They've had enough.'

'Is it possible to regain that popular support?' I asked quickly.

Raed looked at me in surprise but replied just as swiftly, 'The revolution is still going on. The sons of this second phase of the revolution are working hard in the offices we've set up to manage life in our liberated lands – offices for relief, media, finance and statistics. For instance, the statistics office is keeping track of the numbers of people wounded, detained and martyred and documenting what's going on. Every day, our engineers have documented the destruction so that we can calculate the cost of rebuilding our town.

'When donations started coming in from the expats of Kafranbel, we decided to establish an organisation to deliver these resources to everyone. The people who were placed in charge of this were those respected by the townspeople for their honesty, integrity and respect. The idea was to set up a dedicated office for relief operations when the financial office could no longer deal with relief issues because of the mass displacement from the villages to Kafranbel – we had fifteen thousand displaced people and they had to be fed. And any battalions that came to help us, we fed too. We opened the relief office with seven people. When the fighting intensified, the displaced people left and the relief centre has since become this media centre. This is how we've managed to work alone, without resorting to the experience of others. We've generated our ideas ourselves.

'But things are especially difficult, because now we face a danger that's greater than we can bear. All these jihadist battalions and the current chaos, which came out of nowhere – this is a serious obstacle we face. As for me, I'll never give up on our dream. We've accumulated a significant amount of experience, which we need to build on. I will never lose hope, but I can't say it'll be easy to regain popular support.' Raed stopped talking for a moment, then concluded, 'I think that's enough. There's nothing more to say.'

I stopped writing and we each lit a cigarette. The sky glittered with stars and I couldn't utter a single word. Raed was staring at the olive tree by the terrace and nodding to himself. The night's silence was unusual: there had been no explosions. And the crack in my heart felt as if it were growing and growing, with no end in sight.

The customs and traditions in the provinces have always formed a part of the cultural identity of the people, and where women still suffered from persecution this war cruelly compounded it. Then ISIS, the Nusra Front, Ahrar al-Sham and other extremist jihadist battalions came along, imposing further restrictions to obliterate the role of women. We did – and still do – dream of resistance.

Razan's home was cosy and intimate. I realised that like all the homes I'd come to know here, it summed up Syria for me, adding to the bitter nostalgia I felt, the homesickness. Each house was significant in its own way: Abu Ibrahim's house, my main base; the media centres, where we stayed for lengthy periods of time, trapped beneath the shelling; Oum Khaled's house, Ayouche's burnt-out apartment – the houses piled up in fragments in my memory, reduced to rubble by the shelling. Yet we kept on going, functioning as if we were living normally. We constantly flirted with death. The shelling never stopped but we still had to brew the coffee calmly on the small gas stove. This cup of coffee was more important than the idea of life and death on the mornings we woke up to shelling. We still had to look after our appearance. Perform our daily ablutions with the tiniest amount of water. We did what we had to do. Life went on with all its mundane details. Razan and I would wait patiently for our minders to pick us up, so we wouldn't stand out like two foreigners on the streets of Kafranbel.

In January 2011 Razan was arrested for revolutionary activities by a branch of the Political Security in Damascus, on the Syrian border with Jordan. 'The Free Army was in the heart of Damascus,' Razan told me, 'and we were ready for Damascus to fall. The Yarmouk camp was liberated and we used to hold our meetings there.' She was held initially at Daraa prison, a prisoner of conscience among detainees charged with murder, after which they moved her from one place to another. Every day she was moved to a different prison, until she reached Damascus where they eventually released her without charge. But two months later she was arrested again, detained at a branch of air-force intelligence and then released. However, she had never stopped her work. She'd fled across the border and decided to return to Idlib province to work for the revolution.

Razan remained one of the most prominent faces of the revolution and still dreamed of its success, in spite of what was taking place. I saw things differently. It seemed to me that the revolution had entered a ruinous phase and that much of what was happening now was being planned outside Syria with little regard for the revolution that we'd dreamed of. But still, as far as I was concerned, to abandon working on the revolution from within was out of the question.

That morning our colleague Abu Tareq arrived, and waited for me to join him at the end of the dirt path that led to the street from Razan's house. In his forties, Abu Tareq had only stayed in education until the end of secondary school, but had become a relatively affluent man, owning a tailoring workshop and another specialising in mosaics and marble. He had participated in the peaceful demonstrations from the first day of the uprising and enjoyed a good reputation among the locals, who described him as someone you could trust. He proved worthy of their praise, remaining loyal to the revolution and to the people – not that loyalty got you anywhere in these desperate days. Now, he was a military sector commander, with thousands of fighters under his command, and still dreamed of a united Syria, although he said that when Bashar fell, he would put down his weapons and return to his true vocation.

He wanted a civil state, a secular state. 'It's impossible to apply Islamic sharia in Syrian society,' he stressed to me. 'This goes against the nature of our society.' In his opinion, what was happening now was first and foremost a war being waged by the oppressed against a tyrant regime: he didn't want to hear anything about sects and religions. Even though he prayed and fasted and was committed to his religion, he would say, 'It's not the same. We want to build our country, we don't want to ruin it.'

We were to go to Maarat al-Numan that day, which was in an even worse state than I remembered from my previous visits: it was completely devastated. Situated on the front line, the city had been exposed to violent bombardment every day for the past three months. What was left for them to bomb in this ancient historical city that now lay in utter ruins?

The man we were going to meet was an influential leader, an emir, of the militant Ahrar al-Sham movement. Through talking to him, I hoped to understand the way the movement thought. We passed through the danger zone outside town, which I now knew well as I had been to the vegetable market there with Raed to stock up before *iftar*. I lowered my head and held my breath for a few minutes as we passed the sniper district, where the regime's soldiers faced onto the road. Just minutes before we entered Maarat al-Numan, a missile fell, causing a powerful explosion. We didn't stop and continued driving straight ahead.

A problem that had become increasingly obvious in daily life was that an authoritarian power of a different kind had entered the scene and was starting to form a serious obstacle to any civil activism or any attempt to rebuild the shattered society. As we drove through the ruined streets, I thought that a good strategy to sustain a positive relationship between women in Syria and the outside world would be to start with small steps that didn't provoke jihadist battalions such as Ahrar al-Sham. But any interaction between the genders was now prohibited. The matter had been turned into law, and going outside unveiled had become absolutely unthinkable. Any woman without a veil was liable to prosecution and any activist, male or female, risked abduction, murder or arrest. Nevertheless, I refused to despair. I was determined to conduct this interview with the emir of

Ahrar al-Sham, although I had decided that I wouldn't reveal my true identity to him.

On the way we passed the site of the latest explosion. A missile had landed near a school that was under the supervision of the Smile of Hope charity. The shell had pierced one of the walls and part of the roof had collapsed onto the brightly painted chairs and desks. It seemed incredible to imagine that such cheerful colours could exist amid the destruction. The school was an old building encircled by trees, with cheerfully decorated walls. Amidst the rubble I spotted some of the children's artwork – paintings and sketches drawn in soft, delicate lines.

In front of the school entrance sat an old man, lifting his hands up to the sky. Smoke and dust still filled the air. I learned that the old man's son had been hit in the barrage and had died instantly.

'It was a rocket,' said a young man standing nearby.

Rubbish was piled up everywhere, as well as mounds of rubble. Between the destroyed school and the office of the emir of Ahrar al-Sham, the devastation seemed more and more obvious. Litter filled the empty streets and every now and then we'd glimpse a sign of life.

We found Abu Ahmed, the emir of the Ahrar al-Sham movement, sitting in an office which resembled that of a senior civil servant, except that weapons were propped up against the sofa, a cluster of machine guns was lined up behind him, and armed militants stood guard outside. The seats and the sofa in his office were upholstered with black leather. There was a wooden desk, clean and gleaming. Blond with a long, bushy beard, the emir was thirty-eight years old and came originally from one of the villages near Maarat al-Numan. He was of average height and heavyset. After working as a tiler in Lebanon, he had returned to Syria in August 2011, immediately joining the military movement. He hadn't participated in the peaceful demonstrations and had no connection to the civil society movement as, according to him, none of that interested him. Instead, he had enrolled in a military group consisting of fifteen people. Across the way from his office was a stream of families coming to receive humanitarian aid from both the Smile of Hope organisation and Ahrar al-Sham.

The emir didn't ask who I was and spoke to me without looking at my face. Abu Tareq had told him I was writing a book and wanted to see him, and because the emir respected and trusted him he had agreed to be interviewed. He started with basic information and smiled as he addressed Abu Tareq, as if to ease the discomfort of my presence. I asked him to tell me whatever he wanted about himself and about the Ahrar al-Sham movement. I knew that the group were keen to promote themselves so I thought it would be a good way to urge him to talk. The group was an essential part of the armed Islamic resistance and an active player in the north. At my question, he pointedly turned his head and continued to direct the conversation to Abu Tareq. Then, without any greeting, a fighter marched in and interrupted us briefly to tell the emir he'd left three machine guns by the sofa.

I looked down at my blank page. I was nervous, aware that the sound of shelling was close by and that we were at the intersection of a number of combat zones. I couldn't quite come to terms with the fact that I was sitting in the company of an emir of one of the jihadist groups, that I was interviewing him and that – outwardly – I was completely calm. I smiled and tried to draw him out of his reticence. It was midday and I started to feel tense, hot and suffocated. My throat was dry and I suddenly started sweating, but Abu Ahmed finally began to talk and so I started to write.

'I joined the military movement to bring down the regime of Bashar al-Assad and to replace it with God's law in this country,' he told us. 'We have lived under the injustice and criminality of Hafez al-Assad and his son for over forty-four years. Long enough. They used to interrogate me just because I read the books of Abu Tamima and Ibn Qayyim al-Jawziyyah. It happened several times, even though some of my family supported the regime. This is an infidel regime. And what I am doing now is jihad for the sake of God.

'Our group came together for the first time in August 2011. We had just three rifles and one car between us – now we have forty cars and forty tonnes of explosives. We joined forces with Abu al-Baraa, one of the five men who set up the Ahrar al-Sham movement. People said Abu al-Baraa was a *takfiri*, and urged us to disassociate ourselves from him, but we didn't. I was the sixth to join Ahrar al-Sham, so I'm one of the founders and I got to know the other founding emirs well.'

Abu al-Baraa had also been the name of the person who'd made threats against activists when Manhal had gone to the Sharia Court to seek justice for Marcin, although I couldn't be sure it was the same man.

The emir continued, 'We discussed whether we should kill soldiers and decided that if they had defected, we wouldn't kill them, but if they died during the fighting, then it wouldn't be counted against us as a sin and that their deaths would be deemed *halal*, lawful. We planted IEDs in the paths of security patrols. But when the army entered in early 2012, the situation changed. We didn't expect the army to come in and kill us and shell civilians. When the shelling began, it was an operation of annihilation, so we stepped up our strategy accordingly.

'So we stayed, Abu al-Baraa and I, carrying out operations involving detonating IEDs. We would travel about in a Saba car and we'd change the vehicle's colour every two weeks. We became famous for detonating cars and now I'm the Emir of Maarat al-Numan and we have a battalion consisting of one thousand jihadist brothers.'

'But what does the word "emir" mean here?' I asked. 'Why are you called emirs, the leaders of Ahrar al-Sham, the Nusra Front and ISIS?' The title was not traditional in Syria or in the Levant as a whole, and I wanted to know why it was gaining ground.

He stole a glance at me, nodded and replied, 'The emir appoints the military leader and plans the operations, and then there's a legislative official like a judge. In the battalion, we have an advisory body called the Shura Council, but often more weight is given to the emir's decision.'

'Then what's the difference between you and Hafez al-Assad and his son, if it's your opinion that carries the weight?'

'It's nothing to do with me; this is the law. The emir has double the votes,' he answered quietly.

I didn't argue and let him carry on, as I glanced over at the barrels of the machine guns propped next to him.

'The emir is a political leader too,' he explained. 'But our main task is the military operations. We have many jihadist brothers volunteering among the fighters. We don't care about money, but it helps us to recruit those who adhere to the true creed. We don't offer wages.'

I interrupted. 'But I heard that your fighters receive wages and that you have charities and businesses,' I said. 'And this is no secret to anyone.'

He looked me in the eye for the first time and replied in the same measured manner, 'These are what we call "fighters' provisions", and they are payments for their family and their own expenses. As for the charities, they're there to help people.'

'And the businesses?'

He cut across me sharply, 'At the beginning, there were difficulties but we began to win weapons from the spoils of each battle. We did quite well from the army. These were resources stolen from Muslims and they must be returned to Muslims. I bought a number of water tankers here, in Maarat al-Numan, to transport drinking water to people from a well. There's no water or electricity here, and our investment projects have been set up to help the people. We have a long journey ahead and if you support the cause of God, He will help you.

'We have some people with us who work independently of the revolution and we have non-Syrian jihadis who are loyal to us. We also have many Syrians from the Muslim Brotherhood who emigrated and whose children grew up in exile. They've returned to fight with us. Overall, ninety-eight per cent of us are Syrians. There were three from Chechnya but they were originally Syrians whose parents emigrated at the beginning of the sixties.'

Abu Tareq intervened from time to time to contribute a remark or to explain something that wasn't clear. I tried to appear as calm as possible but the atmosphere was becoming increasingly suffocating. Outside, the shelling had quietened down and, for a moment, the world appeared almost peaceful. I rarely experienced quiet like this in the middle of the day. But the smell of leather was making me feel tight in the chest.

'What form would you like the emerging state to take?' I asked.

Now the emir looked me directly in the eyes. 'What we want is the downfall of the tyrant,' he replied.

I repeated the question and he answered with total seriousness, 'Naturally, we want an Islamic emirate. We will have an emir of the believers and a Shura Council.' Then he fell quiet.

'And then?' I prompted.

'And then . . .' he replied, 'there will be laws to protect the sects and the non-Muslims, the *Nasara* – the Christians. It will be unlawful for women to go out without a hijab. Appearing unveiled shall be prohibited; that's the most important thing.'

Abu Tareq had been watching me while I noted down what Abu Ahmed was saying, stealing glances at him as I did so. But when the emir came to the end of this last sentence, Abu Tareq threw me a warning look.

I forced a smile, and Abu Ahmed continued, 'The Alawites can't stay in Syria. Christians will be treated the same way the *Nasara* are treated in Islam, and we declare publicly that we shall reinstate the caliphate of the rightly guided caliphs, the Rashidun.'

'And the Alawites who supported the revolution, and the Druze?' Abu Tareq asked.

'There were only a few Alawites who supported the revolution. Let them leave and we'll fight the Alawites and the Kurds until the last drop of blood.' I was surprised at his mention of the Kurds here, as the Kurds were an ethnic group, not a religious one, and I couldn't understand why there should be any hatred for them. But I carried on writing without saying a word.

'We have twenty-five brothers in the Shura Council,' the emir said. 'We do not recognise the so-called parliament and we will not follow the path of the Muslim Brotherhood, with whom we do not agree.'

I felt drops of sweat trickling down my neck from behind my ears, dripping down to my chest, then my stomach. My fingers were trembling. Any inappropriate movement or reaction to the conversation at this point could prove fatal. I focused hard on the letters of the words I was writing: I was first and foremost a writer and a journalist who had to finish her interview, note it all down, and then get out of there – that was my immediate priority. I needed to push aside that other Alawite woman who was breathing heavily, sweating and trembling – from fear and rage. She could wait till later.

The emir of the Ahrar al-Sham movement continued, 'We and the Nusra Front are broadly in agreement on Islamic doctrine. We disagree on certain issues, but they are courageous men.'

'What's the name of the emir of the whole Ahrar al-Sham movement now?' I asked.

He answered proudly, 'Our elder and emir is Hassan Abboud Abu Abdullah. He was a prisoner who was released in the first months of the revolution. We have important religious elites and from the beginning, back in May 2011, we've worked to include them among us. We were earnest in our work, which was covert initially; we didn't announce the establishment of our group until the end of the year. We are now part of the Syrian Islamic Front. We used to be four factions, which then united to form the Ahrar al-Sham movement. These four were the Islamic al-Fajr movement, Jamaat al-Talia al-Islamiya, Ahrar al-Sham and al-Iman Fighting Brigades.'

'Don't you find it strange that the regime released Sheikh Hassan Abboud at that time specifically?' He looked at me in surprise, so I added, 'The timing of the outbreak of an uprising against al-Assad?'

'No, I don't find that strange.'

I asked him about ISIS and what their position was towards them.

'The brothers of the Islamic State of Iraq and Syria are present here in Maarat,' he replied. 'They have joined us in the fighting and a large proportion of them are immigrants who wish to fight the Nusayri sect, the Alawites that is.'

'We're late and we have to go,' Abu Tareq said suddenly. I nodded. Soon, I thought, we'll finish soon. Abu Ahmed laughed.

'As you wish,' he said.

I put another question to him. 'How do you imagine the situation after Bashar falls?'

'There will be major conflicts. Wars between various factions. I don't give much thought to what will happen after he falls. With God Almighty's permission I will be a martyr. I was wounded with six injuries in a battle, and since the last injury I have only joined in one battle.'

'Is it true that there are now "emirs of war"?'

'Yes, there are,' he replied. 'That's the way it is with war.'

'Does this mean that Syria as a national entity is no longer acceptable to you?' I ask.

'What do you mean?' he answered, surprised.

'I mean that you want an Islamic state – and that means a complete collapse for Syria?'

'No, we're just raising the banner of Islam. Syria will stay as it is, but Islamic. The Alawites will leave.'

'They number more than two million people. And what about the Christians and the other sects?' I asked.

'They can leave Syria, convert to Islam or pay *jizya*, the tax that will be levied on them.'

'And anyone who doesn't leave?' I ask.

'They would meet their fate.'

'Murder?' I ask.

'That is their just reward,' he answered, annoyed now.

'And the women and children?'

'They can leave,' he answered.

'And the Druze and the Ismailites – what will you do with them?' I asked him loudly.

'If they return to Islam then they are welcome, and if they don't, then they'll be judged as infidels. We invite them to the faith, but the Alawites are apostates and must be killed.'

I laughed in an attempt to conceal my nerves. 'But the women and the children . . . the women, what's their sin?'

'The women give birth to children, the children become men and the men kill us!' he answered.

Abu Tareq stood up. 'God keep you, ma'am, please – we must go!' He was looking at me hard and I understood that I was no longer allowed to talk. Although I acted as though I were completely calm, as I stood up my legs were shaking.

'But this isn't a merciful religion, and this isn't God's will,' I said to Abu Ahmed. 'This is absolute evil. It doesn't differ from the evil of Bashar al-Assad.'

Abu Ahmed simply nodded. 'Leave the matters of war to the men, sister.'

As we were leaving, he mentioned plans to teach the children of Maarat al-Numan *tahfiz*, the art of memorising the verses of the Quran.

'I heard that you're interested in education,' he said.

'Very much so, Abu Ahmed,' I replied. 'This is the most important thing.'

'We want to open a school to teach our children to memorise the Quran,' he said.

'May God reward you with goodness, but the Quran is for people's faith, and education is for people's minds, and we need to develop the human mind. Leave God for the heart,' I said.

He shook his head indignantly.

At that moment, I would have revealed my identity if Abu Tareq hadn't silenced me with a glare. We set off quickly in the car. Abu Tareq was left speechless, and for a while neither of us spoke. Once we'd left Maarat al-Numan, I unclenched my fist and wrote down the date in bold ink on the palm of my hand: 4 August.

The transceiver suddenly shrieked into action, and Abu Tareq started to talk to his fighters. He reeled off a lot of numbers and asked about the requirements of the various sections, then told them that he'd see them after *iftar*. Another voice boomed from the transceiver and the numbers were repeated. I asked him if we could pass by the front line and he said we were already in the proximity, but that we wouldn't go up to the top of the hill at the end of the street.

I noticed there seemed to be cats everywhere in the streets. Thin cats and fat cats, strangely plump and swollen. The kind of devastation I'd seen elsewhere could be seen all about us, but here perhaps even more ruinous, merging into a hideous, all-encompassing mass. As we approached the front line, we left the bulk of destruction behind us; the final stage in the formation of these grotesque surroundings was combustion. Everything had gone up in flames; all that remained were iron rods, concrete and rock. A process of purification as the dirt turned to ashes.

There was not a trace of a single house here. Abu Tareq, seven of whose friends had been martyred since the start of the conflict, seemed lost in his own thoughts as he asked me not to get out of the car. 'We can't stay more than a few minutes,' he added. He had barely finished his sentence when the shooting started to get louder from the other side of the front line, and he spun the steering wheel, turning us back in our tracks.

That night was intense. After breaking the fast – with the customary synchronous bombing – we visited a school in the village of al-Dara with the Karama Bus collective, then returned to the centre to talk with a group of rebels and fighters, including a man who had come from Denmark on the trail of Marcin Suder, and who was looking for any clues to his location. He wanted to see me in particular to ask about what had happened.

I had tried to forget that my presence had become known and that it was therefore dangerous for me to remain in Syria. An element of stubbornness made me want to stay on for a while longer as I couldn't surrender easily to the idea that the areas we called 'liberated' had now become forbidden to me, and posed no less of a threat for a woman such as myself than Assad's regime did. In fact, the threat here was definitely worse. Abu al-Majd, the genial Fursan al-Haqq Brigade commander, had told me that I did not need to be afraid where I was, because they were protecting me well. I did feel safe with them, but I also knew it wasn't completely secure. And yet I wanted to complete my work with the women and children.

We stayed up late and by the time I got back to Razan's house, the women were already tucked in and fast asleep. But the noise of children laughing and shouting downstairs interrupted the sounds of distant explosions. It was the sixth day of my stay in the house without electricity or water, and with only rare access to the Internet. We didn't use the generators except when absolutely necessary, in order to save fuel. I couldn't help thinking about those women who had come to the northern regions of the country to work as volunteers in medical relief and in nutrition, having left their homes in America, Europe and areas that had submitted to Assad's forces. Were they in the same danger?

I dropped down onto the nearest available mattress on the floor, and was soon dead to the world. I slept until half past nine in the morning.

That morning we were due to meet Abu Hassan, an emir of the Nusra Front (not to be confused with Abu Hassan of the Kafranbel media centre). I had been trying to meet a representative of the Front for over six months and hadn't yet succeeded. Reaching this emir would be difficult as he was located in a combat zone close to the front line. Despite the fact that he'd been wounded in the leg in the last battle he'd fought in, he insisted on being stationed close to the anti-aircraft weapons. Abu Tareq would therefore be taking me to the village of al-Bara, an ancient historical site, for our meeting. Ibrahim al-Aseel, the volunteer at the centre who gave the rebels media training, would be coming with us.

When I got into the car I wrote the date on my palm: 5 August. I knew the ink would be wiped off by the end of the day and all that would be left would be a blue smudge at the bottom of my palm. But I felt that this latest trip had covered such a long period, I had to do whatever I could to kick-start my memory, which was starting to falter. Each day, I'd write the date at the top of the page in my notebook, but this way I'd also be able to check what day it was simply by glancing at my open hand. I regretted that I hadn't done this from the beginning of this trip, as the black hole in my memory was growing. In fact, two holes were expanding: one in my heart and one in my mind.

On the way to al-Bara, Abu Tareq called three people on the transceiver to finalise the details for the meeting. There had been overwhelming destruction in the village itself. On the transceiver we could hear fighters swearing and cursing. A large battle had taken place between the battalions of the Free Army and ISIS, and Abu Tareq talked us through the events in detail.

'ISIS have hijacked the revolution! We can't just let them get away with what they're trying to do,' he said. Then he added, 'And yet it's an impossible choice: either we focus on fighting Assad's army or we fight the extremist battalions and the mercenaries who've muscled in on the revolution and corrupted it. We're worn out from the sky with the planes, the barrel bombs and the missiles, and from the ground by these Islamist battalions. People are drained.'

The journey to meet the emir was like a voyage in search of hidden treasure. We followed the orders of one of the fighters affiliated to the media centre who was from the Nusra Front, and seemed to take all kinds of circuitous routes before we finally reached the right place. Our quest took us into the heart of al-Bara and out of it again, bringing us eventually to the edge of the village. All the while, the shelling was continuous. This village had been destroyed like so many others.

We pulled up by the side of the road. Over an hour later a car stopped near us and two young men got out. Abu Tareq disappeared with them for some time, then returned and we followed him. We crossed an olive grove and went over a small hill. There was nobody about, apart from a car that drove past with fighters sitting in the boot, young men carrying a black banner reading 'There is no God but God'. They disappeared along a track that branched off in the middle of the olive groves.

It was already midday by the time we arrived and the media representative from the Nusra Front told us we were late. He asked to take our pictures before conducting the interview but I refused: this was a method used by al-Qaeda when meeting journalists and media professionals; they kept the images on file in case they might prove useful one day. But he didn't insist – perhaps because I was only a woman. Later, I told myself, as we set off in the car after the interview, I would tell him my real name but without mentioning anything else about myself. I felt the need to belong to this place and a need to identify myself openly within it, as if this amounted to part of my freedom. Even though I was aware of the risks, my despair over what was happening increased my desire to make a declaration about who I was. Sometimes waves of anger overpowered me, especially whenever we were stopped at an ISIS checkpoint where all its members were foreigners – from Tunisia, Morocco, Saudi Arabia, Yemen and Chechnya. We were just another bunch of Syrians to them, and this made me feel a pang of rage that would propel my objection to the tip of my tongue whenever they asked, 'Who's the woman?' But one of my companions would always answer for me: 'my aunt' or 'my mother' or 'my sister'. This time, I managed to control myself until the very last moment.

We walked across another olive grove until we reached an ancient Roman mausoleum. The architecture was exquisite but it had been struck by a missile. Inside, many stones had been looted and there were only a few remaining. At the far end lay only rubble – the remnants of aerial bombardment. This burial ground was nearly two thousand years old, but the Nusra Front was now using it as a meeting place.

'Who's been looting this place?' I asked the media representative.

'We don't know,' he replied. 'There've been thefts by both sides. That's what happens in war.'

A man came forward from the olive trees. He was of a squarish build, average height and portly, with dark skin. He wore a grey robe and walked leaning on a cane, one leg raised slightly above the ground. This, I discovered, was the local emir of the Nusra Front in al-Bara who went by the name Abu Hassan. I had heard quite a bit about him beforehand and knew that, while people's opinions of him differed, in general he was well liked. He had once worked as a building contractor in Beirut, and also in the Chouf mountains, Jezzine and Deir al-Qamar. He had constructed, repaired and renovated houses in Lebanon for seventeen years.

'Whenever I came back to Syria, and came here to al-Bara, they would arrest me and interrogate me, and accuse me of being a Salafist,' he said. 'Once they held me for seven days before releasing me. But I wasn't interested in politics. We used to only work on contracts with very wealthy clients in Lebanon. My brother was jailed for four years; they released him in May.'

'In the third month of the revolution?' I asked.

'Yes,' he answered.

This testimony concurred with something I had been hearing regularly, and that I'd hinted at during my interview with Abu Ahmed the day before: that Salafists and Islamists were released by the regime during the months of April, May and June 2011. It started to make the repeated claims seem true – that peaceful activists were being tortured, killed and exiled at the same time as these fundamentalist Islamists were being released.

Abu Hassan continued, 'I was being followed. So I went to Beirut four years ago to get a copy of my entry in the public register to use as a form of identification. When events began to unfold in Daraa in March 2011, at the very start of the revolution,

I came back and found that the people had decided to protest against Assad's regime. We held peaceful demonstrations in Jisr al-Shughour, al-Bara and Jabal Zawiya. We didn't carry weapons until June 2011, when they began to shoot at us indiscriminately and started to storm our homes.

'We didn't originally intend to clash with the army – we thought that what had happened in Egypt, Tunisia and Libya would be the same in Syria. Our goals were limited to dealing with the *mukhabarat*, the internal security forces. We regarded the military as our national army and we didn't expect them to bomb and kill us. But after the massacre in May 2011 at the town of al-Mastouma near Idlib, where many civilians were killed, we decided to fight. At that time I only had a hunting rifle, which I took out for weddings and for hunting. We are simple people, as you can see, certainly not famous. But in the revolution we made a name for ourselves.

'The army invaded Jabal Zawiya on the 29th of June and we responded with a simple weapon: the Kalashnikov. When one of the army snipers killed a woman from the Halaq family – a widow – the villagers were incensed and we attacked an army checkpoint. So they shelled our village from their BMP armoured vehicles. We initially thought the army was coming into the village to separate us from the *mukhabarat*, but it turned out that they'd come to support the security forces in suppressing our rebellion. We were amazed to see tanks entering the village. This was an occupation. That's why we – the men – left our homes, while the women and children stayed. And we decided to fight. We were five men facing them.

'This is what it was like in all the villages and towns. It became a public confrontation between the local families on the one hand, and between the army and the *mukhabarat* on the other. Every village armed some of its men to defend their homes and their honour. That's how the revolution began. The justice of our cause gave us faith in our victory and we decided to raid the army checkpoint in al-Bara and seize their weapons, because we didn't possess sufficient funds or arms of our own. We raided the police stations and the branches of the Ba'ath Party and took their weapons, as well as raiding the military recruitment branches and getting their weapons.

'Of course, there were informants among us and we were relatively weak, but we moved on to raiding checkpoints in Jabal Zawiya. We didn't kill members of the *mukhabarat* at the beginning. We used to release them, but that changed later. I travelled between Idlib, Hama and Aleppo to fight. Each PKM machine-gun bullet was expensive – a thousand liras. We didn't have any money and the regime was getting more and more brutal. Every day there were massacres, killings, bombing raids and arrests. We bought weapons with our savings and the profits from the olive season. And we would help each other and begin to get closer as a community, and the dream of victory seemed near. Things changed later.'

'How did they change?' I asked.

'It's a long story,' he replied, 'but the most important thing is that we didn't have any weapons, we were exhausted and most of our men had been killed. A year ago, I decided to join the Nusra Front, and a lot of the defected officers joined up too. But before that, we created the Martyrs of Jabal Zawiya Battalion. And we met some fighters who would go on to form what later became known as the Ahrar al-Sham movement. At that time, July 2011, there weren't the weapons coming from abroad.'

'It sounds like you were a number of armed gangs going round attacking checkpoints, taking their weapons and fighting the regime with them?' I asked.

'Exactly.' He continued, 'The wealthy people in the village told us to buy anti-aircraft weapons and said they'd give us the money for them but we couldn't get hold of any – and, anyway, the problem wasn't with the financing. No one wanted to sell us anti-aircraft weapons. We had a hundred martyrs in our village.

'I got to know a couple of young men, one of whom had been a friend of my brother in prison. They introduced themselves as being from the Nusra Front in the Idlib province. At that time the Nusra Front had no presence in Jabal Zawiya and was limited to Idlib. But they wanted me to join them. So I joined them and, together, we became one force.'

'And ISIS? What's your relationship with that organisation?'

Abu Hassan didn't reply directly. 'ISIS isn't present on the front line,' he said. 'It's in the background. They all used to belong to the Nusra Front. They're foreigners; most of them aren't Syrian. We are a religion of tolerance; we will be merciful with people of other religions. Omar, may God be pleased with him, was merciful. But we want to call people to Islam, and we want to kill Bashar al-Assad.'

'Omar was the first of the *mujtahids* – the early scholars who interpreted the sharia law?' I clarified. 'And you're *takfiris*? You outlaw people as infidels?'

He stole a sweeping glance from my head to my feet, as if he'd just discovered something, and with a wide smile he replied, 'Compared to the others I'm a moderate, miss! What you hear me say doesn't appeal to many people here. The *takfiris* here slaughter and whip people. They have infiltrated some of our groups. I want an Islamic religion that embraces the whole world, but through missionary work.

'In the Nusra Front we want a Shura Council instead of a parliament. We don't accept the coexistence of Christians among us, the *Nasara*. We call them to the religion of Islam. Whoever wishes to enter Islam may do so, and whoever doesn't, will pay a *jizya* tax. We have a "Muslim Treasury" to administrate economic matters. There's no place for Alawites among us.'

As I concentrated on writing my notes, I knew that Abu Tareq and Ibrahim were both keeping an eye on me. They joined in the conversation at times, sometimes addressing me, sometimes Abu Hassan. But right now, I knew Abu Tareq was praying that nobody would touch on anything linked to the awkward subject of my identity.

He continued, 'After the past two and a half years, I can tell you that this is a Sunni–Alawite war, and it will be a long war that will last at least a decade.'

He looked at me and stopped talking. The other six men started to chime in with their opinions, joking and laughing, while I listened.

'They burnt fifty-three men with acid in the village of Bileen,' said one man. 'Just like that! And for what? We'll burn them. We know the whole world wants Bashar al-Assad and that he won't fall, not because he's strong, but because he's backed by Iran, Russia, America and China. But we won't stop fighting him. But when he does eventually fall, I'll leave all of this and go back to my job as a building contractor. I have an olive grove and children waiting for me along with my wife.'

I let the man talk as he went on, 'I went into an Alawite village and I didn't kill the women or the children. I'm against killing. Islam is a religion of tolerance and there is no compulsion in religion. But this will change as time passes. I am a moderate, but my voice and the voice of others like me will not be heeded if the situation carries on like this – and I think it will. That's why I predict a black future. And who will pay the price? Not Bashar al-Assad. The Alawites are the ones who will pay the price. They're infidels and have no religion.'

'You're wrong – they're not infidels,' I replied quickly, glancing at Abu Tareq to make him understand that I wouldn't cross the line.

'How do you know?' said Abu Hassan. 'I know them more than you.'

'I know them a little!' I replied. 'But, Abu Hassan, it seems that the Syrian people don't know each other.'

The conversation moved on to our surroundings. The headstone of a grave nearby was triangular where a shell had struck it, but the area had been targeted arbitrarily, as the olive grove was not a combat zone. One of the men said the graves had been bombed for the sake of looting. A heavyset and fair-haired man who had joined the conversation halfway through, and who was from the Jamal Maarouf Battalion, denied this. However, the young man insisted, 'We can't stay silent about this any more. Antiquities have been stolen, but it isn't only Bashar's army and his *shabiha* who've been doing it.'

'They're all doing it to buy arms,' another man added.

Beneath us, the ground was stirring with miniature battles quite detached from our own: armies of ants marched under our feet.

'And why are you here?' Abu Hassan asked me. 'This book of yours – what use will it serve?'

'I'm planning to publish my discussions with people about the revolution. I think these interviews will give a voice to the voiceless.'

'Will they believe you?'

'That's not important,' I answered curtly.

He looked at me with curiosity. 'Are you from Damascus?'

'What do you think?' I said.

'I don't know, your accent is mixed,' he replied.

'I'm from everywhere,' I answered.

He smiled and added, 'But it's brave of you to come here to us.'

'And what about you, aren't you brave?'

He laughed. 'I'm a man and this is natural.'

'And I'm a woman and this is natural,' I replied, and he stopped laughing.

We left the fighters even though they insisted on offering us hospitality. As we drove off, Abu Hassan said quietly that he would never kill a child or a woman, no matter what the situation cost him. But he also knew that these kinds of things would happen as time passed. And I knew he was a brave man.

'You can tell how brave a man is from his eyes,' I told Abu Tareq when he asked me what I thought of him.

I have to confess that the revolution was teaching me patience and the art of listening. We'd swapped roles, these male fighters and I: it was their turn to do the storytelling. I, in turn, would play with the narrative and turn the world on its head. I could carry on with life because I needed their lives; I needed to turn their experiences into words. I hoped that their narrated stories would repair all this ruin. In the worst case, at least my testimony would remain as proof, evidence of what had happened, so that it wouldn't all be lost to the wind. And so now it was the turn of the emirs Abu Hassan and Abu Ahmed to adopt the voice of Scheherazade in *One Thousand and One Nights* – like Raed had when he told me about the liberation of Kafranbel – and I would be Shahryar, the one who voraciously consumed her tales. But I would be a dual-gendered Shahryar, with a dual role: I would listen, then go back and assume the identity of Scheherazade as I passed on the narrative in turn. Sometimes I'd appear as the one and sometimes as the other; sometimes I would listen and sometimes I would create the story. If it hadn't been for this process – of relaying these stories – I would have stopped returning to Syria, and remained cocooned in my exile. But my claim to this experience was nevertheless a kind of aesthetic fraud, an ugly fraud which I can only hope to redeem through my desire to compose and narrate, and to convey the truth about what was happening. Conveying that truth now is one of the rights of those victims who died for the Syrians' dream of freedom and justice.


I had to go back to Saraqeb. I had been conflicted about the idea of completely leaving the town behind, which I was being driven out of whether I liked it or not. Renting a house in Saraqeb or Kafranbel had become impossible, and staying in Syria to try to live a normal life would have been utter madness. Forcing the rebels to bear the responsibility of my protection, and of accompanying me wherever I wanted to go, had become a burden on them, even allowing for the fact that everyone has the right to practise their own form of madness. I thought about how many people knew I was in Saraqeb. But by now it was the middle of August and my work with the women had to be completed.

On the way from Kafranbel to Saraqeb with Manhal and Mohammed, I continuously photographed the houses, the trees and the sky; and the people moving about these plains, the azure colour of the sky and the pale faces of the children who lined the streets, selling everything you could imagine. At the gates of Saraqeb, the shelling was ongoing and intense. This was normal here. Kafranbel was a relatively safe place, compared with the hell that Saraqeb was facing.

When we arrived at the house, we went immediately down to the basement, where Noura and Abu Ibrahim were already sitting. That night, I didn't sleep. I stayed in my clothes until four in the morning, and eventually went to lie down in the room upstairs with the two old women and Ayouche. I don't know why. When I finally managed to fall asleep for an hour, the shelling was loud enough to wake me up. I was itching furiously from the mosquito bites that covered me, even on my eyelids.

My body felt heavy, as though I could no longer move, but I craved a good scrub. While washing was a problem here, there was just enough water to wipe off the dirt of the last two days. Noura stayed at my side to comfort me, standing near the door to the bathroom. Although the shelling wasn't close, it was continuous. I washed quickly and we made our way to the large family room, which we had to cross the courtyard to reach. A missile dropped nearby as we crossed the courtyard, but we drank our coffee calmly outside with the two old ladies, and I smoked a cigarette. For me, smoking a cigarette in the open air was a dream come true, having resisted the temptation during the daytime in Kafranbel because of Ramadan and the risk of being spotted by the Islamist militants. I felt a flash of sadness because I would be leaving in a few days.

Today was also going to be long, with a tour planned of the women's houses. Nothing much had changed, save the way people were dying and the little they left behind. The same daily details kept repeating themselves: stories giving birth to more stories; evil seeking revenge over evil; the trudging trails of the homeless; and the vacant expression that filled people's faces under the severity of the daily shelling, along with the permanent ashen tinge to their eyes. The look in people's eyes was not new, yet one emotion was plastered to their pupils: horror. Daily routines carried on, with the faces of beautiful widows hidden from the sun, wrapped in each other's arms, creating life out of loss, packing the bags of another death. Nothing increased except the scale of the hatred that mushroomed with the toxins dropped by bomber jets from the sky.

There was nothing new. The same challenges of buying a kilo of vegetables, the same arduous and treacherous journey from the house to the market. A temporary journey to a delayed death and a never-ending cat-and-mouse game with the MiG planes.

And nothing changed in the tours I made of the women's homes and my work with them. Graves were dug and filled in. Bodies were discovered dumped in the valleys and in the hills. Religious shrines were destroyed by the *takfiri* battalions, and new camps for ISIS were built in their place.

And yet, for all this, resistance still coursed through people's veins. There were still soldiers who wouldn't accept being conditionally dependent on the whim of the most powerful countries, refusing to become their pawns. Soldiers, civilian activists and pacifists were being rounded up by ISIS and executed; Syrian media professionals and foreigners were being abducted, killed or held for ransom; and whoever was left was murdered by Assad's aircraft. Fighters in their early twenties were forced to sell their furniture and eat wild plants in an effort to defend their homes.

Here meanings merged. Nothing was clear. Battalions tussled with battalions; the conflict was devouring the revolution. The religious extremist military, with all its factions, had turned into a ferocious many-headed beast. I saw children aged no older than sixteen carrying weapons and disappearing at night among the dark alleys. Gangs of thieves took on the grand names of imaginary battalions, and degenerated into *shabiha* thugs. This was a country in name only, sliced up into areas controlled by rival military brigades, all of them submitting to the absolute power of a murderous sky. But here we carried on with life, regardless. Families plodded on, eking out a living under the lethal sky, among the barbarism of the extremist battalions.

I was going to pack my small bag and leave them soon to head back over the border into exile. We knew – my companions and I – that we weren't partners in death. This partnership we'd formed between us was temporary, and they didn't want me to die. As I was getting ready to leave them, one of the women urged me to stay safe. 'Don't die here,' she warned me. 'Stay suspended between us and the outside world. Be our tightrope, Samar.' I had been watching the women prepare a lavish buffet to bid me farewell, and I looked at her in astonishment. How did this woman, who was over sixty and illiterate, understand me so well? I felt like a rope suspended in space, without beginning or end, and with nowhere for me to settle. Uncoiled, with no solid identity, apart from my language.

A few days before I left, I was still drowning in the detail of death. I had been struck by insomnia and had barely shut my eyes during the last four days of August, which was why I'd discovered the life that went on at night-time, when the streets buzzed with energy once the sky had quietened down a little. It was night that allowed people to leave their homes to prepare for another day. It was at night that I accompanied activists as they cleaned up piles of rubbish on Saraqeb's streets. During the strange and magical night, we witnessed people cleanse their city of the litter to reduce the likelihood of deadly illnesses and epidemics. We passed in the car from one street to another, our headlights switched off for fear of passing planes, travelling between missiles and cluster bombs, to hide in people's homes. We hid in houses opened up for the mourning of dead children, and where young people slept on light bedding, their limbs severed. Then we'd leave and carry on with the cleaning.

Saraqeb's children didn't sleep at night either. They stood in front of the doors to their houses; and I saw them watching the volunteers as they cleared rubbish into a dilapidated car with only three wheels fully functioning, shrapnel having struck its fourth wheel, but which still did the job and grunted along. The smell was revolting and everything that was collected was immediately burnt.

The following day, I carried on moving between the women's homes in the same way as before; nothing more. A daily repetition of the same scene. A place exposed to death. It was only chance that selected the lucky few who would escape this futile game.

As I headed towards the border on the day of my departure, under the glare of the hot sun, I was unemotional. I observed my surroundings and did what I had to do as if driven by animal instinct, finishing my tasks with a professionalism that required two skills: speed and accuracy. Nothing else held any importance. There was no time for sadness. No time for crying. No time for thinking or contemplating. Staying here had disrupted my ability to think. The most we could dream of was to wake up in the morning and discover we weren't buried beneath rubble, or that we had avoided having our heads cut off at the hands of ISIS. So, for that reason, the journey to the border was like a casual day trip, despite us being crammed into the car, despite the heat, and despite the need to stop several times to take cover from mortar shells.

I was quiet and no longer thought about whether I would live or die. I watched the olive groves pass by, and looked at the people on the roads. I understood how death toughens up friendships in the absence of all reason, sense and conscious thought. Here, we realised that slaughter such as this – the very violence that the earth breathed – was the only thing capable of making a decisive break with the history that had preceded it. I was now in the middle of a profound transformation. I knew it; I was touching it and breathing it.

We had to meet one more fighter so I could record his testimony and that was all I focused on. I didn't look into the eyes of the two beautiful young men with amputated limbs who we passed on the roadside, as I usually did. I was engulfed by the intensity of pain and the need to suppress it. What I had to do was separate it from my blood. As though it were a ring of fire I had to avoid. I wouldn't watch the groups of men nearby as I waited next to the car for the fighter to arrive. He was on time. His would be the final testimony I would record.

I had collected over fifty interviews with fighters but this clean-shaven man's story was different. He was referred to respectfully as 'Hajji' and came from the al-Raml Palestinian refugee camp in the port of Latakia, my home city and the heartland of Syria's Alawite population. Latakia was as different and distant socially and culturally from a rural town such as Saraqeb as two stars in two separate galaxies. The son of a taxi driver, the Hajji had been born in al-Raml in 1978, and had attended school in the refugee camp up until he was about eleven years old. Then he had worked at the port. Now he was the commander of the Ahrar Latakia (Free Men of Latakia) Battalion and spent his life on the move, living between the Turkish–Syrian border and Syria's coastal mountainous region, north of Latakia.

I met him at the border and introduced myself. He welcomed me warmly. He was a friend of Maysara's and seemed eager to tell his story. He felt we had now entered a phase of sectarian conflict that would last for the next twenty years, and still Assad's family wouldn't lose. The losers would be the rest of the Alawites, he argued, because the crimes committed by Assad's lot would be committed against the Alawites in turn. There was certainly nothing I could say to persuade him otherwise. He spoke confidently and resolutely, his voice weighed down with hatred and sadness as he recounted his story.

'I used to work at the port as a day labourer,' he said. 'Then Jamil Assad and the Assad family seized control of the port and made us their slaves. I hate the regime and the Alawite sect; they've done nothing but humiliate us. The sons of Munther Assad and

Jamil Assad treated Latakia like their own private fiefdom. They thought the whole of Syria was their farm and we were their workhorses, but in Latakia things were particularly harsh and unjust. We'd hear them – the *shabiha*, the Assad family's thugs, their cronies and sidekicks – we'd hear them constantly cursing us as "Sunni pigs". You're a daughter of Latakia, you know what it's like. For example, the daughter of an officer is untouchable – she could roll even the strongest man's nose in the dirt.

'Between 2003 and 2005, we discovered they were building ten Hussainias in Latakia – congregation halls for Shiite commemoration festivals – and it felt like our religion was in danger because we were seeing this Shiite bloc emerging. For me, it was a matter of doctrine: Sunni or Shiite. That was when we started to meet up and decided that it was unacceptable, something had to be done. I even thought about planning a bomb attack after I saw a sign in Arabic saying "Farsi Language School" in al-Ziraa, which is a Sunni neighbourhood. And they'd already started building Shiite mosques in the Alawite villages – the Iranians were building them. We stayed quiet about that for years. Despite the fact that our religious identity was being suppressed and derided.

'We knew that the Syrian regime had been sending extremists and jihadis to Iraq since the days of Hafez al-Assad, and that our Sunni sheikhs had a good relationship with the regime and were even a part of it. But we didn't want to become extremists, or be part of the regime, so when the Tunisian, Egyptian and Libyan revolutions started, we young people met up and conferred about what we would do.

'Meanwhile, Daraa was on fire with the uprising and there was a massacre. That Friday, at the Mohajireen mosque in the Palestinian al-Raml neighbourhood, we decided to perform a prayer for the souls of the departed. Following it, an enthusiastic demonstration started spontaneously and we marched right up to the door of the security detachment. But they started beating us, so we fought back and set fire to the headquarters. The march continued until it reached the Khaled bin Waleed mosque, then the Saliba neighbourhood.

'Afterwards, we felt like we owned the world. We were able, for the first time, to say: "God, Syria, freedom and nothing else." The next Friday, there were marches from several mosques and twenty thousand protestors came out onto the streets. The army fired at us and around fifteen people were killed; the number of wounded casualties was huge.

'Before the revolution, there were already weapons kicking around in the Palestinian al-Raml district. There were drug dealers, extreme poverty and unemployment. We went underground, covertly planning our next step, organising demos. From the third week, we carried weapons in secret, just in case. They were intended for self-defence and we didn't use them to start with. But after the massacre at Bin al-Alby Square in the Saliba neighbourhood we started carrying guns more openly. That day, we'd agreed to demonstrate peacefully, marching from several mosques to a sit-in on the square. Women and children were carrying the Quran and chanting, "We'll protest until the fall of the regime." After the night prayer, at around eleven thirty, I heard that the army had surrounded the demonstration so I went straight there. People were chanting, "The army and the people are one," and "Peaceful, peaceful, peaceful." The army ordered them to disperse and they refused, so the army fired at them, intensively – live ammunition. Two hundred people, including women and children, were slaughtered that day. I was a witness. The bodies piled up on top of each other. Anyone standing on the balconies of the buildings nearby, who saw what had happened, was killed too.

'A sixteen-year-old girl grabbed a colonel by the chest, so he ordered a soldier to kill her. When the soldier refused to kill her, the colonel shot the soldier and then shot her.

'At exactly eleven forty-five at night, a fleet of cars arrived and carried off the corpses and within minutes fire engines had washed the whole area and there was no sign left that anything had taken place. That was on the 17th of April 2011. We decided that day that armed resistance was the only solution. We started to get hold of weapons, Kalashnikov rifles and machine guns, and began to go out on marches with them to defend the protestors. We used them as well to stop army forces and *mukhabarat* officers from entering our camp, the Palestinian district. We held out for six months this way.

'But we were weak and there were informers everywhere. We no longer had enough weapons and they were firing at us continuously. I was travelling about on a motorbike, sleeping half an hour a day. I was completely exhausted. And I never slept in the same place twice or went back to somewhere I'd stayed previously. After surviving three assassination attempts, I learned to be careful.'

The Hajji didn't stop. He was angry, stern and different somehow from many of the fighters whose testimonies I recorded: he clearly loved life. He wanted to live. He admitted he didn't want to marry so that he could remain free, and he smiled; but he was still angry as he continued his story.

'In the camp, people were helping each other out, sharing aid donations, but there were problems. A lot of people were taking drugs, so we banned drug-taking. Looting became widespread so we posted watchmen between the houses to provide security. I asked everyone to open up their homes to each other and we continued to protest and to prevent the army from entering the quarter. We started a shift rota for guarding the entrances and exits of the camp, even from the direction of the coast. And every Friday, we would come out of the mosques and march. We were more than ten thousand people out protesting.

'We established an independent state in the Palestinian al-Raml neighbourhood and were able to run our own affairs for six months, and we set up our first military council. That was in the fourth month of the revolution. I was a field commander. I had experience with munitions because I've been using them for years and I'm a bit of an aficionado.

'The situation wasn't good in the al-Sakantoury neighbourhood either. Like us, most of the boys were uneducated and unemployed, or manual labourers and taxi drivers. A skirmish erupted between their district and ours. We only had dynamite whereas they had gunboats and Dushka machine guns. They attacked us. After that, we handed out weapons to people for free. Some of our young guys were keen to attack them too, but I stopped them because we didn't have the capacity and I thought we should wait until someone sent us support. To be honest, I was waiting for the Free Army and for the other regions to help us, but neither happened. I felt like we'd been tricked and left on our own. We had three thousand five hundred bullets, ten rifles and a machine gun, and we decided we would resist until we die, that we wouldn't surrender.'

The Hajji sighed. He was chain-smoking and clearly trying to gauge my reaction to what he was saying. I carried on writing, ignoring his glances.

'Our plan was to meet any attack head on. We were relying on a purely defensive strategy to stave off the army for as long as possible, since we were just a neighbourhood in a city in a country controlled by the army. We distributed our fighters so that they could keep a lookout in the alleys they lived in. That was our mistake. We lost control over them. They didn't follow the orders they'd been given and started to shoot at soldiers and tanks.

'We were able to resist from dawn until the afternoon of the following day, helped by the nature of the alleyways in the camp. The army's boats shelled us from the sea and tanks shelled us from the coast, and they attacked the camp and reached the taxi rank. They came in with armoured personnel carriers and posted snipers on the roofs and between the buildings. We killed forty-five of their men and they killed thirteen of ours. We rounded up the women and children in Ein Tamra Street to evacuate the camp. My mother and sister were among them. We attacked the army checkpoint so we could accompany them out. We didn't sleep or eat for four days. We resisted and fought, but when the army reached the al-Sakantoury neighbourhood next to us, thousands of people fled. We stayed in deserted buildings and building sites. We had to keep moving about, hiding in the houses.

'During this time they arrested forty-five young men in the Raml neighbourhood, but we got away. We escaped across the Turkish border to the Yelda refugee camp. I had six hundred men with me who I was responsible for and I didn't know what to do. I didn't have any money to give them. I was lost, so I went to Antakya where I received a second shock when I realised that others had staked a claim to the leadership of the military and civil campaign instead of me. This revolution has been one long string of betrayals, lies and backstabbing.

'I met with countless officers and presented my battle plans to them. I received various amounts of money for weapons and was careful not to launch into anything before getting assurances that the supply lines would stay open. The suppliers promised to bring us weapons by sea but I said no. I knew that would be impossible.

'I asked everyone for help and I didn't get any, and I felt like the burden of responsibility was getting harder to bear. The whole world was letting us down and the fighters and battle commanders were seized with despair. We couldn't find anything to eat and we barely slept. I rallied the fighters who had come to Turkey with me and told them that whoever wanted to go and fight on any front line was free to go because I didn't have the weapons. At the beginning of 2012, I returned to the battlefield in the Mount Kurd region and stayed there until the battle of Mount Doreen in July.

'We were in the heart of the mountains. Every day we planned a new attack on a checkpoint or security detachment and we would steal cars because we didn't have any money. I ordered my men to kill the driver if he was an Alawite. Some people opposed me and were angered by my commands. I can't help bearing a grudge! I had a very bitter experience of Alawites when I worked in the port.'

He stopped talking. I knew that he was watching me to see my reaction. I didn't lift my head, gripping the pen in my hand.

'And then what happened?' I asked.

He didn't answer. Several minutes of silence passed. I lifted my head and stared right at him. He was looking at me unblinking. I continued to look at him fixedly.

'Carry on,' I insisted, and he continued talking to me with the same intense look.

'Before the planes started to bomb us, the battles were straightforward and we were advancing. But things changed after the aircraft began bombing us. This happened from the al-Hafa battle onwards, and after the battle of Doreen I had no ammunition left and we were on our own under the bombardment. I left the guys in the mountains and returned to Turkey, where I secured money and weapons before returning to the battlefield. I smuggled the weapons from the Kurdish mountains to the Turkmen mountains in the province of Latakia.

'The first battle there was on Jebel 45, a peak in the range, and the second was in Nab al-Murr at the Kessab border crossing. We entered an Alawite village, Bayt Uthman, which was more or less deserted. There were only a few young men left so we killed them. We took the chickens to eat and our men stole whatever food they could find for the battalion. They burnt down some of the houses and left the rest. After a while, Jebel 45 was sold out by one of the battalions. We were shocked when the army returned to Jebel 45, which the regime had used as an observation point in the past. There were more betrayals. The front lines were being sold out as soon as they were liberated. People were trading during battles, right at the front line, trading with our blood. We became dejected, we started to lose confidence and we no longer knew who was a traitor and who we could trust. Whoever could bolster the coastal battle with weapons controlled the fate of the fighting. This was around the time of the battle of al-Zaeniya. We besieged Regiment 135 for two hours and killed a lot of them.'

'You talk about killing so easily and cheerfully. Are you a murderer?' I asked.

'Yes, I've murdered people,' he said, looking at me angrily. 'I'm defending our rights. But I won't kill you.'

'Maybe not, because we're on the Turkish border. You're being careful. If we were elsewhere in Syria you would have killed me!'

'I won't kill you,' he replied. 'With the torture that's ahead, I feel pity for you. Killing you would be mercy! You're in an unenviable situation and you're cut off from reality. What's happening here is nothing but a religious war!'

I stared into his eyes once again. I wanted to see him as he spoke about me.

'Yes,' he added, 'I feel sorry for you and I hope you'll stay far away from this vile war. I know of an Alawite soldier who defected and later committed suicide in a battalion of the Free Army.'

'Did he commit suicide or was he killed?' I asked him.

'He definitely committed suicide. That was early on. I'll tell you the story of something that happened to me at Mount

Arbaeen in Idlib province, seeing as you like stories. I took fifteen men with me to the Foronloq Forest region. We'd found out about the regime army's movements in the area. There was a cliff ahead of us. We reached a large open area at the heart of the range, between three peaks. Shellfire was pouring down on us like rain from every direction, so we hid between some rocks. I told the guys to follow me, and we screamed at the soldiers, "Defect, soldiers, defect! We are your brothers." Their only reply was to curse us, then both sides started to exchange insults. I shouted at them to surrender because we'd cut them off, and when they just swore at us we shot at them. You wouldn't believe how exasperated I was because we were Syrians killing Syrians. But what else could we do?

'We withdrew, but they managed to encircle us and began shooting with Dushkas and sending over mortar bombs. Somehow we managed to get out of there and survive. We thought we were going to die. That battle stays with me more than any other, because we were close enough to hear each other.

'During the battle of al-Zaeniya, we didn't leave a single man alive. There were corpses strewn ahead of us as far as the eye could see. We left the bodies out in the open, where some of them were ripped to shreds by wild dogs before the army could get there with their trucks to collect the corpses.

'After al-Zaeniya, my battalion's headquarters was in the Turkmen mountains and we followed the command of the 10th Brigade, which was under the central command of the Free Army. I stayed in the trenches in one of the deserted Alawite villages, which we controlled for three weeks. Three other battalions joined mine and we advanced by fourteen kilometres into the regime-controlled area. After three months I asked for some support from central command. I was within range of the regime, facing continuous shelling and exposure to snipers. It was suicide for us to be in that situation and yet no one else agreed to advance with us. The other battalions stayed in the nearby village of Kandasiya. When I felt that my men and I risked being sold out and left to die, I informed the military council that I was going to withdraw, and I did. After that my debts piled up, so I sold the mortar and the Russian weapons in order to repay them. I went back to the central command headquarters and placed myself under their authority. My battalion is now called the Ahrar Latakia Battalion. I only go to the front line with them when I'm ordered to. We're now based near Mashqita, fifteen kilometres away from the city.'

'But you don't think the fighting on the coast is a genuine battle?'

'No, it's not genuine,' he answered. 'I think the foreign countries want the Syrians to fight among themselves – that's why they made us turn on each other and then ran. I learned about this from a professor who was fighting with us. That's why I'm now more depressed than ever because so much Syrian blood will be shed for nothing.

'Another strange thing is that ISIS is present on the coastal front but not on the other front lines. There're more than five hundred and fifty of their fighters in that area, and they're just watching now. I don't know what they'll do next! Ahrar al-Sham also have a presence and we, the sons of Latakia who want a national Syrian state, are being driven out! And what's even stranger is that ISIS are the ones killing off members of the Free Army now. They're doing that instead of fighting the regime. A while ago, they came with Grad rockets and wanted to attack a populated Alawite village. I refused, but they'll do it one day and may even bomb Latakia. I told them to beat it. The ISIS fighters were Tunisian, Libyan and Saudi Arabian. Things have occasionally got a bit nasty between us – I've got into a fight with them once or twice.'

'Hajji, what will you do after the fall of the regime?' I asked. He laughed until he was red in the face, then looked at me with a sly expression.

'It won't fall any time soon,' he said. 'We have a long journey ahead. We need twenty years for the war to end and I don't know what will happen after that. But I'm certain I won't survive till then, which is a shame, because I love life. But I'm always in the front line. I'm as good as dead. If there was someone to lead us properly then our prospects would look much better.'

The meeting with the Hajji, the last of the fighters whose testimony I recorded, drained the last reserves of my concentration. The absurdity and the pain of what was happening seemed to cloak me in a haze of nothingness as I walked along, taking my final steps towards the border crossing.

Yet all the contradictions, stacked up in my mind and around me, failed to shake me out of the animal simplicity of my movements, as I was towed along by the queues of people shuffling forward like livestock, mere shadows of themselves. Here, the flow of life and acceleration of death had brought these two opposites hurtling towards each other on a collision course. Always in such close proximity, it had become difficult to distinguish between life and death in this swollen river of shuffling souls fleeing from bombs to a misery awaiting them of asylum, poverty, homelessness. A contrasting queue on the other side of the border flowed in the opposite direction, a stream of fighters surging to meet death as the bridge to eternity in their presumed paradise. Arms brokers, arms traffickers, human traffickers, human arms laden with weapons of death. Here was the point where these two streams crossed. I watched them as I moved forward in my daze.

At this final border crossing, I was surrounded once more by the swarming crowds of terrified humans desperate to escape. Wounded fighters and representatives of humanitarian organisations. Reporters of broadcasting networks, foreign journalists. Victims with missing limbs hopping among multitudes of women and children. Yet the mass of people trudged forward without any sense of curiosity, like extras in a film being goaded on by the director, their eyes staring straight ahead. Anxious but erratic. Giddy from the heat of the sun. This same scene had repeated again and again at each crossing point I'd used to steal in and out of the country. Hordes of people departing as if it was the Day of Judgement.

Atma camp was much the same. The number of barefoot children had increased since I'd last passed through, as had the density of scattered tents and armed checkpoints, mostly manned by jihadis and ISIS soldiers. Until that time, the end of August 2013, ISIS had maintained a cordial relationship with the other jihadist factions like the Nusra Front and Ahrar al-Sham. Later, the situation would change: ISIS would enter into a war with them and it would become clear that its campaign had no boundaries; it was an organisation dead set on establishing a future state.

The penultimate checkpoint that stopped us belonged to ISIS too. Four young men brandished their guns, pointing them into the air, standing to attention with their legs apart, ready for action. Two of them were completely masked and the other pair revealed only half of their faces. They weren't Syrian. I remained as calm as I could when I saw them, staring at a fixed point in front of me on the road, and I paid little attention to what they wanted or what they asked my companions. Their accents were strange and I didn't understand what they were saying. I only noticed how arrogant and confident they seemed, how loudly they shouted.

They moved as though they were the lords and masters of the place, and signalled with their hands, allowing us to pass.

The final checkpoint at the entrance to Atma camp was manned by Ansar al-Islam fighters. The role of guarding the camp was now being shared out among the armed battalions. On both sides of the border there were trucks packed with wooden boxes that contained weapons. A shipment was being carefully offloaded from one of the trucks as we passed. This was happening in broad daylight on the border, in plain view of all the crowds of old men, women, children . . . and traders, smugglers, regime henchmen and journalists. At the edge of the olive grove on the Turkish side, young men of different nationalities were sitting under the sun. They were fighters waiting for their turn to enter the country and join the fray. They also weren't Syrian.

My friends accompanied me right up to the border – the same point we had come through at the beginning of my trip. Maysara joined me in the queue, where we became part of one of those human columns, straight out of a Goya painting. It took over an hour for us to pass the crossing point. Next to me, a beautiful girl was being swept along by the people surrounding her. She was around fourteen years old, give or take a year, and her mother was at her side. The girl, whose name was Fatima – a common name for girls here – told me she was leaving Atma camp to get married. Her father had been killed in the bombing, and she was the eldest of six sisters. I asked her about her future husband and what he did for a living. She said he lived in Turkey but was Jordanian by nationality and that she would live in Antakya because he worked in trade between Amman and Turkey. I didn't try to find out how old the man was, not wanting to embarrass her. When Fatima asked me what I was doing there, I told her a white lie – that I was from Jabal Zawiya. She became silent and paid me no attention after that.

But I saw Fatima again later as I was crossing to the other side, where a hire car was waiting for her. She was met by a man who was in his early sixties or maybe even older. His forehead was marked with the *zebiba*, the sign of the devout – a hard patch of skin on the forehead from touching the ground during prayer, and he wore a white abaya gown. I was near enough to call out to her.

'Your husband?' I asked. The husband seemed to recoil into himself.

'Hmm,' Fatima replied in a small voice, stealing a glimpse at me before turning her back.

Sweat was dripping from the official who was recording people's names. I was still dressed in my black clothes, covered from head to toe. The long line of women, men and children stretched out behind me, an uncountable number of people waiting for their turn under the heat of the sun, not one of them with any identification papers. Behind me, a woman was carrying a baby in her arms, trying to calm him by singing gently. I turned to her. The baby's arms were wrapped in white gauze from his shoulders to the tips of his fingers. I lowered my gaze and stared down as the official recorded my fake name, the one I would depart with. Just then, I remembered the first time I'd travelled under a pseudonym, when I'd fled my family home in 1987 at the age of sixteen and a half, and I laughed. I have borne many names in my short life as I've travelled back and forth from my exile.

The official looked up, annoyed by my laughter. 'Let us laugh with you,' he said. But he glanced only briefly at my face before I went through, passing over it like every other face he'd seen.

I myself didn't know why I was laughing. It was a habit I'd picked up from the young fighters: I would start laughing whenever I felt suffocated. I laughed even more loudly.

'You wouldn't laugh. If I told you, you wouldn't laugh!' I said to myself.

Then I stepped forward and looked over to the opposite side where I would soon be in Turkey.

My companions were still there on the Syrian side, standing back from the crowds, watching me through the line of people. As I left, I tried not to prolong the moment of parting; one wave was enough. They waved back. At my side, Maysara didn't utter a word as my tears fell. I would probably never see these young men again. I waved once more.

'I feel like a cartoon character crying these buckets of tears,' I said.

Maysara quietly signalled to me to follow him. I turned my head for the last time now; I had to be as steady as possible as I crossed to the other side. The men watched me until I finally disappeared from their sight.

After seeing the child bride leave with her new husband, old enough to be her grandfather, I was seized by one thought: the thought of my dear little enchantress Aala, Maysara's middle daughter. I started planning the stories I would tell her when I reached the family's flat in Antakya, and how I would describe the house in Saraqeb to her and what we had done in her absence – Noura and I, her aunt Ayouche, and the two old ladies. I plotted how I'd act out those stories, perform them for her, the story of each character in this book. I pondered how I would tell this little survivor the tales of her neighbours and relatives, since they were all relatives of a kind in Saraqeb. I tried to organise the details in my mind before I reached their new home. I needed to reach some sort of ending with Aala, who would one day grow up and tell the story of her own escape and of living in asylum. Or maybe she wouldn't tell anyone, but would attempt to forget it and not try to uncover anything about her childhood.

The car drove us alongside the border, where Syria lay to our left. Now I was the enemy and my blood ran hot with revenge against all the murderers. I was a fragmented, fissured being who had uprooted herself and adapted to growing in new soil, only to uproot herself once again. I was both seeking an identity and escaping from an identity. Someone who lived in airport lounges and on train platforms, driven out, driven far from this place. The impossibility of staying shook me violently out of my dream of returning. Now, though, I tried to make myself accept once and for all that I was leaving for exile. I was leaving behind me this land drenched in ruin, soiled with secrets and conspiracies, sacked by marauding *takfiri* militants. The lands that the Syrians had liberated with their blood, the villages and towns of the north, were occupied once again. This was no longer liberated land, nor was it even Syrian. Our dreams of revolution had been hijacked. The powerful countries of the world now played out their own battles in this space, moving their armed battalions like pawns, financing and stocking imaginary front lines. In full public view, the border from Turkey gaped wide open to all kinds of fighters, and to weapons streaming in from a number of sides. Who were the people financing ISIS? Who were the people financing the Nusra Front? Who was assassinating the commanders of the Free Army? Who was killing the journalists and pacifist activists? What was causing this abduction of the revolution, this transformation of it into a religious war? These questions hung in the air.

As for me, I would reach Paris within the next two days, and this scene before my eyes would fade. Our car would disappear into Turkish territory and we would go, Maysara and I, back to their house, where Aala would be waiting for me with her rich store of tales, which would not end until I left Antakya airport on a flight to Istanbul. In turn, I would give her news of her neighbours, of the young rebels, and I would lie a great deal. I wouldn't tell her about the bodies of her friends, the children who died. I would say an elegant, neat farewell and promise her that I'd be back in a few months' time.

In my previous book, *A Woman in the Crossfire*, I dipped into the first layer of hell, with my account of the beginning of the revolution and its first four months. This second testimony had dragged me in even further, into a deeper abyss. And now, as I resurfaced into exile once again, I found not much had changed. This still didn't feel like a real exile. It hadn't altered its state to accommodate the full-on commotion of the accelerated events I'd experienced. Exile perhaps wasn't even the right word: it needed redefining, I needed to go back to its root meaning. For this exile crammed full of the fleeting images of social media was no longer what exile had meant in its original sense. Modern technology had transformed the whole concept into something completely different. Even in exile, people today were no longer cut off with such finality from their places of origin. Instead, those places remained present and accessible in so much as it was still possible to interact online with those left behind and communicate about events as they happened. In this respect, exile no longer entailed such an intense sense of loss of identity as it had before the emergence of the Internet.

And so the border disappeared behind us. I found myself imagining that if the physical mass that is me could be broken up somehow into atoms floating in space, leaving me as free as a soft sheet swaying in the breeze, it would be wonderful. I would be content to seep from physicality into nothingness. And then, in that moment, I remembered that we had reached the end of August, that I might never return, that my country was occupied and the sky was occupied, and I became motionless, heavy as a marble statue. I stared hard, unblinking, back at the void of the border.

# EPILOGUE

I completed the first draft of this manuscript at the end of September 2014. I put down my pen after my final departure from the country and it was months before I felt able to start writing up my experiences. At the time, I felt it was pointless to write; even to talk about what was happening seemed absurd and frivolous. My fingers seized up and my mind froze. This mental block, or emotional paralysis, kept me from going back to my notes, from digging out the interviews. It seemed impossible to confront my feeling of futility. The enormity of the injustice and the daily massacres had left me speechless. I needed an eternity to regain my ability to write.

Writing is a route to awareness through its complex relationship with death. It is a reproduction of life, courageously challenging death. But it also represents defeat in the face of death, because ultimately death, with all its complicated questions, is both the impetus of writing and its source. And yet it's a valiant defeat. I hadn't understood the inevitable overlap between writing and death before now.

A year has passed since my final exit from Syria, where surely the sheer scale of the mass exodus of the people will go down in history. I keep a close eye on developments from afar. Doesn't everyone? You flick through images, scan the news and keep in touch with whoever is still stuck there – but what does it mean? What does it achieve? The essential piece of the puzzle is missing. To read about barrel bombs and shells falling for ten consecutive days in the city that you've lived in, Saraqeb, doesn't in any way resemble actually living with those explosions crashing all around you. Saraqeb has been bombed with barrel and cluster bombs every single day for over a year now. To see the corpses piled up under the rubble isn't the same as touching them; the smell of the earth after a cluster bomb doesn't come out and hit you from the photos and videos shared by the scant few activists who are still alive and documenting what's happening. Where is the stench of burning, the panic in the eyes of terrified mothers or the hush of the brief, shocked silence after an explosion? All these images connect us to what's happening instantaneously, but what actual meaning do they relay? They mean nothing except more madness. Because such two-dimensional images fuse the reality with the imagined and reduce level-headed logic to futile absurdity, blurring the divisions of life and death themselves.

The outside world won't believe that what is happening in Syria – which the whole world is witness to – is nothing but the international community's desire to see its own salvation. Other people are dying instead of them. Something prompts their desire to track life as it is extinguished before their eyes. They are the survivors and that's enough. It's a carnal instinct like lust. Voyeurs the world over are getting a kick from watching Syria's desperate fight for survival – a scene composed essentially of the heaped-up corpses of Syrian victims. The world merely watches on – apart from embroidering and sensationalising the contrived spectacle of the war between Assad and ISIS, until that scarecrow has grown into the fearsome monstrosity they needed to assuage their absent conscience. What is happening is nothing new in the history of humanity, but now it's unfurling in public view, the blood spilling before our eyes and on to our hands. With savage images that make cold-hearted monsters of us, the global media machine churns out a barbarous conveyor belt of updates that ensures each victim is forgotten as soon as the next one comes along, breeding a nauseous familiarity through the magnitude of death. We consume the news then toss it out with the rubbish.

This is what the Syrians have become in four years. A peaceful popular revolution against a dictator tumbled headlong into an armed mutiny against army and state, before the Islamists hijacked the stage and turned the Syrians into puppets in a proxy war, ISIS playing the leading role in this morbid theatre of blood. Islamic State of Iraq and Syria (ISIS), the fundamentalist faction that emerged on the scene in April 2013, is now a state in itself and a de facto occupying power. The foreign fighters who flow across the Turkish border have become the automatons of death and destruction. Everything is caught up in the iron grip of violent radicalism.

ISIS occupies Syrian cities. The US-led coalition bombs them almost coquettishly, then runs away meekly. Meanwhile, ISIS and its allies advance unscathed and the massacre continues. The whole world is obsessed with 'Islamic State', while Assad's aeroplanes continue to hurl bombs down on civilians in the provinces of Idlib and Damascus, Homs and Aleppo. The world seems to be waiting for the murky spectre of ISIS to become clear, to crystallise, while innocent civilians continue to fall under the regime's mortar fire and the swords of the Islamist militants. The cogs of international deliberation slowly grind, as the blood pours, as millions of people are displaced, and millions become refugees. Syria will never be the same again – it has been hanged, drawn and quartered.

I stay in touch with the rebels and the women on the inside. Mohammed still hasn't left Saraqeb. He still refuses to leave the country to get the medical treatment he needs. He still can't see with one eye. In our last conversation, he told me that when he's outside Syria he feels suffocated. He and the others have started to dig underground caves to sleep in at night and in the morning they drag victims out from the rubble, document the violations and help the people where they can. Suhaib, the nephew of the family, has also dug his heels in, refusing to return to Europe where he used to live.

'I'll die here; I'll never leave,' he said.

Maysara and his wife and family are still in Antakya. My dear little Aala has a new brother and a happy life with her siblings. They are learning Turkish and go to school. Maysara goes back to Saraqeb every now and then.

Raed Fares survived an assassination attempt and is still being threatened by ISIS and armed *takfiri* groups, but refuses to leave Kafranbel. The other men I know have also refused to leave – Abdullah, Khaled, Ezzat, Hammoud, Abu Tareq and Abu Waheed – they all cling to their dream of staying. The scope of their work has changed, but they all repeat the same mantra: 'We'll die here; we'll never leave. This is our land.' They won't submit, they say; they're still adamant they'll resist the lure of funding from the *takfiri* battalions. Ahmed and Abu Nasser are also still fighting, but Ahmed was wounded in a battle. Abdullah married and has become a father. He hasn't had his leg seen to properly and still limps. Manhal settled in Turkey, but then decided recently to return to Saraqeb. He went back and joined the rebels again. Razan left Kafranbel. She refused to wear the hijab and now lives in a Turkish city near the Syrian border. At the time of writing, there is still no news of Marcin.

Abu Ibrahim and Noura – my generous hosts – finally left their house in Saraqeb and went to live on a farm on the plains far from the shelling. But the missiles still reach them and a massacre took place in the vicinity. Ayouche moved to the farm with them, as did the old mother and the aunt. A month after they'd all settled there and she'd lost her old home, the aunt, that beautiful old lady, died. Yet Abu Ibrahim refuses to leave Saraqeb completely and

Noura, who loves him dearly, told me via Skype that she won't ever leave her husband behind, despite the fear and panic that still grip her. She says that she has lived with him and she will die with him.

These are just some of the protagonists in one of the greatest tragedies of the twenty-first century – and their suffering is the overwhelming proof of humanity's moral fall from grace. They went to their revolution full of dreams of freedom and justice. They paid the price of their miscarried dreams heavily in blood. These are the sons of the great Syrian epic that I will never forget. Even in Paris, where beauty bursts out of the smallest of details, I still feel ugliness killing me. It nestles deep in my chest. This city hasn't yet been able to extract me completely from my land; the feeling of exile, of homesickness, that I thought I would expel from my life, that I thought I could resist, still predominates. Before this experience, I didn't think much about the definition of exile as an exceptional status that squeezes the narrow confines of a person's identity, be it their language, nationality, religion, or their geographic location. As far as I was concerned, my text and narrative were my identity – that's how I used to see it. For more than twenty years, stories constituted the only realm I believed in, but I have discovered, after a year of living in exile, that exile is exile and nothing else. It means walking down the street and knowing that you don't belong there.

Here in exile, I've learned how to walk and think in my sleep: asleep, or maybe already dead? What's the difference? Either way I'm detached, absent from reality. I touch my body; I don't recognise my fingers, and my narrative seems foreign beyond recognition. Did I ever belong to it? Perhaps I belong to it more, the deeper I sink into my exile.

# APPENDIX

## A Brief Note about Alawites and Sunnis
### by Samar Yazbek

The Alawites are a sect of Shia Islam, which has its own secretive religious teachings and recognises twelve Imams (legitimate successors to the Prophet Mohammed). They have suffered a difficult history of persecution, displacement and pogroms, because some orthodox Sunnis have regarded them as infidels and heretics.

Sunni Islam is the largest sect in Islam, to which the majority of Muslims belong, and its legislation and traditions are based on the Quran and the Hadith, the teachings of the Prophet. They recognise only four Imams: the leaders of the four official schools of Sunni Islam which emerged after the death of the Prophet.

The Alawites follow the Imam Ali bin Abi Talib, the cousin of the Prophet Mohammed, and do not accept the authority of Sunni Islamic traditions. They have their own theological traditions, of which the most important is the idea of the separation of religion and state. They were known by many names before the nineteenth century, including the Nusayris, but the status of the Alawites in Syria changed when Hafez al-Assad, the father of Bashar al-Assad, came to power, because he was able to harness the community and its difficult history to his own advantage, enforcing their allegiance. Although many opponents of Hafez al-Assad were in fact Alawites and spent many years in prison under his rule, he filled the ranks of his army with them and he impoverished much of the community, forcing many of them into his security services, and corrupting some of them through positions in the army and the state. Hafez al-Assad dispensed with the important religious authorities and made use of the Alawite religion for his benefit, and for whatever helped him and his family stay in power. When the revolution began in Syria, the Alawites generally sided with Bashar al-Assad.

# SELECT GLOSSARY

Arabic place and personal names can vary widely when rendered in English due to the usage of different transliteration conventions. In this book, the translators have sought to use the spellings which are mostly commonly found in the British media and in online maps and resources.

**Abaya:** a robe-like garment that covers the entire body, with the exception of the feet, face and hands.

**Ahrar al-Sham:** a militant rebel group rumoured to have ties with the transnational fundamentalist group Muslim Brotherhood.

**Alawite:** a religious sect of Shia Islam, based in Syria and believed to have been founded during the ninth century.

**Alhamdu lilah:** an expression of relief, meaning 'praise be to God'.

**Allah:** the Arabic word for God.

**Allahu akbar:** a common Islamic Arabic expression meaning 'God is great'.

**Ba'ath Party:** the political party that has governed Syria since a coup brought the Ba'athists to power in 1963. Bashar al-Assad is both the party's Regional Secretary and the state president.

**Bedouin:** an ethnocultural group of people descended from nomads who historically inhabited the Arabic and Syrian deserts. Derived from an Arabic word meaning 'desert dweller'.

**Caliphate:** a form of Islamic government led by a caliph, a leader of the Muslim community regarded as a successor of the Prophet Mohammed.

**Druze:** a monotheistic religion incorporating Gnosticism, Neo-platonism and various philosophies, evolving out of Ismailism, an offshoot of Shia Islam.

**Emir:** a title of high office, whose literal meaning is 'commander', 'prince' or 'general'.

**Fatwa:** an authoritative ruling on a point of Islamic law, based on religious scripture.

**Free Army** (also known as the Free Syrian Army): rebel forces fighting the regime. Comprising diverse battalions and brigades, including military defectors from the Syrian Army and moderates.

**Fursan al-Haqq** (also known as Liwa Fursan al-Haqq): 'The Knights of Justice' rebel brigade, a subgroup of the Free Army.

**Hadith:** collections of the teachings and sayings of the Prophet Mohammed, based on oral reports.

**Hajj:** an honorific title given to a Muslim person who has successfully completed the Hajj (pilgrimage) to Mecca, often used to refer to an elder.

**Halal:** (of food and drink) prepared in accordance with Islamic law. In more general terms, any object or action that is 'allowed' or permissible according to Islamic law.

**Haram:** an act that is sinful and forbidden by Allah.

**Hijab:** a veil covering the head and chest, worn by women in the presence of adult males outside the immediate family.

**Iddah:** the period of time a woman must observe after the death of her husband, or divorce, during which she may not marry another man.

**Iftar:** the evening meal with which Muslims break their daily fast during Ramadan.

**Imam:** the person who leads prayers in a mosque. Also the title of various Muslim leaders.

**ISIS** (also known as Islamic State, ISIL and DAESH): an Islamic extremist rebel group and self-proclaimed caliphate controlling areas in Syria and Iraq, with affiliates in other areas of the Middle East, Africa and Asia.

**Jihad:** a term broadly referring to religious duty and the struggle against those who do not believe in Allah. Controversially interpreted in some contexts as 'holy war'.

**Jinn:** supernatural creatures in Arabian mythology, which can appear in human or animal form.

**Jizya:** a tax levied on the non-Muslim adult male subjects of an Islamic state, according to certain criteria.

**Khimar:** a head covering or veil typically concealing the head, neck and shoulders.

**Kurds:** an ethnic group spanning parts of modern-day Iran, Iraq, Syria and Turkey, with a history of persecution.

**Mazut:** heavy, low-quality fuel often used for heating.

**Muezzin:** the official at a mosque who proclaims the call to prayer.

**Mujahideen:** plural form of *mujahid*, the term for one engaged in jihad.

**Mukhabarat:** security forces or intelligence agencies.

**Nasara:** a group mentioned in the Quran as holding the doctrinal belief that Jesus was the son of God, and therefore identified with modern-day Christians.

**National Coalition of Syria:** coalition of opposition groups founded during the Syrian civil war.

**Nusra Front** (Jabhat al-Nusra): a militant rebel group allied to al-Qaeda and designated as a terrorist organisation by various bodies including the United Nations.

**Quran:** the central religious text of Islam, held to be a revelation from Allah.

**Ramadan:** the ninth month of the Islamic year, during which fasting is observed from sunrise to sunset.

**Rawafid:** pejorative term meaning 'rejectors', applied to those the speaker believes to have rejected legitimate Islamic authority and generally used to refer to Shiites.

**Salafism:** conservative movement within Sunni Islam that has become associated with a strict and puritanical approach to Islam and militant jihad.

**Shabiha:** armed militant supporters of the Ba'ath Party and al-Assad's regime.

**Sharia:** Islamic law.

**Shia:** the second largest denomination of Islam, who regard Ali, the fourth caliph, as Mohammed's first true successor.

**Sufism:** a mystical and ascetic dimension of Islam in which knowledge of God is sought through direct personal experience.

**Suhoor:** the meal consumed in the early morning before fasting until sunset during Ramadan.

**Sunni:** the largest denomination of Islam, differing from Shia in its understanding of the Sunnah (the traditional portion of Islamic law based on the Prophet Mohammed's words and acts) and its acceptance of the first three caliphs.

**Syrian Army:** troops fighting on the side of Al-Assad's regime.

**Tahfiz:** learning the Quran by heart.

**Takfiri:** a Muslim who accuses another Muslim (or an adherent of another Abrahamic faith) of apostasy.

**Wallahi:** phrase meaning 'I swear to Allah' or 'by God' to make a promise or express truthfulness.

**Yallah:** phrase meaning 'come on' or 'let's get going'.

**Zebiba:** Arabic for 'raisin', a dark circle of calloused skin created by repeated contact of the forehead with the prayer mat during daily prayers. Regarded as a sign of piety.